the
military advantage

the military advantage

by Lynn Vincent

LearningExpress

New York

Copyright © 2001 LearningExpress, LLC.

All rights reserved under International and Pan-American Copyright Conventions. Published in the United States by LearningExpress, LLC, New York.

Library of Congress Cataloging-in-Publication Data:
Vincent, Lynn.
  The military advantage / Lynn Vincent.—1st ed.
  p. cm.
  ISBN 1-57684-363-2 (pbk.)
  1. Retired military personnel—Employment—United States.
  2. Veterans—Employment—United States. I. Title.

UB443 .V56 2001
650.14'086'970973—dc21

                                        00-067427

Printed in the United States of America
9 8 7 6 5 4 3 2 1
First Edition

For more information or to place an order, contact LearningExpress at:
900 Broadway
Suite 604
New York, NY 10003

Or visit us at:
www.learnatest.com

CONTENTS

CHAPTER 8:

CHAPTER 9:

CHAPTER 10:

CHAPTER 11:

Preface

People choose a tour—or a career—in the military for a variety of reasons . . .

- Some like the idea of leaving home to visit or live in other parts of the world.
- Others join the military to help pay for college.
- Still others see military service as a way to earn a living while learning vocational skills.
- Finally, some folks join the armed forces out of a sense of duty and patriotism.

Whatever your reason for considering or joining the military, you're in good company. Some of our nation's most admirable citizens are military veterans of distinction. Senator John McCain, for example, is a former Navy pilot who was shot down over Vietnam and held prisoner for five years by the North Vietnamese. Senator McCain recently rose to prominence during his 2000 bid for the Republican nomination for the presidency. General Colin Powell, after leaving his position as Chairman of the Joint Chiefs of Staff during Operation Desert Storm, is now chairman of America's Promise, one of the nation's most successful community service organizations. America's Promise mobilizes people from every sector of American life to build the character and competence of America's youth.

General Powell and Senator McCain are just two very public examples of people who chose to join the military. But successful military veterans populate mainstream American business as well. For example, Clarence Briggs, a former combat infantry commander, now heads a Fayetteville, NC–based web-hosting business called Advanced Internet Technologies (AIT). Along with a group of his Army buddies, Mr. Briggs founded AIT in 1996. His company was the first to challenge a near-monopoly by another tech firm in the arena of Internet domain-name registration. Today, Mr. Briggs' company hosts more than 100,000 domain names, occupies a 93,000-square-foot office building, and employs more than 100 people, 80% of whom are former military personnel. AIT's business revenue in 2000 was an estimated 15 million dollars.

Last year Mr. Brigg's firm launched a "business incubator." In business, an incubator is a developmental enterprise that trains people with specific niche expertise in the goal of spinning off successful subsidiary businesses. The military is the ultimate people-incubator: It trains experts and equips them with tools for later personal, educational, and financial success. But not every military servicemember takes advantage of that training. This book tells you how *you* can.

The Military Advantage will show you how to make the most of military service— first, by serving your country with honor, courage, and commitment; and second, by taking advantage of civilian education and career opportunities afforded by military service. In the next ten chapters, you'll learn how to:

- Put your best foot forward during your military career
- Earn a college degree while on active duty
- Finance your college education
- Match your military experience with civilian career options
- Market your military skills to civilian employers
- Execute a successful transition from military service to a great civilian job

If you're in the process of deciding whether to join the U.S. Army, Navy, Air Force, Marines, or Coast Guard, you've got an exciting decision on your hands. If you're already serving in America's armed forces, you've got exciting opportunities on your hands.

In either case, this book is for you, so let's get started!

the
military
advantage

CHAPTER 1

What Is the Military Advantage?

FROM EDUCATION TO LONG-TERM FINANCIAL BENEFITS, MILITARY SERVICE OFFERS BIG REWARDS

What is the "Military Advantage"? Armed forces recruiters are trained to answer that question so convincingly that you sign on the dotted line. Maybe your recruiter enticed you with the "thousands of dollars for college" you'd get if you joined the military. Or maybe he tempted you with on-the-job training—in the red-hot field of computer technology, for example. Those selling points for military service may have been recruiter-speak, but in both cases, they also were the truth. Still, the answer to the question "What is the Military Advantage?" is more multifaceted, extending not only into the realms of education and career, but also into personal development and even financial opportunity.

Below, I've outlined four broad categories of advantages the military offers everyone who signs on the dotted line. If you're already serving in the armed forces, keep reading to make sure you're getting your contract's worth. If you're still considering military service, you ought to keep reading, too—you may find something your recruiter didn't tell you.

THE EDUCATION ADVANTAGE

In today's increasingly technical workforce, a college degree can be your gateway to a bright career future. And there isn't a more flexible, cost-efficient environment in which to earn your degree than the U.S. military. You'll learn more about pursuing and financing a college education in later chapters. For now, take a look at the Military Advantage in education.

EDUCATIONAL GUIDANCE

All active duty servicemembers enjoy access to free education guidance counseling through their base or post Education Offices (EO). EO professionals provide assessment and counseling services to help servicemembers chart a course to a college degree. EO professionals also help servicemembers find degree programs that best match their career interests, time constraints, and the logistical requirements of their military jobs.

FLEXIBLE PROGRAMS

Over the past three decades, the Department of Defense has created a host of flexible programs designed to help military servicemembers earn college degrees despite frequent deployments and rapid-tempo operational commitments. Through distance learning, cooperative community college programs, online classes, traditional classroom courses, and even college courses offered aboard ships and submarines, every servicemember can earn college credit while on active duty. The military offers access to an array of degree and training programs that will meet the educational goals of virtually every member. You'll learn more about education options in Chapter 4.

REAL PEOPLE

Air Force Senior Airman Joseph DePorter wanted to earn a B.S. in Finance. Rather than pursue his goal through nontraditional avenues like distance learning or correspondence courses, he attended traditional classroom courses at University Nevada Las Vegas. "I considered nontraditional programs," DePorter said, "but I wanted a more traditional business degree because I like the career itself and wanted to master the subject matter." On the other hand, Bruce

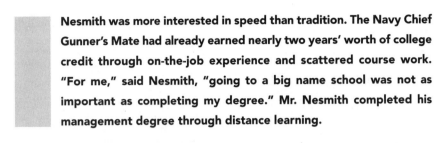

Nesmith was more interested in speed than tradition. The Navy Chief Gunner's Mate had already earned nearly two years' worth of college credit through on-the-job experience and scattered course work. "For me," said Nesmith, "going to a big name school was not as important as completing my degree." Mr. Nesmith completed his management degree through distance learning.

FINANCIAL ASSISTANCE

At this writing, the Montgomery GI Bill (MGIB) program provides military veterans with nearly $20,000 that can be used toward degree and certificate programs, flight training, apprenticeship/on-the-job training, and correspondence courses. The program provides monthly payments for up to 36 months; military veterans can use the funds for up to 10 years after release from active duty. But the MGIB isn't the only way military servicemembers can finance a college education. Tuition Assistance (TA) is a program available to all active duty servicemembers. Through TA, the military will pay for up to 75% of all tuition costs incurred by an active duty member attending an accredited institution. In Chapter 5, you'll learn more about military options for financing a college education.

ON-THE-JOB TRAINING

Whether it's administrative management, computer electronics, or gas turbine repair, every military servicemember is trained in a specific vocational or professional skill. That training—completed while gaining practical work experience—can give technical military job candidates an edge over fresh-from-college civilian job applicants.

"Today's employers want candidates who can hit the ground running," says military career transition specialist Bernard Marstall. "Theory courses offered in college are important. But in technical or industrial maintenance and repair fields, practical work experience will help a job candidate rise to the top of the heap."

THE POST-MILITARY CAREER ADVANTAGE

Thousands of employers have a positive view of candidates who have experience gained during military service. Many also actively recruit veterans for the special skills and work habits they've acquired. Below, the advantages civilian firms find in military job candidates are explained.

PROBLEM-SOLVING ABILITY

In basic training, military members are expected to follow orders and speak only when spoken to. But from the moment they report to their first permanent military assignment, they're trained to take the initiative in tackling problems of all stripes: logistical, operational, and supply. The military is a results-oriented organization that demands rapid, proactive decision making. When confronted with a problem, military members are expected to establish a game plan, marshal the necessary resources—which often are limited—and overcome the challenge. In the civilian economy, that kind of initiative and problem-solving ability equates to dollars saved.

"Employers value veterans' ability to produce solutions," says Joseph M. Land, Sr., a Navy veteran who now works as a civilian career counselor. "A candidate who can solve problems quickly and efficiently can be a valuable asset to a company."

WORK ETHIC

Many employers look for the "soft skills" ingrained in military veterans—skills like courtesy and attention to detail. But the soft skill that tops the wish lists of many hiring managers is the solid work ethic instilled by military service.

"The biggest thing is the military work ethic," said Debbie Dunn, regional manager for the Eastridge Group, a San Diego staffing firm. "Things like attendance and punctuality. Military people tend to have a more disciplined work ethic."

The cornerstones of a solid work ethic are an integral part of military life: respect for authority, a strong sense of duty, punctuality, and diligence are all part of a serviceperson's training. These traits are equally important to the civilian employer, but are not a necessary part of every civilian employee's background or training. A civilian employer can expect a former servicemember to demonstrate these intangible skills. As these skills become less evident in the civilian population as a whole, employers find former servicemembers to be especially desirable candidates.

REAL PEOPLE

Sibia Neurosciences, a biotechnology research firm in La Jolla, CA, was seeking a new senior staff assistant, but the qualities they sought were hard to find all rolled into a single applicant. Not only did the firm want a candidate with solid organizational skills, but also one

who could communicate diplomatically with scientists and managerial personnel. They found their ideal match in Thomas Scott, a former Air Force personnel specialist. Scott had been wondering how his military experience would play in the non-military marketplace. What he learned was that his military experience made him a very attractive candidate.

"I had four interviews the same day," Scott remembers. "Both the human resources coordinator and a company vice-president told me they felt military service instilled good communication and organizational skills. They also said they felt military personnel were very dedicated to their jobs."

ADAPTABILITY

Another soft skill in high demand is adaptability. Human resource managers often screen job candidates for organizational fit, that is, the potential of new hires to fit in at a company, and create maximum productivity with minimum disruption. Military servicemembers, who transfer to new organizations on a regular basis (from an aircraft squadron to a ship to a training unit, for example), are taught to learn policies and procedures quickly at any new unit, and align their actions accordingly. Some civilians mistake this ability to change for lockstep group-think. But many employers recruit military veterans precisely because they are able to adapt to new environments quickly. As one hiring manager at a major U.S. high-tech firm put it: "Around here, you have to be able to turn on a dime."

ADVANCED TRAINING

Armed forces veterans arrive in the civilian job market as some of the most thoroughly trained job candidates around. Your military training involves not only schools and courses related to your particular job specialty, but also training in areas that are hot topics in corporate America, like occupational safety and human relations. For employers, this can mean you're a more well-rounded candidate than someone who just graduated from college with a new degree and no real-world work experience.

ATTENTION TO DETAIL

Even a single military tour can turn a freewheeling individualist into a stickler for details. That's because an "off" moment in combat can cost lives. That's the underlying reason for seemingly nit-picking rules such as how many inches from your eyebrows the brim of your hat must fall. Many civilian hiring managers view such attention to detail—whether it's acquired through experience in meticulous record-keeping or spotless housekeeping—as a great asset, particularly in administrative and technical fields.

TEAMWORK

Here's what happens in boot camp: One guy in the platoon doesn't make his bed properly, so Drill Sergeant A rips the sheets and blankets off everybody's beds while Drill Sergeant B disciplines the entire platoon with a 10-mile hike. As with the emphasis on attention to detail, this kind of military training also has an underlying goal: teaching servicemembers to work together in pursuit of organizational goals. From the moment you first don a uniform, teamwork is a defining principle of military service. Not only do servicemembers learn the concept through practical experience, but also through classroom training in team-building and cooperative approaches to job accomplishment.

Corporate managers value a prospective employee who has demonstrated the ability to work with others, instead of operating as a lone gun.

PLANNING AND ORGANIZING

Even the most junior military personnel are handed project responsibility early in their careers. While such projects may not have far-reaching impact, they still require the member to establish objectives, evaluate resources, create action steps, and plan timelines. Through senior supervision and practical experience, service-members develop the skills required to plan and organize operations and projects that meet organizational goals. In a civilian company, that kind of skill saves both time and money.

SAFETY AWARENESS

Employers pay employees millions of dollars each year for injuries claimed under workmen's compensation insurance. Many such injuries result from preventable on-the-job accidents. Companies also must comply with state and federal occupational safety and health (OSHA) requirements. Compliance efforts can be costly, so a safety-savvy workforce can be a plus to civilian employers. Military personnel receive monthly—sometimes even weekly—safety training. Such continuing awareness of safety regulations and concerns can be a big plus in civilian companies, particularly those involved in hands-on work like manufacturing and technical repair.

SECURITY CLEARANCE

For some employers, finding an employee who can do the job isn't as difficult as obtaining a security clearance for a new hire. In fact, a security clearance can be so expensive and time-consuming that some employers would prefer to hire a candidate with an active clearance, then train him to do his new job, than hire a qualified candidate with no clearance. Even if a high-level security clearance is not of immediate value to a civilian employer, your ability to obtain that clearance shows a civilian employer that you have a clean record.

THE PERSONAL DEVELOPMENT ADVANTAGE

The military is more than just a job. It's a culture, and a way of life. As such, military service can help develop in people a variety of positive characteristics that can have a lifelong impact.

SELF-DISCIPLINE

The United States Marine Corps is world-famous for its emphasis on rigid discipline and strict allegiance to an organizational code. But the Corps isn't the only branch of service that young adults join to gain skills in self-discipline. The other service branches—Army, Navy, Air Force, and Coast Guard—also cultivate self-discipline in their members. Whether it's learning the self-motivation to roll out of bed before dawn, or gaining enough grit to run a mile uphill with a 50-pound pack on your back, the self-discipline gained in military service translates for many into a lifelong habit.

REAL PEOPLE

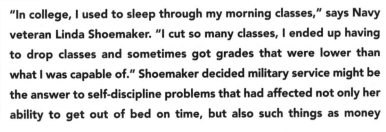

"In college, I used to sleep through my morning classes," says Navy veteran Linda Shoemaker. "I cut so many classes, I ended up having to drop classes and sometimes got grades that were lower than what I was capable of." Shoemaker decided military service might be the answer to self-discipline problems that had affected not only her ability to get out of bed on time, but also such things as money

management and completing projects on deadline. **After eight years of naval service, she still procrastinates on some projects, but "the military helped me learn to plan ahead and get things done on time."**

LIFELONG FRIENDSHIPS

The phrase "old Army buddy" isn't just a cliché. While serving in the military, many people develop friendships that last a lifetime. These relationships often cross cultural and even international boundaries and that's an opportunity many people would never have were it not for the global nature of military service.

TRAVEL

"Join the Navy, See the World" goes an old Navy recruiting slogan. It may have been a slogan, but it wasn't far off the mark. From Italy to South America and from Thailand to Japan, military members are afforded the opportunity not only to visit foreign cities, but also to live in them.

CULTURAL APPRECIATION

A service career ensures that you will work with people from a broad cross section of American cultures, as well as with people from countries around the globe. For today's employers, who must be concerned with equal opportunity and anti-discrimination regulations, the ability to get along with all different types of people is an important trait.

DIVERSE EXPERIENCES

Here's a revelation service members often have when visiting back home after a couple of years in the service: "Everyone here is doing the same old thing." The chain of small towns that connect the American coasts is the backbone of our nation. While small towns offer security and continuity for their residents, they can sometimes limit opportunities for diversified experiences. A military tour or career can open a whole new world of life-shaping work and personal experiences.

THE FINANCIAL ADVANTAGE

The military is not known for stellar rates of pay. But once you ascend above the grade of E-5 (a sergeant in all services, except for the Navy and Coast Guard, where an E-5 is a Petty Officer Second Class), you can make a decent living. And beyond pay, the military offers substantial financial benefits in terms of cost savings on everything from food to health care.

HEALTH CARE

While serving on active duty, comprehensive medical and dental care is available to servicemembers at no cost. It's also available to their immediate families for free or for very little cost (say, $12 for a visit to the family doctor). In an era where non-military families can pay between $300 and $500 per month for health insurance, that's a huge financial benefit. Should you retire from military service, your health coverage will continue at a cost substantially below that of civilian health care plans.

COMMISSARY AND EXCHANGE PRIVILEGES

Shopping in military commissaries—the equivalent of civilian grocery stores—will save you about 30% on your grocery bill. While that may not seem like much if you're single, it will equate to hundreds of dollars annually if you decide to raise a family. And that translates into paycheck money you can spend on something else. For young adults considering or embarking on a military tour, the idea of actually staying in long enough to retire from the armed forces might not even be on the radar scope. But consider for a moment that you might stay on active duty for 20 years. If you do, your continued access to military commissaries, and to base and post exchanges (the equivalent of civilian department stores), will give you access to lower prices on brand-name goods, including high-end electronic equipment, tires, furniture, clothes, even toys for the kids. Plus, at military exchanges, you don't pay state sales tax. On big-ticket items, that perk alone represents significant savings.

VETERANS HOME LOAN GUARANTY

Is buying a home in your future? Under conventional home financing, a buyer must put down between 5% and 10% of the home price to qualify for a mortgage loan. But military veterans are entitled to use the Veterans Administration (VA) Home Loan Guaranty program. The VA guaranty program, designed to protect the lender against loss, is intended to encourage lenders to offer veterans loans with more favorable terms. With the current maximum guaranty, a veteran who hasn't previously used the benefit may be able to obtain a VA loan up to $203,000 depending on the borrower's income level and the appraised value of the property.

Other benefits include the flexibility of negotiating interest rates with the lender and the elimination of monthly mortgage insurance.

The VA Home Loan Guaranty Program is a substantial financial benefit to veterans. When other home buyers are saving for years to scrape together a down payment, veterans are able to proceed to purchase with zero down.

SUMMARY

In this chapter, you've learned why this book is called "The Military Advantage." You've learned about flexible education programs and college financing options. You've read about the military-instilled traits that civilian employers covet. You've learned about personal advantages like travel and exposure to diverse cultures. And you've seen how military service can offer financial benefits that range from health to home. From education to career, from personal development to financial opportunity, the advantages of military service extend far beyond the primarily economic benefits and advancement opportunities usually associated with civilian jobs. In the next chapter, you'll learn how to put your best foot forward in a military career.

CHAPTER 2

Getting In, Moving Up

HOW TO GET YOUR MILITARY CAREER OFF TO A GREAT START

Now that you've read a little about the "Military Advantage," you're ready to find out more. Each year, the U.S. armed forces hire more than 350,000 new enlisted and officer personnel. Do you want to be one of them? If so, you'll need to know:

- What it takes to join the military
- What to consider before you join
- How to succeed once you're in

That's what we'll cover in this chapter.

ENLISTED SERVICEMEMBERS

In order to join one of the five services—Army, Navy, Air Force, Marine Corps, or Coast Guard—enlisted personnel must sign a legal agreement called an enlistment contract. An enlistment contract usually requires:

- Eight years of military service, of which two to six years are spent on active duty with the balance spent in the reserves.
- The military to provide the agreed-upon job, rating, pay, and cash bonuses for enlistment in certain occupations, as well as medical and other benefits, occupational training, and continuing education.
- Enlisted personnel to serve satisfactorily for the specified period of time.

Requirements for each service vary, but certain requisites are the same across all branches. To join the U.S. military, a person must be between the ages of 17 and 35 (17-year-olds must have the consent of a parent or guardian). Air Force enlisted personnel must enter active duty before their 28th birthday. Each enlistee must be a U.S. citizen or immigrant alien holding permanent resident status. Enlistees must have a birth certificate and may not have a felony record. Applicants must pass both a written examination—the Armed Services Vocational Aptitude Battery—and meet certain minimum physical standards such as height, weight, vision, and overall health. All branches require high school graduation or its equivalent for certain enlistment options. In 1999, over 9 out of 10 volunteers were high school graduates. Single parents are generally not eligible to enlist.

ADVANCE RESEARCH

So far so good, right? But hold on: Just because you meet the requirements above doesn't necessarily mean the military is a good fit for you. Before you sign on the dotted line, take some time to research and explore. First, are you cut out for military life? To get a better idea of the answer to that question, see how many of the following questions you can honestly answer with a *yes*.

- Can you accept low starting pay?
- Would you like to be stationed overseas?

- Would you be willing to transfer to a new location at a moment's notice?
- Can you accept long and often irregular working hours?
- If you find you don't like military service, can you accept the fact that you can't just quit?
- Are you willing to travel, sometimes spending extended periods separated from your family?
- Can you be happy living aboard a ship or submarine?

If you answered "yes" to most of those questions, you may be made of the right stuff to flourish in a military lifestyle. But is there a military job that fits your current needs and future goals?

Never jump blindly into just any military job. Such a leap of faith won't necessarily block future success, but it's better to research and plan a military career track before you enter the service. What kind of work interests you? Which service branch offers the most attractive program in that field? Do you qualify for that program? If not, can you go out and get the education and experience you need, then join?

Here's another important question: Does the career field you're interested in have a future—both in the military and in the private sector? What does the promotion track look like? Is there a clear path to higher rank, or is the field top-heavy, making advancement difficult? Don't ask recruiters these kinds of questions—their job is to get you to join, and they may not be too worried about helping you select an upwardly mobile career field. Also, don't rely on websites that promote military service. For example, www.militarycareers.com is an excellent source of military career field information, but the data there is relentlessly positive and does not reflect natural, cyclical changes in promotional opportunities and duty location related to specific career fields.

If you know someone already serving in the military, ask them to help you research current opportunities. School counselors can also be helpful. Another way to find out the current status of career fields is to check with active duty military career counselors working aboard bases and posts. They have access to current career field information. *The Occupational Outlook Handbook*, available at the Bureau of Labor Statistics website (www.bls.gov), also discusses the job outlook for civilian occupations that are related to military jobs. (The next chapter of this book also contains a detailed discussion of which of today's military specialties can lead to a successful civilian career.)

THE ASVAB

Selection for a particular type of training depends on the needs of the service, your general and technical aptitudes, and your personal preference. The military uses an aptitude test, called the Armed Forces Vocational Aptitude Battery (ASVAB), to help determine your placement in a military job. Test scores largely determine an individual's chances of being accepted into a particular training program. Because all prospective recruits are required to take the exam, those who do so *before* committing themselves to enlist have the advantage of knowing in advance whether they stand a good chance of being accepted for training in a particular specialty. If you aren't sure what kind of specialty suits you, it may be a good idea to take the ASVAB first, then go over your career field options with a recruiter. A recruiter can schedule you for the ASVAB without any obligation on your part to then follow through and join the service.

HELPFUL HINT

You can boost your ASVAB score—and broaden your career field choices—by preparing for the test. LearnATest.com offers a complete online practice ASVAB with instant scoring and personalized recommendations to help you improve your score.

SIGNING UP

If you decide to join the military, the next step is to pass the physical examination and sign an enlistment contract. Before signing, be sure you've chosen the enlistment options that are right for you. This includes:

- Length of active duty time
- Monetary bonuses
- Types of training you'll receive (If the service is unable to fulfill its part of the contract, such as providing a certain kind of training, the contract may become null and void.)

Remember, it is *before* you sign the enlistment contract that you're in the driver's seat. So be sure you're taking advantage of all your options. Not sure you want to serve for four years? Check to see if the service branch you've chosen is offering two- or three-year enlistments. (You many want to check with more than one recruiter.) Do you want to be trained as a jet mechanic? Make sure it's written into the contract.

The spoken word of your recruiter does not bind the military after you enlist—only the written contract does. And here's a note to the wise: Recruits without specific occupational training schools written into their contracts receive on-the-job training at their first permanent duty assignment. This is not a particularly good situation. To avoid time spent mopping floors on active duty while trying to get into a particular technical school, sign up for specific training when you enlist.

DELAYED ENTRY

All services offer a "delayed entry program" by which an individual can delay entry into active duty for up to one year after enlisting. High school students can enlist during their senior year and enter a service after graduation. Others choose this program because the job training they desire is not currently available but will be within the coming year or because they need time to arrange personal affairs. Delayed entry can create a useful window during which you can "get your ducks in a row"—including personal affairs and the provisions of your enlistment contract— before you head off to basic training.

WOMEN AND COMBAT

Women are eligible to enter most military specialties. Although many women serve in medical and administrative support positions, women also work as mechanics, missile maintenance technicians, heavy equipment operators, fighter pilots, and intelligence officers. Only occupations involving direct exposure to combat are off-limits to women.

ENLISTED ENTRY AT A GLANCE

Here's a basic rundown on programs under which enlisted members can join the military:

Delayed Entry: **Enlistee can delay entry into active duty for up to one year.**

Buddy Program: **Friends may join together, may be stationed together, and may also enter the service at a higher rank. For example, two sailors joining the Navy under the Buddy Program might enter at the rank of E-2, instead of the normal starting paygrade of E-1. This means they would earn more money from the start.**

Guaranteed Training Enlistment Program: Enlistee is guaranteed a specific training program and military occupation as a condition for enlistment.

Advanced Rank Enlistment Program: Enlistee enters the service at an advanced rank, usually E-2 or E-3, based on prior civilian experience or college education.

Enlistment Bonus: Enlistees who select critical occupational specialties may be eligible for cash incentives for signing.

WHAT NEXT?

Okay, so what happens after you sign the contract? New enlistees head for recruit basic training, also known as boot camp. For 6 to 12 weeks you'll learn military skills and protocols—and probably do a whole lot of push-ups. After boot camp, most recruits head for technical schools where they learn the basic skills for their chosen military occupational specialty. The formal training period generally lasts from 10 to 20 weeks, although training for certain occupations—nuclear power plant operator, for example—may take as long as a year.

JOINING AS AN OFFICER

Officer training in the armed forces is provided through the Federal service academies (Military, Naval, Air Force, and Coast Guard); the Reserve Officers Training Corps (ROTC) offered at many colleges and universities; Officer Candidate School (OCS) or Officer Training School (OTS); the National Guard (State Officer Candidate School programs); the Uniformed Services University of Health Sciences; and other programs. All are very selective and are good options for those wishing to make the military a career.

SERVICE ACADEMIES

Federal service academies (the Naval Academy, Air Force Academy, Coast Guard Academy, and West Point) provide a four-year college education leading to a Bachelor of Science degree. Midshipmen or cadets are provided free room and board, tuition, medical care, and a monthly allowance. Graduates receive regular or reserve commissions and have a five-year active duty obligation, or longer if entering flight training.

To become a candidate for appointment as a cadet or midshipman in one of the service academies, most applicants obtain a nomination from an authorized source (usually a member of Congress). Candidates do not need to know a member of Congress personally to request a nomination. Nominees must have an excellent academic record, college aptitude test scores above an established minimum, and recommendations from teachers or school officials. They must also pass a medical examination. Appointments are made from the list of eligible nominees. Appointments to the Coast Guard Academy, however, are made on a competitive basis only, and nomination is not required.

COLLEGE GRADS AND DIRECT COMMISSIONING

Armed forces recruiters often visit colleges seeking students near graduation who are interested in joining the military. Students pursuing technical degrees, such as mathematics or computer science, are highly sought after by officer recruiters. But liberal arts degrees may also be acceptable depending on armed forces manning levels. (Students interested in joining the military may also visit recruiting offices to learn what types of degrees recruiters are currently seeking.) College graduates can earn an armed forces commission by joining the military, then completing a 13-week OCS or OTS program in the Army, Navy, Air Force, Marine Corps, Coast Guard, or National Guard. After completing training, newly commissioned officers generally must serve a specific period of obligated service on active duty. Here are some specifics regarding different kinds of officer entry:

- People with training in certain health professions may qualify for direct appointment as officers. In the case of health professions students, financial assistance and internship opportunities are available from the military in return for specified periods of military service.
- For professionals already trained and qualified to serve in other special duties, such as the judge advocate general (legal) or chaplain corps, direct appointments also are available.
- Commissioned officers in each branch of the armed forces may also take advantage of flight training. In addition, the Army has a direct enlistment option to become a warrant officer aviator.

SUCCEEDING ON ACTIVE DUTY

Few people would dispute the idea that the military is a terrific stepping-stone to future civilian success. In fact, that's one way the government attracts and recruits our all-volunteer force. Meanwhile, military service members who do sign on the dotted line commit to doing an important job: That is, making the strongest and most respected military force on the planet even better. Career military members sometimes resent soldiers, sailors, airmen, and marines who are only marking time until their degrees are complete and their contracts are up. This chapter is about staying focused on the present while keeping one eye on the future. Here are five tips to help you manage your military career for active-duty success.

1. APPEARANCES COUNT: KEEP YOUR UNIFORM SHARP

Even in the private sector, maintaining a sharp professional appearance has its advantages. It can affect the way peers, superiors, and subordinates perceive you—even the way they relate to you. In the military, a sharp appearance may be even more important.

"The first way I judged a soldier's professionalism was by the way he wore his uniform," says former Marine Corps Captain David Gerweiner. "My evaluation didn't end there, but that's where it usually began."

It may sound like judging a book by its cover, but Gerweiner isn't the only one who feels that way. Military members serving in leadership roles often say they can tell a lot about servicemembers' self-image, sense of commitment, and even organizational skills, by the appearance of their uniforms. The details of this part of military life might be hard for newer servicemembers to get used to. To see things like haircut regulations, the way shoes are laced and shined, or the proper placement of ribbons and pins as important may seem, well, a little ridiculous. But there's purpose behind it.

"It's about creating a cohesive unit," notes Gerweiner. "It's about attention to detail, and the right and wrong way to do things." Those concepts translate into other realms—safety, for example. An aircraft mechanic who's consistently sloppy in the way he looks may also be sloppy about work habits. And while a misplaced uniform ribbon won't kill anyone, a misplaced wrench might.

Set the example for your military co-workers: Use your uniform to project a sharp, professional image.

2. BE A TEAM PLAYER

"Teamwork is the thread that keeps the military community tied together," says former Army helicopter pilot Bill Gaul, president of the Destiny Group, a San Diego-based military-to-civilian career transition firm. "A true sense of camaraderie is developed and encouraged as soon as you enter the military; it's reinforced throughout your career."

Indeed, team building is a key to the success of the U.S. military. During peacetime, every project and mission accomplished—from mundane maintenance tasks to complex multi-service training exercises—is the result of a team effort.

In order to be an effective coach or leader, says Gaul, you must also know how to be a team player: "Whereas business schools may stress the importance of individual contributions, the military training you receive recognizes the synergy of a well-trained team, working together toward a common goal. The responsibilities you learn while in the military as part of a team make you much more mature than your civilian counterpart at a much younger age." Make sure that you are a team player in all aspects of your military career.

3. BUILD PROFESSIONAL KNOWLEDGE IN YOUR OCCUPATIONAL SPECIALTY

There are people who know their jobs, and then there are those who not only know their jobs, but who constantly strive to improve the depth and breadth of their professional acumen. The military provides a variety of opportunities to build your professional know-how. Local and service-wide training manuals exist for nearly every job specialty, as do other manuals and publications that go beyond the basic knowledge needed to accomplish the daily routine. In addition, the military offers advanced formal training in a variety of career fields, as well as peripheral training—like leadership classes or inventory management—that can enhance professional depth across a range of fields.

Often overlooked by servicemembers, such training—as well as study pursued on an individual basis—can help you develop the ability to solve complex technical problems, develop new solutions for your work team, and meet requirements for qualification and promotion early and with distinction. Your peers and superiors will appreciate that kind of professionalism—and that appreciation is sure to show up in written evaluations of your performance.

"Strive to become a 'recognized expert,'" says former Air Force Master Sergeant Jim Lowell. "Be the person in your unit that people turn to when they need reliable answers on questions important to mission accomplishment."

4. PURSUE OFF-DUTY EDUCATION AND SPECIAL PROGRAMS

The military encourages off-duty education to foster post-military success; but service leaders also know that educated soldiers, sailors, airmen, and marines contribute to a more well-rounded military force. Special duty programs, such as special operations, recruiting, warrant officer, and commissioning programs can also build your career, distinguishing you as a professional who stretches beyond required minimums.

Here are some examples of special programs:

- **Special operations** teams take on dangerous and difficult missions, including offensive raids, demolitions, intelligence, search and rescue, and other missions from aboard aircraft, helicopters, ships, or submarines. Due to the wide variety of missions, special operations forces team members are trained swimmers, parachutists, and survival experts, in addition to being combat trained.

- Each year, the military services enlist approximately 200,000 young men and women. Attracting young people with the kinds of talent needed to succeed in today's military is a large task. **Recruiting specialists** provide information about military careers to young people, parents, schools, and local communities. They explain service employment and training opportunities, pay and benefits, and service life.

- **Warrant officers** are technical and tactical leaders who specialize in a specific technical area; for example, one group of warrant officers is Army aviators. Although small in size, they've got big responsibilities: Warrant officers receive extended career opportunities, worldwide leadership assignments, and increased pay and retirement benefits.

Remember: Attending college and undertaking special programs not only helps build your career, it helps build a better military.

5. BE A TEN-PERCENTER

In the civilian world, there's a saying: 10% of the people do 90% of the work. In the team-oriented structure of the military, nine out of ten workers seldom get a free ride. Still, it's true that some servicemembers are more motivated than others to excel.

"Be a ten-percenter," advises Danny Vincent, a Navy air traffic control chief stationed aboard the USS *Boxer*. Vincent says being a "ten-percenter" means taking the initiative to solve problems, improve procedures, and accomplish tasks on or before deadline. It means pursuing extra responsibilities, planning and prioritizing with skill and foresight, and performing top-quality work. "Be the person," says Vincent, "that others can count on to do the job right every time."

SUMMARY

In this chapter, you've learned the basics about joining the military, including the differences between enlisting and entering the service as a commissioned officer. You read about basic requirements like age, health, and citizenship. You also learned the different channels through which officers and enlisted personnel can enter the service, as well as what to look for in an enlistment contract. Finally, you learned a few basics about what it takes to build a successful armed forces career. In the next chapter, we'll take a look at how to choose a military career field that will help you build a future civilian career.

CHAPTER 3

Choosing a Military Career Field

SELECTING A MILITARY CAREER PATH THAT BUILDS TOWARD A POST-MILITARY FUTURE

More than 1.2 million people serve in the U.S. armed forces. Whether serving for a single tour or a 20-year career, every one of them learns real-world skills that will later transfer well into the civilian job market. Even members serving in combat occupations that seem to have no civilian equivalent learn valuable soft skills, like punctuality and a solid work ethic, or support skills, like record-keeping, workplace safety, and systems maintenance.

To get those skills in the armed forces, you have to select a specific job, or what the military calls an occupational specialty. With scores of military occupational specialties to choose from, how do you make your pick? Personal aptitudes and interests will, of course, narrow down your choices considerably. For example, you'll learn below that the health care field is one of the hottest career fields in the country—and will be for some time to come. But if you have absolutely no inclination to work in a health-related or medical profession, it won't matter to you how many jobs are available. You're simply not cut out for that kind of work.

Still, though your interests and natural aptitudes may reveal what you don't want to do for a living, you still may not have a clear picture of what you do want to do. If that describes you, you may want to undertake a little comparison shopping before selecting a military career field.

First, we'll look at broad occupational categories available across some or all service branches. Then, we'll examine civilian job market projections extending through 2008. By comparing the two, you may be able to select a career that not only suits your interests and aptitudes now, but that will also translate into a great post-military career.

MILITARY OCCUPATIONAL GROUPS

Both officers and enlisted service members can work in any of the career fields described below. In most cases, enlisted members E-1 through E-6 perform the daily, hands-on technical tasks associated with the work described. Senior enlisted personnel at the ranks of E-7 through E-9 manage and supervise operations, plan budgets, and oversee mission accomplishment at division and department levels. Commissioned officers working in the fields below plan and direct mission accomplishment at the division, department, and organizational levels.

Administrative—Administrative occupations include records maintenance, reporting, and file maintenance in specialized areas such as finance, accounting, legal, maintenance, or supply.

Combat specialty—Combat occupations, such as those involving artillery, infantry, and special forces, normally specialize according to the type of weaponry or combat operation involved. For example, the Army employs artillery specialists, the Marine Corps employs tank gunners, and the Navy trains and deploys special operations personnel called SEALs.

Construction—Military construction occupations include personnel who build or repair buildings, airfields, bridges, foundations, dams, and other structures. All kinds of trades and technical specialties are represented in this job category, including carpentry, electrical work, plumbing, and metalworking. The construction occupations also include engineers and other degreed building specialists, both of which are usually commissioned officers.

Electronic & electrical equipment repair—Personnel working in these occupatio.. specialize according to equipment type. The military employs people as electronic and electrical equipment technicians working in all kinds of fields, including avionics, communications, computers, weapons systems, and navigational aids.

Engineering, science and technical—In this occupational category, members specialize in areas like information technology, space operations, environmental health and safety or space operations.

HELPFUL HINT

If you're already serving in the military and are not happy in your current field, it still may not be too late to make a change. Under many circumstances, active duty members can change occupational fields. Those circumstances vary widely among service branches and individual occupational specialties. If changing active duty career fields is something you'd like to consider, check with your unit, department, or command/post career counselor for guidelines that apply to your situation.

Health care—In this field, enlisted personnel assist degreed medical professionals, providing clinical and administrative support. They may work in patient care, assisting doctors, dentists, and nurses. Or they may perform technical and administrative tasks like operating diagnostic equipment, conducting laboratory analyses, dispensing medications, or maintaining medical records. Officers in this field provide specialized health services including patient examination, diagnosis and treatment, therapy, and rehabilitative treatment. Note: The Marine Corps does not employ its own health care workers, but obtains health care services from Navy personnel.

Human resource development—In this field, specialists recruit, train, and place qualified personnel. Armed forces recruiters, for example, provide information to the public about what it's like to serve in the armed forces. Personnel specialists collect and record information about pay, training, job assignment, health, and promotions. Training specialists provide instruction in both job-specific and general topics. Officers working in the human resources field plan for military manpower needs and development policies related to military personnel.

Machine operator and production—Technicians and craftsmen working in this field operate industrial equipment, machines, and tools that fabricate or repair structures, materials, and equipment. For example, a welder may manufacture metal parts for a ship or submarine. They may also operate ships' boilers, nuclear plants, or gas turbines.

Media and public affairs—Personnel working in the media and public relations field develop and disseminate information about military personnel and operations through a variety of print and broadcast media. Some work as journalists, covering military events for base or post newspapers; others work in public affairs offices, acting as liaisons between the public and specific military units. Public relations specialists may also act as foreign language interpreters and translators.

Protective services—Protective service personnel provide security for military installations and enforce military law. They may work as security guards, base police, or in military correctional facilities. Some protective service workers specialize in criminal investigation or disaster management.

Support service occupations—People working in support service occupations provide subsistence services like food preparation, housing management, and counseling. Religious program specialists are considered part of the support specialist occupational group. Support services support the morale and well-being of military members and their families.

Transportation and material handling—Personnel who work in this field ensure that cargo and passengers are transported safely via aircraft, ship, or auto. From gunboats to heavy trucks, they operate all kinds of different vehicles and vessels. People involved in cargo transport also learn to operate material-handling equipment like cranes and forklifts.

Vehicle and machinery mechanics—The American military is one of the largest consumers of equipment in the world. It takes thousands of mechanics to maintain and repair it all. The military employs aviation mechanics, heavy equipment mechanics, powerhouse mechanics, marine mechanics, and mechanics who repair heating and cooling systems, just to name a few.

Officer Occupational Groups—Military officers sometimes work in an occupational group classified as executive, administrative, and managerial. These personnel oversee and direct military operations in areas like finance, accounting, health, administration, and supply. An additional occupational category for officers is the professional specialty category. Officers in these occupations work in fields that would be considered professional, white-collar occupations in the private sector. Examples of such jobs include attorney and engineer.

That's a general overview of available military job specialties. Your next step: Compare available military careers with growing private sector professions.

HOT CIVILIAN CAREERS

Since the late 1990s, corporate recruiters have been struggling with a tight labor market, meaning there are more job openings than qualified workers to fill them. The Bureau of Labor Statistics's (BLS) employment projections released in December 1999 characterize the U.S. economy as marked by "moderate growth, low unemployment, and improving productivity" that will continue to spin off new jobs for workers at all educational levels. How many new jobs? More than 20 million by 2008.

But more jobs doesn't mean more available workers. Across the nation, employers are struggling to find enough good employees, and that's good news for service members in career transition. Exit the military with solid training and a marketable skills set, and that tight labor market may mean for you a short job search.

But what constitutes a marketable skills set? Obviously there is more demand for some types of workers than for others. Check out the table on page 28: It shows 20 promising career choices culled from the BLS's projections of the 30 fastest-growing occupations and the 30 jobs with the largest numerical growth. Then, read on to learn specifics about hot fields for the coming decade.

THE BIG JOB PICTURE

According to the BLS, professional specialty occupations, like teachers, counselors, computer engineers, and healthcare occupations are projected to grow the fastest and add the most jobs. Technicians and related support occupations also will mushroom during the coming decade.

The fastest job growth will occur in jobs requiring an associate's degree or higher. While jobs requiring at least a two-year degree accounted for just 25 percent of all jobs in 1998, by 2008, they account for 40 percent of all job growth.

TOP 20 MILITARY CAREERS

OCCUPATION	NUMBER OF JOBS HELD		AMOUNT OF CHANGE		QUARTILE RANK	REQUIRED EDUCATION AND TRAINING
	1998	2008	# OF JOBS	%		
Computer Technology						
Systems analyst	617,000	1,194,000	577,000	94	1	Bachelor's degree
Computer support specialist	429,000	869,000	440,000	103	1	Associate's degree
Computer engineer	299,000	622,000	323,000	108	1	Bachelor's degree
Computer programmer	648,000	839,000	191,000	29	1	Bachelor's degree
Healthcare						
Registered nurse	2,079,000	2,530,000	451,000	22	1	Associate's degree
Medical assistant	252,000	398,000	146,000	58	3	Moderate-term on-the-job training
Education						
Teacher, secondary school	1,426,000	1,749,000	322,000	23	1	Bachelor's degree
Teacher, elementary school	1,754,000	1,959,000	205,000	12	1	Bachelor's degree
College or university faculty	865,000	1,061,000	196,000	23	1	Doctoral degree
Social & Human Services						
Social worker	604,000	822,000	218,000	36	2	Bachelor's degree
Social & human service asst.	268,000	410,000	142,000	53	3	Moderate-term on-the-job training
Protective Services						
Correctional officer	383,000	532,000	149,000	39	2	Long-term on-the-job training
Financial Services						
Securities, commodities, and financial services sales agent	303,000	427,000	124,000	41	1	Bachelor's degree
Management						
General manager or executive	3,362,000	3,913,000	551,000	16	1	Work experience + bachelor's degree
Engineering, natural science and computer information systems manager	326,000	468,000	142,000	44	1	Work experience + bachelor's degree
Administrative/Clerical						
Office and administrative support manager	1,611,000	1,924,000	313,000	19	2	Work experience in related occupation
Blue Collar						
Truck driver, light and heavy	2,970,000	3,463,000	493,000	17	2	Short-term on-the-job training
Blue-collar worker supervisor	2,198,000	2,394,000	196,000	9	1	Work experience in related occupation
Sales and Marketing						
Marketing & sales supervisor	2,584,000	2,847,000	263,000	10	2	Work experience in related occupation
Legal						
Paralegal and legal assistant	136,000	220,000	84,000	62	2	Associate's degree

*Quartile rank indicates which quarter of all wage earners this particular job's salary falls under (by 1999 median hourly

"Technological advances are driving this market," says Mimi Collins, communications director with the National Association of Colleges and Employers. Employers see college graduates as "more trainable and technologically savvy" than non-college job applicants. "In a tight labor market, employers are snapping up educated candidates who show aptitude and training them for specific tasks, even though their degree may not be in a field related to a particular opening. And technical people have something else going for them—their skills are up-to-date."

COMPUTER-RELATED OCCUPATIONS

Computer-related positions top the list of growing degreed occupations. (For example, the number of computer engineers is projected to double by 2008.) The computer industry is, of course, the fastest growing industry in the national economy. As the price of computer equipment falls, more businesses are expanding their computerized operations, creating a need for employees who can manage such technology. Expanding Internet technologies and subsequent integration into most areas of commerce also is fueling a rising demand for skilled professionals who can develop and support Internet, Intranet, and web applications. In addition, the increasing number of information management applications (such as customer databases used by financial services institutions) is creating demand for staff who can manage those systems.

Available openings in computer-related jobs are expected to more than double over the next seven years, reaching 3.5 million by 2008. Analysts attribute the job boom to advances in technology, falling technology prices, and the pervasive influence of the Internet across nearly every industry. Even in manufacturing, where overall job growth is slowing to a crawl, more than four out of ten new workers who are hired to support goods-production will be computer systems analysts, engineers, and scientists.

Below are descriptions of two computer-related private sector occupations, as well as the job prospects in those careers over the next seven years.

COMPUTER SUPPORT SPECIALISTS

Computer support specialists provide technical assistance, support, and advice to customers and users. They troubleshoot and interpret problems and provide technical support for hardware, software, and systems. In addition, computer support specialists use automated diagnostic programs to detect and analyze system malfunctions. Employers prefer candidates for these positions to hold an associate's degree, but solid work experience in a related occupation is also a strong selling point. By 2008, more than twice as many computer support specialists will work in the United States than did in 1998.

COMPUTER PROGRAMMER

Computer programmers write, test, and maintain the programs that run computer systems. Programmers are often grouped into two broad categories. *Applications programmers* usually focus on business, engineering, or science. They usually write code designed to handle a specific job within an organization. *Systems programmers* maintain and control computer systems software, making changes in how the overall system processes information, and controlling the operation of peripheral components like printers or individual workstations.

The number of programming jobs in the United States is expected to grow by nearly one-third during the next decade. But as computer technology has become more sophisticated and the complexity of programming has increased, so have employers' expectations. Conventional programming languages like COBOL have been edged out by advanced function- and object-oriented languages like Java, C++, and Visual Basic. Job prospects for programmers will be best for college graduates who are up to date on the latest technologies. But prospects will be even better for candidates who have both a degree and cutting edge experience. Military candidates who plan ahead are in a great position to offer both.

RELATED MILITARY OCCUPATIONS

How does military experience with computers apply? The U.S. military is one of the largest consumers and storehouses of computer data in the world. As a result, an increasing number of military job specialties involve computer programming, engineering, operation, and repair. Some military specialties translate directly into the civilian marketplace; some are more easily marketed in the private sector when bolstered by corollary civilian certifications. Here are examples of military jobs that can prepare you for a civilian career:

COMPUTER SYSTEMS OFFICERS

- Prepare data processing plans and budgets
- Develop and monitor contracts for data processing equipment and services
- Translate military objectives and needs into computer systems requirements
- Design and maintain computer software and databases
- Plan and oversee the installation of new equipment
- Direct teams of computer systems specialists and computer programmers

COMPUTER PROGRAMMERS

- Determine and analyze computer systems requirements
- Code programs into current computer languages
- Design, test, and debug computer programs
- Review and update old programs as new information is received or changes are needed

COMPUTER SYSTEMS SPECIALISTS

- Identify computer user problems and coordinate to resolve them
- Install, configure, and monitor local and wide area networks, hardware, and software
- Compile, enter, and process information
- Provide customer and network administration services, such as passwords, electronic mail accounts, security, and troubleshooting

REAL PEOPLE

Tom Phillips offered employers the best of two worlds. The former Army radio/communications security technician launched his job search three months before leaving the service in November 1998. "Most recruiters were looking for technicians with five years of experience or a two-year degree," says Phillips. "I had both." The first day he applied for technical openings via e-mail, 20 eager employers wrote back to say they were interested. Phillips says he had colleagues who were transitioning at about the same time he was. The difference? They had technical experience, but no degree. The result? They got hired, too—but at substantially lower salaries.

CORRECTIONS

The BLS projects substantial job growth in the field of corrections. The number of correctional officers is expected to grow nearly 40% to more than half a million by 2008. Correctional officers supervise people who are incarcerated in local and county jails awaiting trial or who have been convicted of a crime and are serving sentences in jails, reformatories, or penitentiaries. Some correctional officers work for the Immigration and Naturalization Service, overseeing detainees and criminal aliens. Correctional officers have no law enforcement responsibilities outside the institution where they work.

The BLS projects not only thousands of new jobs for correctional officers, but also thousands of openings in existing jobs. Many such openings will be generated by high employee turnover. Understandably, the work can be stressful. Correctional institutions sometimes find they have difficulty attracting and keeping quality employees because of the difficult nature of the work and relatively low salaries. The middle 50% of corrections officers earned between $22,930 and $37,550. However, the upper end of that range can be quite competitive considering that most jobs in the field are concentrated in rural areas with low costs of living.

Some military members, particularly those that are interested in work related to law enforcement, may find corrections to be an attractive career field. No college degree is required and federal, state, and local corrections departments provide training for new hires. A number of military occupational specialties provide good preparation for the field. The armed forces employ active duty police and security forces to protect lives and property on military bases. The Coast Guard patrols U.S. coastal waters, apprehending smugglers and illegal immigrants. Here are two examples of military jobs that would provide excellent preparation for corrections work:

LAW ENFORCEMENT AND SECURITY OFFICER

- Direct the enforcement of military law
- Supervise the arrest, custody, transfer, and release of offenders
- Plan and direct criminal investigations and investigations of suspected treason, sabotage, or espionage
- Plan for the security of military bases and office buildings and direct security procedures
- Manage military correctional facilities

LAW ENFORCEMENT AND SECURITY SPECIALIST

- Guard correctional facilities and conduct searches of inmates, cells, and vehicles
- Perform fire and riot control duties
- Investigate criminal activities and activities related to espionage, treason, and terrorism

Most civilian applicants in the corrections field have had no opportunity to gain prior experience. Clearly, former military law enforcement and security specialists are in a great position to outshine competing job candidates.

SOCIAL SERVICES

Social work is an attractive field for people who want to make a positive difference in the lives of others. Due to an aging population, continuing interest in crime prevention, and the need for professional intervention in the lives of AIDS patients, the mentally ill, and families in crisis, employment in the social services field is expected to grow much faster than the average in other industries. For example, the BLS projects a one-third increase in the number of social workers and an increase of 56% in the number of human service assistants.

SOCIAL WORKER

Social workers help clients who face a life-threatening disease or social problems like inadequate housing, unemployment, serious illness, substance abuse, or, in the case of children, neglect or abuse. They counsel clients and refer them to other agencies that can provide assistance with specific needs. School social workers help parents, teachers, and students cope with problems. Today, many social workers provide services in health care settings run by managed care organizations (HMOs). About four out of ten work for government agencies. The minimum educational requirement for a social worker is a bachelor's degree in social work, but advanced degrees are quickly becoming the standard for many positions. Master's degrees in social work are necessary for positions in health and mental health settings. In addition, demand has increased for social workers with specific certifications such as Licensed Clinical Social Worker (LCSW).

HUMAN SERVICE WORKERS AND ASSISTANTS

Many people would love to work in a helping profession like social work, but don't have the time to complete the necessary college degrees. Human service workers and assistants work with many of the same types of people in need, but provide services on a less clinical level. Such workers can be employed, for example, as case management aides, social work assistants, substance abuse counselors, life skills counselors, or gerontology aides. Human service workers and assistants work in most of the same settings as do social workers, including psychiatric hospitals, rehabilitation programs, health care settings, and residential- and day-treatment programs. A bachelor's degree is usually not required for such positions, but employers do look for applicants with relevant work experience or education beyond high school. The military can provide both.

RELATED MILITARY OCCUPATIONS

While the armed services employ civilian social workers and counselors such as those who work in the Navy's Family Service Centers, the military trains and employs active-duty social workers, caseworkers, and counselors who perform many of the same functions. Military social workers generally are commissioned officers, but caseworkers and counselors can come from the enlisted ranks.

MILITARY SOCIAL WORKERS

- Counsel military personnel and their family members
- Supervise counselors and caseworkers
- Survey military personnel to identify problems and plan solutions
- Plan social action programs to rehabilitate personnel with problems
- Plan and monitor equal opportunity programs
- Conduct research on social problems and programs
- Organize community activities on military bases

MILITARY CASEWORKERS AND COUNSELORS

- Interview personnel who request help or are referred by their commanders
- Identify personal problems and determine the need for professional help
- Counsel personnel and their families
- Administer and score psychological tests

- Teach classes on human relations
- Keep records of counseling sessions and give reports to supervisors

Military social workers, caseworkers, and counselors receive from 8 to 26 weeks of formal training. Such training, added to any earned degrees, plus practical on-the-job counseling experience can help make military applicants attractive to civilian social services employers.

HELPFUL HINT

Some service members in transition need to add real-world credibility to their resumes, but don't have the time to invest in a degree program. There's good news: Some community colleges offer certificate programs that can be completed by taking as few as three courses. For example, California's Orange Coast Community College offers electronics-related certificates for working technicians—one in microcomputer repair, and another in testing and troubleshooting. Check with admissions counselors at community colleges in your area to learn whether a certificate program is available that might spruce up your professional knowledge—and your resume.

TEACHING/EDUCATION

The number of jobs for teachers is expected to grow steadily through the coming decade. While growth percentages are not as steep as in some other career fields, the BLS projects about 200,000 new teaching jobs at the elementary school, college, and university levels. More than 300,000 new positions will emerge in secondary schools. While public school teachers must hold at least a bachelor's degree, complete an approved teacher credentialing program, and be licensed, many states offer alternative licensing programs for hard-to-fill positions.

At the elementary and secondary levels, teachers provide the tools and environment for students to learn foundational academic subjects like mathematics, language, social studies, and science. In addition, teachers at these levels instruct students in other subjects like athletics, music, art, and the use of computers. Special education teachers provide instruction for students with a variety of disabilities. For all elementary and secondary school teachers, the job outlook varies by geography and subject specialty. Some locations, like inner cities and remote rural areas, have a tough time recruiting and keeping good teachers. Teachers with licensure in advanced fields like chemistry and physics are also hard for many school districts to find. According to the BLS, teachers with multiple subject certifications—particularly in math and the physical sciences—who are willing to go where the jobs are will be valued candidates in the country's educational system.

At the college level, instructors are more specialized. Not only do they teach students in narrow disciplines (mathematics, physical science, or literature, for example), but they also keep up with developments in their field—or even create developments in their field through research and the preparation of scholarly papers. College and university faculty also consult with business, government, and community organizations. Job prospects at the college and university level will be better in fields like computer science, engineering, and business where instructors, who are often qualified for (and accept) lucrative nonacademic jobs, are more scarce.

RELATED MILITARY OCCUPATIONS

The military provides a wide range of training and education for its members. Military personnel, usually commissioned officers, teach classes in such academic subjects as engineering, physical science, social science, and nursing. Enlisted military instructors teach subjects that are related to their military occupations specialties, and also general subjects like leadership and management, safety, and substance abuse prevention.

MILITARY TEACHERS AND INSTRUCTORS

- Develop course content, training outlines, and lesson plans
- Prepare training aids, assignments, and demonstrations
- Deliver lectures
- Conduct laboratory exercises and seminars
- Give tests and evaluate student progress
- Diagnose individual learning difficulties and offer help

Experienced military instructors who hold at least bachelor's degrees in particular academic fields must, in most cases, complete state teacher certification and licensing programs in order to apply for jobs at the elementary and secondary levels. This is not true at the college and university level, however, where subject matter expertise and teaching experience alone can get a candidate hired, at least on an adjunct (or part-time) basis. Non-degreed military instructors who wish to pursue teaching at any level should consider pursuing a bachelor's degree while still on active duty.

TROOPS TO TEACHERS

The Troops-to-Teachers program seeks to improve American education by providing "mature, motivated, experienced, and dedicated personnel for the nation's classrooms." Translated into plain talk, that means American public schools want *you*, the military veteran. Troops-to-Teachers provides counseling and assistance to help military servicemembers identify employment opportunities in education, as well as teacher certification programs.

All military and Coast Guard personnel, reservists, veterans, Department of Defense, and Department of Education civilian employees who did not separate prior to October 1, 1990, are eligible to receive support under this program. If you want to teach academic subjects, you must have a bachelor's degree. Candidates who wish to teach vocational subjects (like electronics, computers, or construction trades) are not required to have a degree, but must be able to document their skill level and expertise. For more information on Troops-to-Teachers, visit the website at www.doded.voled.mil.

SELF-EMPLOYMENT

Ever dreamed of owning your own business? More and more workers are choosing that option. As companies increasingly hire outside vendors to accomplish everything from advertising and public relations to research and payroll, more and more Americans are finding ways to earn a living by supplying a service niche. The niches are varied: The BLS says the number of self-employed executive, administrative, and managerial workers will increase by 361,000, and more than 500,000 service workers and professional specialty workers will call themselves their own boss by 2008.

RELATED MILITARY OCCUPATIONS

Many military trades and technical fields could translate to self-employment. Computer technicians, machinery repairmen, security systems installers, and construction workers all have successfully launched businesses as contractors or self-employed technicians and repair persons. A servicemember with administrative experience could start a secretarial or resume service. A person with experience overseeing military occupational safety and health programs could market himself as an occupational safety and health consultant. One note: Before deciding to open your own business, check with professional associations to see what kinds of certifications and licenses the civilian world requires of consultants and businesses operating in your field.

Today's technology, including remote communications and electronic delivery of services, makes self-employment a real possibility, even for people who don't have a lot of start-up money. For more information on self-employment, visit the Small Business Administration website at www.sba.gov and the Service Corps of Retired Executives (SCORE) at www.score.org.

HEALTHCARE

The number of available jobs in the healthcare field is skyrocketing. Of the top 20 fast-growing jobs, 8 are in healthcare. According to BLS economist Douglas Braddock, the trend reflects several economic factors including an aging population, increased demand driven by advances in medical technology, and a wealthier citizenry that can afford better care. Some developments, like Medicare caps and the spread of managed care, will curtail job growth in certain healthcare sectors (general practice physicians in private practice, for example). But alternative delivery occupations like nursing aide and home health aide, which decrease in-patient care and office visits, will blossom as a result. In addition, a variety of technical positions will see rapid growth, including audiologists, nuclear medicine technologists, and occupational therapists.

REGISTERED NURSE

The position of registered nurse (RN) is the largest healthcare occupation of all, with more than two million jobs. At a projected growth rate of 23% over the next decade, the field is expected to add nearly half a million new openings. That makes registered nurse one of the top ten largest-growth occupations in the country.

Registered nurses provide direct patient care, promote health, prevent disease, and help patients cope with illness. They work as health educators, teaching and interacting with families and patients and serving as community health advocates. Registered nurses may have different specialties and work environments. For example, *office nurses* work in physicians' offices, surgicenters, and clinics, while *public health nurses* work in government and private agencies and places like schools and retirement communities.

In all states, nurses must graduate from a nursing program and pass a national licensing examination. In 1998, there were more than 2,200 entry-level RN programs.

MEDICAL ASSISTANT

Like the position of RN, the medical assistant profession is expected to be one of the top ten fastest-growing career fields during the coming decade. Medical assistants perform routine clinical and administrative tasks. Growth in the field will be driven by an increase in the number of full-service outpatient medical facilities (like clinics and group practices) that need the flexibility a medical assistant can offer by providing both clinical and administrative services.

Clinical duties, which can range from recording vital signs to performing on-site lab tests, vary according to what the law in each state allows. Administrative duties include greeting patients, completing medical histories, updating and filing medical records, completing insurance forms, and billing and bookkeeping. Most employers prefer to hire graduates of medical vocational schools. Former military medical personnel can use military education benefits to enroll in such schools and emerge with both the necessary civilian education and years of practical work experience.

RELATED MILITARY OCCUPATIONS

The military also employs registered nurses. All hold the same types of degrees and certifications as civilian RNs. Military RNs often are able to cross directly into civilian nursing. The hospital corpsman is another type of patient-care provider in the military.

HOSPITAL CORPSMEN

- Examine and treat patients
- Interview patients and record their medical histories
- Take patients' temperature, pulse, and blood pressure
- Prepare blood samples for laboratory analysis

- Keep health records and clinical files up to date
- Give shots and medicines to patients

Performing many of the same functions as a licensed practical nurse or LPN, corpsmen often require very little additional training to become certified civilian LPNs. And they have a world more experience than most LPNs coming straight from academic nursing programs. Some corpsman enter RN programs while on active duty.

In addition to nursing duties, enlisted medics and hospital corpsmen may specialize in a wide range of medical technology specialties, such as cardiovascular technician, dietetic technician, laboratory technician, physical therapy assistant, radiologic technician, and many others. Many of these fields will also afford military candidates stellar career opportunities in civilian health care.

Enlisted military medical workers may also specialize as medical records technicians.

MEDICAL RECORD TECHNICIANS

- Fill out admission and discharge records for patients entering and leaving military hospitals
- Assign patients to hospital rooms
- Prepare daily reports about patients admitted and discharged
- Organize, file, and maintain medical records
- Type reports about physical examinations, illnesses, and treatments
- Prepare tables of medical statistics
- Maintain libraries of medical publications

SUPERVISION AND MANAGEMENT

Half a million more management professionals will enter the American workforce in the next decade. These management professionals hold more titles than meet the eye. There are, of course, chief executive officers. But executive vice president, owner, partner, office manager, or superintendent are all also job titles that fall into this category.

GENERAL MANAGERS AND TOP EXECUTIVES

The responsibilities of top managers include setting goals and policy for an organization, either at the corporate or departmental level. Some managers oversee the effectiveness of a company in a specific area, such as property management, sales, purchasing, finance, information management, or administrative services.

Most military officers and senior enlisted members perform these kinds of duties. In the private sector, most employers prefer to hire managers who have both a bachelor's degree and work experience in the industry in which the company does business. Some military management jobs—such as management of property, information, or administrative services—translate well into the private sector. Still, military members who are interested in pursuing high-level civilian management jobs should seek part-time or volunteer opportunities in private sector industry.

Facility manager is another type of management position that the BLS says will experience strong growth through 2008. Facility managers plan, design, and manage the physical workplace. Their jobs include operations and maintenance, project planning and management, facility safety communication, quality assessment, and human and environmental factors. Again, most officers and senior enlisted military members will gain experience in one or several of these management areas. Unlike those hiring general managers and executives, employers seeking facility managers don't necessarily require candidates to have a bachelor's degree.

Still, a degree is helpful. One mistake servicemembers often make is planning to pursue "some type of management job" after their service careers. If you plan to stay in the military long enough to gain management experience, plan a little further ahead: Earn at least an associate's degree and arrange to lock in some real-world experience in a specific industry.

BLUE-COLLAR WORKER SUPERVISORS

Though this profession is expected to grow more slowly than other occupations, at a rate of just 9% through 2008, we include it here for two reasons: 1) Even at such a small growth rate, the sheer number of workers in the field will yield nearly 200,000 new jobs over the next decade; and 2) Huge numbers of military members are well qualified to land in one of those jobs.

Blue-collar worker supervisors manage workers, equipment, and materials to elicit maximum productivity. They also:

- Ensure that machinery is set up correctly
- Schedule or perform repairs and maintenance work

- Create work schedules
- Maintain production and employee records
- Supervise the work of other technicians and craftsmen
- Monitor work progress and quality

Military members in literally hundreds of occupational specialties perform precisely the same duties. Technicians and craftsmen in the armed forces who enjoy their trades may want to move into civilian supervisory positions after completing their military careers.

HELPFUL HINT

For more detailed information on specific occupations, check out the *Occupational Outlook Handbook (OOH)* on the BLS website at www.bls.gov. The online version of the *OOH* is searchable by industry and by specific occupations. To compare civilian occupations with military occupations, search for careers that interest you at www.militarycareers.com. Sponsored by the Department of Defense, militarycareers.com provides information on hundreds of military occupations, including job duties, training provided, and special requirements like health status and education.

LAW

PARALEGAL AND LEGAL ASSISTANT

Because paralegals increasingly perform many legal tasks formerly accomplished by attorneys, the profession is expected to grow by an astonishing 62% over the next decade. Paralegals assist attorneys in a variety of ways, including:

- Preparing for closings, hearings, trials, and corporate meetings
- Investigating the facts of cases and ensuring all relevant information is considered
- Identifying appropriate laws, judicial decisions, and legal articles
- Analyzing and organizing information relevant to cases and preparing written reports

- Assisting corporate attorneys with matters related to company employees, finances, or any pending corporate litigation

RELATED MILITARY OCCUPATIONS

The military employs active duty legal specialists and court reporters to assist military lawyers and judges. Such specialists perform legal research, record legal proceedings, and prepare legal documents. In addition, they:

- Research court decisions and military regulations
- Process legal claims and appeals
- Interview clients and take statements
- Prepare trial requests and make arrangements for courtrooms
- Maintain law libraries and trial case files
- Type text from stenotyped records, shorthand notes, or taped records of court proceedings
- Prepare records of hearings, investigations, court-martials, and courts of inquiry

Military legal assistants complete six to ten weeks of instruction in legal terminology and research techniques, preparing legal documents, high-speed transcription, and military judicial processes. Some civilian paralegals gain their education through on-the-job training. But an increasing number of law offices prefer graduates of postsecondary paralegal training programs. While the legal knowledge and technical skills of a military legal assistant might not transfer directly into the practice of civilian law, the military member has a distinct advantage: the opportunity to pursue postsecondary paralegal training while on active duty, then market that professional certification along with years of on-the-job legal know-how.

SUMMARY

In this chapter you've learned what military occupations are available. You've also learned how those jobs compare with civilian jobs projected by the Bureau of Labor Statistics to grow over the next decade. By comparing the two, you can chart for yourself a military occupational path that promises to lead to a successful post-military career. In the next chapter, we'll discuss options for pursuing a college degree while serving on active duty.

CHAPTER 4

Get with the Program

EARNING A COLLEGE DEGREE ON ACTIVE DUTY

Fact: According to the U.S. Bureau of Labor Statistics, jobs requiring at least a two-year college degree accounted for just 25% of all jobs in 1998. But by 2008 they'll account for 40% of all job growth.

Fact: In a recent survey by the Information Technology Association of America and Virginia Polytechnic and State University, 83% of companies say they require bachelor's degrees for all or most computer-programming positions.

Fact: In 1999, Michigan State University researchers surveyed 320 employers to find out which ones planned to hire college graduates. Fully half of employers surveyed said they planned to hire more candidates with degrees than they had the year before.

"There will be more job opportunities for students in the future," says Philip Gardner, director of the Collegiate Employment Research Institute at Michigan State, "especially for students that have the academic credentials employers are looking for."

The question is, what are you doing about your academic credentials?

If you're waiting to finish your military career before you start your college education, you're throwing away thousands of dollars—literally. Yes, you may have signed up for the Montgomery GI Bill. And yes, you may have $40,000 in college cash waiting for you at the end of your service career. But did you know the military will also pay for you to attend college while you're still in? That's right: Through a program called Tuition Assistance, the military will pay for 75% of your tuition expenses for every accredited college course you take while on active duty.

Look at it this way: For every dollar you spend on your own education, the military will pay three more. So, for every $100 you don't spend on college while on active duty, you're throwing away $300 to which you're entitled! But no one is going to make you enroll. Pursuing a college degree while on active duty takes initiative, and you're the one who must initiate the process.

This chapter will help by teaching you:

- College terminology and types of degrees
- How to get started on your active-duty college education
- What military programs are available to assist you

IT'S A FACT

The Department of Defense Directive, "Voluntary Education Programs for Military Personnel," establishes that tuition assistance will be made available for personnel serving in all branches of military service. Under Tuition Assistance (TA), a service member pays 25% of tuition costs and the military pays the other 75%. As of April 2000, the annual TA limit for any one servicemember during one fiscal year is $3,500. Tuition assistance will be covered in detail in Chapter 5, but for now crunch these numbers: Under the current TA limits, you'd pay less than $1,200 for $4,600 worth of college education!

NO EXCUSES

"But," you may be protesting, "I'm going to constantly be relocating and going TDY or TAD (temporary, short-term assignments to locations other than your permanent station). I work weird hours and I'm working hard to get qualified in my new job assignment. By the time I'm qualified, it'll be time to transfer again and I won't have time to start school."

Those are all good excuses not to get started on a college education. But they're still just that: excuses. Thousands of senior servicemembers retire every year after making those same excuses for 20 years. Know what? Those veterans—with 20 years of experience in everything from personnel management to information technology—have a tough time getting good jobs, for the reasons mentioned at the beginning of this chapter. Employers are looking for degreed job applicants to fill their prime openings.

"Technological advances are driving this job market," says Mimi Collins, communications director with the National Association of Colleges and Employers. Employers perceive "students coming out of college [as] more trainable and more technologically savvy" than their noncollege job market competitors. "In a tight labor market, employers are snapping up educated candidates who show aptitude and training them for specific tasks, even though their degree may not be in a field related to a particular opening."

Another incentive to attend college is that it increases your promotion and pay potential while you're still serving on active duty.

All the excuses in the world won't change the civilian job market once you get out. Fortunately, the military has set up education programs that work around the hardships that generate those excuses. For the constantly deployed student, there is distance learning. For the continually transferred student, there are portable degree plans. For those who work the graveyard shift, there are college classes offered online 24 hours a day.

So the military has your time and money bases covered. In other words, there is no good excuse not to enroll in college. So let's get started.

EDUCATIONAL LINGO

As you enter the postsecondary world of professors, semester hours, and GPAs, certain terms will come up again and again. Call it academic jargon or call it "edspeak," here are a few definitions you'll need to know as you go along.

Accreditation. Accreditation is something like the Good Housekeeping Seal of Approval. It refers to the system of reviewing and recognizing educational institutions for a particular level of performance, integrity, and quality. When a school is "accredited," it means it has earned the confidence of the educational community and the public. Since there is no universal accrediting body in the United States, accreditation can sometimes factor into transferability. The nature of a school's accreditation affects its reputation and the perceived value of degrees it confers. There are numerous accrediting bodies, but there are six regional bodies that are the most widely respected and accepted in the educational community. Those regional institutional accrediting bodies are:

- Middle States Association of Colleges and Schools (MSA/CHE)
- New England Association of Schools and Colleges (NEASC-CIHE)
- North Central Association of Colleges and Schools (NCA)
- Northwest Association of Schools and Colleges (NASC)
- Southern Association of Colleges and Schools (SACS)
- Western Association of Schools and Colleges (WASC Sr./Jr.)

Don't be afraid to ask about a school's accreditation. It's better to find out that school's standing in the educational community before you take courses there than to take courses there and find out later that they won't transfer to another school of your choice.

HELPFUL HINT

Some professional or specialized programs have their own accrediting bodies. For example, the American Bar Association grants accreditation to law schools. These forms of accreditation may sometimes be more important than regional accreditation. If you are entering a professional or specialized education program, check with professional associations in that field to learn which accreditation future employers value most.

Semester Hours vs. Quarter Hours. Most colleges and universities operate on either a semester system or a quarter system. The semester system is a lot like most high schools' systems, with a fall semester and a spring semester. When an institution also offers a summer semester, the entire program is known as a "trimester" system. Schools operating on the quarter system break the academic year into four parts, typically named for seasons of the year (fall quarter, winter quarter, and so on).

Most schools measure their courses in terms of "hours"—either "semester hours" or "quarter hours," depending on how the school arranges its academic year. The list below describes the basic differences between the quarter system and the semester system.

THE SEMESTER SYSTEM

- A typical course is worth three hours' credit, though this varies widely.
- To earn a bachelor's degree in a traditional semester program, a student would typically take 15 hours' credit (usually five courses) each semester.
- A student completing a degree on the semester system would generally attend two semesters per year for four years to complete the 120 semester hours required for a baccalaureate.

THE QUARTER SYSTEM

- A bachelor's degree earned on the quarter system normally requires 180 quarter hours.
- To earn a B.S., a student would need to complete about 45 quarter hours during each year of college.

So, you may be asking, what's the big deal?

For the traditional, go-to-one-school-and-graduate-four-years-later student, the difference between quarter and semester hours isn't a big deal. But for you, the college student serving on active duty, the difference can wreak havoc with your educational efforts. Military students tend to amass credits from numerous schools and a variety of nontraditional sources like work experience and testing. Adding them all up at the end can be a little like counting pies with slices missing to find out how many whole pies you have—you may not end up with an even number. Because quarter and semester hours do not necessarily translate one-for-one, the military student approaching degree completion can find himself one-half of one semester hour short of the number of total hours required to graduate. That could mean devoting a whole extra quarter or semester—and the accompanying cash—to taking an entire three-hour class just to make up the half-hour difference. The moral here: While navigating the tricky waters of military educational pursuits, it's critical to keep track not only of the number of courses you're taking, but also what type of credits you're earning.

Residency. Most colleges and universities establish residency requirements. Residency means that, in order to earn a degree from a particular school, you must actually complete a minimum number of courses given by that school, notwithstanding how many transfer credits you may have. Residency is important to colleges for a number of reasons. First, when a school confers a degree upon a student, the institution is guaranteeing that the student has been educated according to that school's standards. Second, colleges charge students money for their classes. It wouldn't make financial sense for a school to allow a student to spend the bulk of his or her education dollars at another institution, then transfer in at the last minute so that the receiving college awards the degree.

Residency and transferability are no big deal for most traditional students, who may attend one, maybe two schools at most. But for military students, who often attend as many schools as they have fingers, issues of residency and transferability must always be kept at the forefront when charting a course to a degree.

Transferability. "Transferability" refers to whether or not credit you've earned will be accepted, or transferred, to your college transcript, by a receiving college when you change schools. For example, a college might set limits on the number of credits you can transfer in, or rule out a specific course because its content doesn't meet that college's standards. Transferability is of primary importance to the part-time military student, who will probably attend multiple schools during the course of earning a degree. While charting your course to a degree, it's important to carefully examine transferability each step of the way. Failure to do so can result in wasted time, wasted money, and the necessity of repeating courses you've already completed in some other form.

TYPES OF DEGREES

For the purposes of this book, we'll consider three main types of degrees: associate's, bachelor's, and master's. In a traditional college program, those degrees take approximately two, four, and six years respectively to earn. But regardless of the *chronological* time normally required to earn a particular degree, each requires a specific number and type of credit hours. Here's a basic overview:

There are three broad categories of college courses: general education, major courses, and electives:

- Most colleges have general education requirements, mandated either by the state or an accrediting body. General education normally includes basic subjects like math, English, oral communications, social studies, and science. These studies form the foundation of most degrees, regardless of a student's major, or specialized field of study.
- Major courses are those that a student is required to take in order to earn a specific degree. For example, a computer science major might be required to complete Introduction to Programming, Java, and C++.
- Electives are courses that enrich your college experience by letting you branch out and take classes that may not be required for your degree, but that you just find interesting. Most degree programs have a certain number of credit hours set aside for electives.

Associate's, bachelor's, and master's degrees each require successively more—and more specialized—courses. Here's how they break down:

- *Associate's degree* = 60 semester hours (SH), or 90 quarter hours (QH). Typically, half of these credits must be general education courses, and the other half a mixture of major courses and electives.
- *Bachelor's degree* = 120 SH (180 QH). A student pursuing a bachelor's degree (or baccalaureate) may or may not have completed an associate's degree first. If he or she has, some (or all, if the student's planned right) of the associate's degree coursework may count toward completion of the bachelor's degree. A bachelor's degree usually includes 30 hours of general education, 60 hours of major courses, and 30 hours of electives. Some programs are more rigorous and require more major courses and fewer electives.
- *Master's degree* = Number of credit hours varies. While both associate's and bachelor's degrees fall into a category called undergraduate education, the master's degree is the first graduate-level program. Master's degree candidates, who must already have completed a bachelor's degree, normally go through a rigorous application procedure in order to be accepted to a school's program. Pursued full-time, most master's degree programs take from two to three years to complete.

EDUCATION OFFICES: WHAT THEY CAN DO FOR YOU

Military students who launch their college careers without first stopping to map out their route can end up wasting both time and money backtracking or redirecting their educational programs.

Fortunately, the military has provided a one-stop shop for its members who aspire to college degrees. Your base or post education office (EO) offers absolutely everything you need to chart an efficient, economical course to a quality degree.

HELPFUL HINT

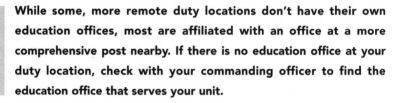

While some, more remote duty locations don't have their own education offices, most are affiliated with an office at a more comprehensive post nearby. If there is no education office at your duty location, check with your commanding officer to find the education office that serves your unit.

WHAT'S AVAILABLE

The degreed civilian professionals at your EO have comprehensive knowledge of military education resources, the financial benefits available for your college education, and can also help you explore your career options. Here are some of the ways they can assist you.

COLLEGE PLANNING

- Your EO can help you decide what type of degree program is right for you. Do you need a bachelor's degree to create your best future, or will an associate's degree be enough for your particular field? Are you able to attend traditional classroom courses, or does the nature of your military duty require more creative alternatives? Have you already earned a significant amount of college credit, or do you need a degree program that starts from scratch? These are all questions that counselors at your EO can answer. All you have to do to take advantage of their expertise is to make an appointment with them.
- Your EO will evaluate and document your military educational experience. A form called the DD-295 serves as an official transcript of

your military training and experiences. Many colleges will award you credit based on training and education you complete in the military. For example, if you've already completed a military meteorology course, a college may count that as general science credit. Or, if you've completed a military leadership course, you may earn management credits. Sometimes, colleges will award you elective credit for some of your military training. In order to earn *any* credit from military educational experiences you must first have a DD-295 to submit to the college or university where you're enrolling. Your EO will help you get that form prepared.

• Your EO will evaluate your military work experience in view of college credit. Did you know you are eligible for college credit simply for having done your military job? For more than 50 years, the American Council on Education (ACE) has produced publications that have been the standard for recognizing on-the-job learning acquired by service-members and translating that learning into equivalent college credits. These ACE guides (there's a version for every service branch) offer detailed descriptions of every military occupational specialty, along with ACE's specific recommendations on the number and type of credits colleges ought to award servicemembers based on the details of those job responsibilities.

For example, the ACE recommends that a Navy Electronics Technician First Class (E-6), who has trained and served as an instructor, be awarded 42 semester hours in academic categories like science, teaching, and management. Would that sailor actually receive those credits? That depends on the policies of the institution where he or she applies. A student may receive some, all, or none of those credits. But certain schools, like those in the Service Members Opportunity Colleges network described later in this chapter, are very generous about awarding credit for military work experience. Your education office will help you document your experience so that the college you apply to can evaluate it for credit.

• Your EO will show you which colleges and universities offer the type of degree program in which you're interested. After helping you evaluate your educational experiences to date, and how your military experience may translate to college credit, your EO can help you choose the college or university that best meets your need. Your EO carries manuals describing literally thousands of programs offered by colleges, universities, and vocational schools.

Examination Programs: Your EO offers examination programs that can help you earn college credit. You'll learn more about those, including DANTES and CLEP exams, later in this chapter.

Career Exploration: Don't know what you want to study because you're not sure which postmilitary career you'll pursue? Your EO offers career-exploration tools. Your EO can administer a variety of interest surveys and career assessment resources including:

- The Holland Self-Directed Search
- The Kuder Occupational Interest Survey
- The Strong Interest Inventory
- The Myers-Briggs Type Indicator
- Campbell Interests and Skills Survey

The Kuder, Holland, Strong, and Campbell surveys are designed to help you learn your aptitudes and interests and find out how your aptitudes mesh with specific occupations. The Meyers-Briggs Type Indicator helps identify your personality type. This information may give clues to your ideal work environment by indicating how you fit in with others on a work team.

HELPFUL HINT

Most military servicemembers put off exploring options for a post-military career until late in their service careers. By that time, most use the resources offered by base or post career transition centers. But, while transition centers can help servicemembers transition out of the military into civilian jobs, they do not help members get the education and training they may need to land the job of their dreams. Now is the time to start planning your second career, and your EO is the place to do it. By using your EO *early* to help you in postmilitary career planning, you won't face the struggle faced by many servicemembers: arriving at the end of your military career unprepared for a successful civilian one.

Adult Education: Did you struggle in high school, or just feel you may need some assistance in academic basics like reading and math before moving on to college? Your EO can plug you in to adult basic education classes. Once you complete the classes, your EO can administer basic tests to prove your accomplishments to any college that requests it.

Certification Materials: Let's say you're a mechanic and would like to seek national certification in your field. Your EO offers test preparation guides for a variety of national certification exams, including:

- Automobile Technician
- Medium/Heavy Truck Technician
- Engine Machinist
- Collision Repair and Refinish Specialist
- Parts Specialist

In a vocational career field, becoming a nationally certified professional can make the difference between an employer hiring you—or the other guy.

Distance Learning: Your EO can direct you toward programs that can help keep you moving toward a college degree no matter how often you move around the globe. There are dozens of nationally accredited distance learning programs that offer courses you can complete without ever setting foot in a traditional classroom. Your EO can help you decide which one is right for you. Distance learning is covered in more detail later in this chapter.

TWO BIG MISTAKES

"There are two huge mistakes military students often make," says former Navy education counselor Linda Henry.

Many servicemembers, she says, put off enrolling in college because they haven't yet decided on a major. "Not a good move," says Henry. "While you make up your mind, your time to complete a degree while you're still in the service is flying by. Instead, consider taking transferable general education courses from a reputable school. You'll almost certainly need them for whatever major you eventually decide to pursue."

The other mistake is just the opposite: deciding, "Hey, I'm going to start on my degree!", then enrolling willy-nilly in a random batch of classes. "That's a little like taking off on a cross-country driving trip without first pulling out a map," Henry says. "Without advance planning, you may run out of time and money before you reach your destination."

That's where your military education office comes in. No matter which branch of the military you're serving in, your base or post education office is your absolute, no-excuses first stop on your journey toward a college education. Not only can your education office help you chart the most efficient path to a quality degree; it can save you a lot of time—and maybe most importantly—a lot of money.

NONTRADITIONAL EDUCATION

If it weren't for nontraditional education, many servicemembers wouldn't be able to get an education at all. But what is nontraditional education? It might help to first define traditional education. Traditional education means attending daytime classes in an on-campus classroom, having a live instructor, juggling books, homework, and class schedules, taking midterms and finals, and receiving—if all goes well—a decent grade report at the end of the term.

Nontraditional education is everything else. And for the military servicemember, everything else covers a wide range of options. As a servicemember, you can earn credit through testing, through military courses you've already taken, and simply by having certain levels of expertise in your occupational specialty. Since most servicemembers are part-time students and regularly move from one spot on the planet to another, such options can mean the difference between having the time to earn a degree while on active duty—or not.

WHAT'S OUT THERE

Credit through examination: Ever wished you could just prove you know enough about, say, freshman English, to avoid sitting through an entire semester of it? Good news: You can! Military base education offices offer two types of testing that can earn you college credit. The first is called CLEP, which stands for College Level Examination Program. A nationally administered program, CLEP tests come in two types, General and Subject exams. CLEP General exams cover general education requirements taught in the first year at most colleges. Your ability to pass a CLEP General exam shows, theoretically, that you already possess the knowledge that most colleges would teach in such a course. Each of the five General CLEP exams— English, Social Science, History, Science, and Math—is worth six credit hours of college credit. These General exams, if accepted by a receiving college, typically satisfy requirements for the first two semesters of study in that particular discipline. For example, a student who passed the CLEP General exam for English would be considered already to have passed two semesters of freshman English. (Note: Different schools treat CLEP exams differently; more on that below.)

CLEP Subject examinations cover other courses typically taught during the first and second years of college. CLEP Subject exams are generally worth three credit hours each.

Military education offices administer a second type of testing for college credit: DANTES exams. DANTES (Defense Activity for Non-Traditional Education Support) publishes more than 100 subject examinations. Topics, which run the gamut from technical to artistic, include subjects as diverse as Foundations of Gerontology and the History and Interpretation of English Literature. (A complete listing of available DANTES examinations is included in the back of this book.) The number of college credits you can earn for each test vary according to the depth of the subject matter and the scope of the test.

Why test for credit? Testing for credit works well under a number of circumstances.

- Some students take a CLEP or DANTES test when they are just a credit or two shy of completing a degree and don't want to commit the time or money to sitting through one class for an entire term.
- Others test for credit when a course they need for their degree program isn't available to them through other, traditional means because of duty location or commitments.
- Still others take tests when they simply, as mentioned earlier, have a lot of accumulated knowledge in a particular subject area.

But beware: Policies on accepting tests as credit vary widely from one institution to another. For example, while most schools accept some types of credit by examination, very few accept all available tests. Further, let's say you pass the CLEP General exam for English and enroll at a school that awards you credit for it. If you transfer to another school, that credit doesn't necessarily transfer with you. Your new institution will reevaluate that CLEP exam based on its own credit-granting standards. If that school doesn't accept CLEP tests as credit and you want to earn your degree at that school, you could find yourself required to take freshman English in your senior year.

Your military education office can provide you with study guides for both CLEP and DANTES exams. Both types of exams are free to active duty servicemembers.

Distance Learning: Colleges and universities have long offered correspondence courses, in which students received instruction through books or tapes, then completed and mailed in assignments and exams. Distance learning operates on the same principles, but includes a greater number of educational delivery channels, most notably the Internet. Now, in addition to courses in print, and on audio- and videotape, you can take classes in which lessons are posted on a school's website; you communicate with your instructor via e-mail.

Another Web-enabled option: courses taught live in online chatrooms. Suddenly, it doesn't matter whether you're stationed in Iowa or the middle of the Indian Ocean. You can sit in on live college courses and receive instruction in real time. That's precisely why distance learning is an indispensable option for some service members stationed in remote locations. Without it, their educational pursuits would grind to a halt every time they deployed or were put on a bizarre work schedule that didn't allow time for classes.

But distance learning isn't for everyone. Studying and learning independently requires self-motivation and the ability to meet incremental goals and deadlines. If you're the type who puts everything off until the last minute, or who can't produce without supervision, distance learning may not be for you.

If you do consider distance learning as a way to earn credit, remember: Alternative course delivery is offered by both traditional and nontraditional schools. If your military responsibilities will often take you far afield, shop around for a school that either offers its own distance learning options or will accept transfer courses you complete via distance learning through other institutions.

Experiential credit: As discussed earlier in this chapter, many schools award servicemembers college credit for experience obtained in their military occupational specialty.

TRADITIONAL OR NONTRADITIONAL EDUCATION: THE PROS AND CONS

The opportunity is out there: A degree can be earned, in large part, through training you've already completed, testing, and other nontraditional options like distance learning. In a very real sense, you could graduate from college without ever setting foot in a college classroom. But once you've earned a degree in this way, how will employers screening resumes view it? And if you go on to apply to a traditional graduate school, how will master's program admissions counselors evaluate the worth of a heavily nontraditional degree? Is one degree as good as another?

"From an academic standpoint, people in the admissions field may be a little skeptical about some nontraditional degrees," says Dwana Broussard, a guidance counselor at Nellis Air Force Base, Nevada. "In some cases, the curriculum may not be as strong, especially when the program targets working adults who want to update their knowledge, or earn a degree for career advancement."

University of Colorado at Boulder professor Margaret Eisenhart said a non-traditional bachelor's degree would be "a slight, but not insurmountable detraction" for an applicant to her institution's master's program. Deborah Losse, associate dean of the Arizona State University's graduate college, says her staff would screen an applicant's nontraditional transcript to "see whether the courses and time spent looked similar to other [traditional] university programs." Losse recommends that servicemembers considering going on to master's programs contact grad schools they might attend to see how a nontraditional degree would be evaluated—before completing their bachelor's degree through nontraditional means.

As for future employers, some look harder than others at whether your degree comes from a "name-brand" school. For many companies, a degree is more a checklist item than a quality issue. But Jim Beirne, director of university recruitment for Minneapolis-based General Mills, said he views all elements of a candidate's prior life experience as an indicator of future performance. Beirne says a degree from a school known for awarding credit for nontraditional educational experiences might not cause a job candidate to be screened out. But the candidate would need to have other strong points for General Mills to screen him in.

In general, students who plan to enter professional fields like teaching, medicine, or law should try to enroll in more traditional college programs. Also, students who plan to enter postmilitary careers not related to their military specialty would do better to attend schools that offer substantial classroom and practicum time, since they won't have related work experience to bolster their resumes. If either of these scenarios applies to you, check with potential employers to find out how they view nontraditional curricula—before settling on a degree program.

OPPORTUNITY KNOCKS: SERVICE MEMBERS OPPORTUNITY COLLEGES

Worried about enrolling in college because you know you're going to transfer soon or often? Do you want to enroll, but fear losing credits you've already earned because of school residency requirements? The military has those—and other—bases covered with Service Members Opportunity Colleges. Through SOC, about 1,300 colleges and universities offer servicemembers educational advantages that help overcome the special difficulties associated with pursuing a degree while in military service—like changing duty assignments and transferring credits.

All SOC schools agree to abide by a set of guidelines designed to preserve credit earned by servicemembers. Since military personnel are often forced to attend numerous schools because of the mobile nature of their military careers, SOC schools agree to:

- Limit the amount of course work students must take at a single college to no more than 25% of degree requirements.
- Design transfer practices to minimize loss of credit and avoid duplication of course work.
- Award credit for military experience as recommended by the American Council on Education.
- Award credit for national testing programs such as CLEP and ACT-PEP.

The SOC program, which is administered from Washington, D.C., is your military education "agent," working as a liaison between the Department of Defense and higher education organizations and institutions across the country.

While all SOC schools agree to abide by the four general requirements outlined above, about one in ten also belongs to one of three degree networks, each of which is specific to the Army, Navy, or Marine Corps. The Air Force, which awards credit for military schools and experience under the Community College of the Air Force program (CCAF), participates in SOC, but does not have its own degree network. (You'll learn more about CCAF later in this chapter.) Air Force members may, however, participate in the networks of other service branches.

SOC degree networks provide service members with a global stepping-stone to a degree. You can enroll at one home college, then take courses at any other school within the network—whether at a school's actual campus or at an overseas adjunct facility—without fear of losing credits. Courses you take at any network college are accepted by your home college, then integrated into your transcript.

Once you successfully complete six credit hours at your home college, the real progress begins. You can then request an official evaluation of your prior learning experiences, including military schools and military work experience. Your home college will award you college credit based on recommendations published by the American Council on Education. For example, boot camp counts toward physical education requirements. Technical training you completed to enter your military job specialty may count toward math or science credits, and so on. Your home college may, according to its transfer policy, also accept some or all of any college credits you've earned.

All of this information will then be integrated into a student agreement, or degree plan. Your student agreement will show how much of your degree you've already earned through both traditional and nontraditional means, as well as which requirements you still need to meet. A student agreement, which is valid within your service's degree network until graduation, is a critical tool that helps you:

- Find the shortest path to degree completion.
- Avoid duplicating credit already earned through work experience.
- Avoid wasting time and money taking classes that won't count toward your degree.
- Choose nontraditional or distance learning options when your military duties make traditional classroom courses unavailable.
- Keep moving steadily toward degree completion no matter how many times you transfer.

Most SOC colleges require students to establish academic residency with them in order to receive that school's degree. This means a servicemember must take 25% of his or her degree program with the home college.

Nearly 30 associate's and bachelor's degree programs are available within the SOC networks. Students who want to pursue a curriculum not currently offered within a network may request to participate in SOC as a "Non-Network" student. Using this option, SOC colleges can offer the same evaluation and guarantees as they do for networked curricula.

COMMUNITY COLLEGES

Community colleges are a great solution for servicemembers who are trying to determine "the next step" in their education. More than 10 million students—or 45% of all U.S. undergraduates—populate the country's 1,100-plus community colleges. Such schools award nearly half a million associate's degrees and 300,000 two-year certificates each year.

Community colleges are a good deal for servicemembers for three main reasons: atmosphere, flexibility, and cost.

Norma Kent, communications director at the Washington, D.C-based American Association of Community Colleges, says community colleges emphasize a "warmer, more welcoming atmosphere." Such responsiveness works well for military servicemembers, who are often new in town or returning to school after a lengthy layoff. Since classes are generally smaller than at four-year institutions, instructors can provide more personal attention to each student.

Community colleges also offer what Kent calls a flexible, user-friendly environment. The average age of students at two-year institutions nationwide is 29, and many attend school while holding down full-time jobs. To accommodate working students, including active duty servicemembers, most community colleges offer a wide selection of evening and weekend classes. Compressed or "mini" semesters also work well for servicemembers who need to squeeze in a course or two between operational commitments. Many community colleges work closely with education offices at area military bases, and often offer courses on bases and posts.

For many servicemembers, cost is a big hurdle to pursuing off-duty education. Community colleges are a great way to get started on a degree program without breaking the bank. According to the American Association of Community Colleges (AACC), the average annual tuition for a full-time student is $1,518—a fraction of the cost of four-year colleges. But, like 64% of all community college students, most military servicemembers attend school part-time and will pay per-class tuition rates.

Still, per-class rates are microscopic compared to four-year schools. For example, the San Diego Community College system charges just $13 per unit for in-state residents—that's less than $40 for a three-unit class. And many community colleges will extend in-state tuition rates to active duty servicemembers.

To learn more about community colleges in your area, visit your base or post education office, or see "Schools" in your area Yellow Pages. Also, see the resources section at the end of this book.

CCAF

While Air Force members are eligible for all the same benefits as those in other service branches, they also have a little something extra going for them: the Community College of the Air Force (CCAF). CCAF is the largest multicampus community college in the world. With more than 119 affiliated schools and 7,000 faculty members in locations all over the planet, CCAF offers enlisted members of the Air Force, Air National Guard, and Air Force Reserve an opportunity to earn an associate's degree in applied science without cost. The program is designed so that members can earn a degree even while frequently relocating due to changing duty assignments.

CCAF is accredited by the Southern Association of Colleges and Schools/Commission on Colleges. Each degree program relates directly to an Air Force Specialty Code (AFSC), which means each is specifically related to an individual career field. CCAF offers 66 degree programs in five career fields:

- Aircraft and missile maintenance
- Electronics and telecommunication
- Allied health
- Logistics and resources
- Public and support services

Degree programs require a minimum of 64 semester hours, most of which you can earn through training and work experience acquired while serving on active or reserve duty, or while serving in the Air National Guard. For example, physical education credits are satisfied by completion of basic training; career field-specific technical education is satisfied by completion of entry-level and advanced technical courses within a servicemember's Air Force specialty. CCAF enrollees may meet general education requirements, like oral communication, math, and social science, by taking courses at regionally accredited schools and transferring them to CCAF, or through testing. Servicemembers who meet degree requirements at civilian institutions must pay for those courses as required by the individual institution. Often, Tuition Assistance (TA) can be used to offset these costs. (More on TA in Chapter 5.)

Air Force members may enroll in CCAF after being assigned an AFSC. From the time of enrollment, students have six years to complete their degree. To learn more about CCAF visit your base education office or the CCAF website at www.au.af.mil/au/ccaf.

SUMMARY

In this chapter you've learned college terminology and why concepts like residency and transferability are important to military students. You've learned what options are available for military servicemembers to pursue a college degree, including community colleges, distance learning programs, and Service Members Opportunity Colleges. You've read about base and post-educational offices and how they can work for you. In addition, you've learned the difference between traditional and nontraditional education. Hopefully, with all that knowledge under your belt, you have no excuses left to postpone college.

In the next chapter, we'll discuss a topic in which most college students are keenly interested: how to pay for it.

CHAPTER 5

Financing College

HOW TO PAY FOR COLLEGE WHILE YOU'RE IN THE SERVICE—AND AFTER YOU'RE OUT

You've heard the recruiter pitches: Join the military! Get $40,000 for college! Maybe that's even why you joined. But did you know that even though that $40,000 is waiting for you when you leave the service, there are many other sources of financial aid you can tap—some while you're still on active duty?

FINANCING COLLEGE ON ACTIVE DUTY

ACTIVE DUTY OPTION 1: TUITION ASSISTANCE

Tuition Assistance (TA) is the best option for active duty college financing. Through TA, the military will pay for 75% of your tuition expenses for every accredited college course you take while on active duty. That means you only have to spend $500 to get $2,000 worth of education. Or, to put it another way, for every dollar you don't spend on your own education while on active duty, you're throwing away three matching dollars!

All servicemembers (officers, warrant officers, and enlisted) on active duty, and Army National Guard and Army Reserve members on active duty, are authorized to participate in the TA program. In fiscal year 1999, the Department of Defense implemented a Tuition Assistance (TA) policy that is uniform across all the military services. Servicemembers may receive a maximum total yearly amount of up to $3,500 at a rate of 75% of tuition costs, or up to $187.50 per semester hour, whichever is less.

HOW TO GET TA

Before obtaining TA, you usually must visit your base or post education office. After discussing your educational goals and plans with a counselor, you can obtain tuition reimbursement through a series of easy steps. The nature and order of the steps involved may vary by service branch and duty location, but the following general procedures normally apply:

- Your education counselor will provide you with the appropriate claims forms for TA.
- The counselor will explain TA procedures, requirements for TA reimbursements, and, if necessary, any active duty service obligation officers will incur by accepting TA.
- Depending on the service branch, the counselor will have you sign a statement of understanding for tuition reimbursements, indicating that you understand your TA benefits and obligations, and how the program works.
- You then obtain the approval of your unit commander or leading supervisor, indicating that your unit is aware of your participation in off-duty education.
- You return your TA claim forms to the education office prior to course enrollment for the education services officer's authorization signature.
- Now you're ready to enroll in the college courses you have discussed with your counselor. Usually, this is accomplished by taking your TA claims form to the appropriate representative at the college where you'll be enrolling, then following standard class enrollment procedures.

HELPFUL HINT

Spouses stationed overseas with active duty members are eligible for Spouse Tuition Assistance. See your base or post education office for details.

ACTIVE DUTY OPTION 2: SCHOLARSHIPS

So TA is paying 75% of your college tuition. Did you know you can use scholarships to pay for the other 25%? That's right: Active duty military members are as eligible as any other citizen to apply for scholarships.

Scholarships come in many forms. The type most people are familiar with are those based on athletics or academic performance. But there are many scholarships available that aren't tied to either of those things. Some are based instead on religious affiliation, ethnicity, service-branch membership, organizational membership, residence in a particular city, and so on. The point is there are literally thousands of different kinds of scholarships. You just have to find out which ones you qualify for.

"Most students—especially veterans—think they have no chance of getting a scholarship. That's not true," says Terrence Thomas, founder of GI Bill Express.com (www.gibillexpress.com), a website that provides free information on college financing for military members and veterans. In fact, says Thomas, your military experience is an advantage you can use to get "a leg up" on competing applicants. "Talk about the many places you have lived, obstacles you've had to overcome in the service, professional achievements, medals you've earned," Thomas advises. "You might want to grab your performance evaluations and use those as a starting point. Once you put down all the exciting and challenging things you have done during your military career, you will be impressed, as will the reader of your application."

But Thomas warns that diligence is the key to landing scholarship money: "If you are trying to earn a scholarship, find out the qualifications, note the deadline, then apply, apply, apply."

How do you find scholarships? Dozens of scholarship search services dot the Internet, and the library is full of books on landing college aid. Just remember: Websites like gibillexpress.com, www.fastweb.com, and www.doded.voled.mil provide this information free of charge. There's never a need to pay for scholarship data.

ACTIVE DUTY OPTION 3: MONTGOMERY GI BILL

I'll explain the Montgomery GI Bill (MGIB) in detail later in the chapter. But I mention it here because, unbeknownst to most, you can use your MGIB benefits while on active duty. It's not a good idea, but you can do it if you want to. The reasons why it's not a good idea are complicated, but here it is in a nutshell: MGIB benefits are paid in months to veterans who are attending college. In other words, if you are out of the service and attending college, you are eligible to receive 36 months worth of benefits—essentially, one month's benefit is equal to your total MGIB entitlement divided by 36.

But the Veterans Administration will not fund full-time study for service-members on active duty. So if you use your MGIB on active duty, you will be receiving part-time benefits (around 250–300 dollars a month at this writing), instead of full-time monthly benefits. At most private schools, part-time benefit amount will pay for as little as a single credit hour. Tuition Assistance, on the other hand, pays 75% of your expenses, part-time or otherwise. For active duty members, TA is usually the better deal.

FINANCING COLLEGE AFTER YOU LEAVE THE MILITARY

THE MONTGOMERY GI BILL

The Montgomery GI Bill–Active Duty, called "MGIB" for short, is the best means for financing your post-military college education. The MGIB program is managed by the Veterans Administration. The program provides up to 36 months of education benefits to eligible veterans who had their military pay reduced by $1,200 ($100 per month for the first 12 months). Servicemembers are offered the option to sign up for the MGIB during basic training. Normally, this is a one-time offer. Servicemembers who elect not to sign up for the MGIB are not afforded another opportunity, except under special circumstances. Such circumstances include certain, but not all, instances of involuntary separation (a member is forced to leave the service before expiration of contract), and selection by a member of certain early separation options.

MGIB benefits can be used for:

- College or business schools
- Technical or vocational courses
- Correspondence courses
- Apprenticeship/job training
- Flight training

There are four categories of servicemembers who are eligible for MGIB benefits. The series of dates in the category descriptions below can seem overwhelming, but do read them carefully to be sure you are eligible. The following servicemembers are eligible for MGIB benefits:

- Those who entered on active duty after June 30, 1985, and had their military pay reduced by $1,200. This voluntary contribution toward your education is nonrefundable.
- Those veterans with remaining education entitlement under the old GI Bill on December 31, 1989, who were on active duty for any number of days during the period from October 19, 1984, to June 30, 1985, and continued on active duty from July 1, 1985, through June 30, 1988. Military pay is not reduced for veterans qualifying under this category. These veterans may receive Chapter 30 payment plus one-half of the old GI Bill payment.
- Those veterans who originally declined to participate or who were not eligible to participate in Chapter 30. If you were involuntarily separated from service after February 2, 1991, you must have chosen to participate in Chapter 30 before military separation. If you voluntarily separated under SSB or VSI after December 5, 1991, you may be eligible for Chapter 30.
- You also may be eligible for MGIB benefits if you were serving on active duty on October 9, 1996 and you had money remaining in a VEAP (Veterans Education Assistance Program) account on that date *and* you elected MGIB by October 9, 1997. Or you entered full-time National Guard duty under title 32, USC, between June 1, 1985 and November 28, 1989, *and* you elected MGIB during the period October 9, 1996, through July 8, 1997. You must also have had military pay reduced by $100 a month for 12 months or made a $1,200 lump-sum contribution.

HELPFUL HINT

Your GI Bill is a benefit you earn by serving. Your GI Bill is generally not considered financial aid, and does not count against you when you apply for other forms of financial assistance.

HOW MUCH DOES THE MGIB PAY?

The monthly benefit paid to you is based on the type of training you take, length of your service, your category, and whether or not the Department of Defense put extra money in your MGIB Fund. (This extra money, which the VA may occasionally add to your account should funds become available, is called a "kicker.") You usually have ten years to use your MGIB benefits, but the time limit can be less, in some cases, and longer under certain circumstances. The benefit amount also changes based on changes in the maximum total value of the MGIB benefit. To learn the current value and monthly benefits, visit www.va.gov or call 1-888-GI-BILL-1.

VETERANS EDUCATION ASSISTANCE PROGRAM (VEAP)

Each year there are fewer servicemembers who fall under the pre-MGIB education benefits plan called the Veterans Education Assistance Program (VEAP). But since there still are a significant number of VEAP-eligible servicemembers who may be reading this book, I've included an overview of this benefit.

Members who first entered active duty between January 1, 1977, and June 30, 1985, were able to voluntarily contribute to an education account to establish eligibility. The initial contribution must have been made by March 31, 1987. The maximum contribution for each participant is $2,700. Department of Defense funds equal to twice the contribution are added to the veteran's account. Veterans have ten years from the date of release from active duty to use VEAP benefits. Eligible members may use VEAP benefits to pay for:

- College
- Correspondence courses
- Flight training
- Apprenticeship or job training
- Cooperative training

The amount paid for each different type of training or education listed above varies widely. Details are available at www.va.gov.

WHO IS ELIGIBLE FOR VEAP?

You may be eligible for education benefits under these programs while still on active duty if:

- You entered active duty for the first time after December 31, 1976, and before July 1, 1985.
- You enrolled in and contributed to VEAP (or had money contributed for you by DOD) before April 1, 1987, and have at least three months of contributions available. For an elementary or high school program you need at least one month of contributions available.
- You served for a continuous period of 181 days or more.
- You completed your first active duty commitment.

Some servicemembers are eligible to receive MGIB benefits based on prior eligibility for another education benefits program called the Vietnam Era Veterans' Educational Assistance. If you fall into this category, you are not eligible for VEAP.

OTHER POST-MILITARY COLLEGE FINANCING OPTIONS

Financial aid options differ based upon your status entering college and what type of aid you want to receive. Aid comes in three forms: scholarships, grants, and loans. We've already talked about scholarships. Let's take a look at the other two.

GRANTS

The best thing about a grant is, of course, that you don't have to pay it back. Grants are available from three main sources: the federal government, your state government, or the school you attend. Most grants are need-based. They depend heavily on your income (or your parents' income, if you are still considered a member of their household) prior to your enrollment in school. To determine your eligibility for state and federal aid, you must fill out a government form called the "Free Application for Federal Student Aid." You can obtain a FAFSA application at the school of your choice or by visiting www.fafsa.org. At that website, you can either complete an online application or request to receive an application through the mail. Using the FAFSA, the federal government will calculate and notify you of your eligibility for federal (and state, if you fill out a state grant application) grants.

LOANS

Student loans are available to pay for the costs of college that exceed your ability to pay out-of-pocket or through grants.

"Many students are frightened by student loans," says GI Bill Express.com's Thomas. "But we recommend that if you find a school that you like and all other sources are tapped, a loan is not a bad option. Consider it an investment in yourself."

Loans come in two forms: subsidized and unsubsidized.

Subsidized Loans: If you have a subsidized loan, the federal government will pay the interest (not the principal) while you are in school. Six months after departing school, you must begin repaying your student loan—interest and principal. And there is one little catch to keep in mind: It doesn't matter whether or not you graduate—you still have to repay the loan.

Unsubsidized Loans: In an unsubsidized loan, the federal government does not pay interest on your loan while you are in school. While repayment does not begin until six months after departing school, the interest starts accumulating the minute you sign for the loan.

STAFFORD LOANS

Money for loans can come from a variety of sources. The federal loan for students, called the Stafford Loan, is funded in two ways:

- By private lending institutions, such as banks, credit unions, and savings and loan associations. These loans are guaranteed against default by the federal government.
- By the U.S. government directly to students and their parents through their schools (called direct lending).

All Stafford Loans are either subsidized or unsubsidized. To receive a subsidized Stafford Loan, you must be able to demonstrate financial need. All students, regardless of need, are eligible for the unsubsidized Stafford Loan. Under the Stafford Loan program, dependent undergraduates—those still considered by the Department of Education to be attached to the household of another taxpayer (usually parents)—may borrow up to $2,625 their freshman year, $3,500 their sophomore year, and $5,500 for each remaining year. Independent students are allowed to borrow an additional unsubsidized $4,000 the first two years and $5,000 the remaining years. Graduate students can borrow $18,500 per year, although only $8,500 of that is subsidized. Stafford Loans have variable interest rates. The rate is capped at 8.25% or less, depending on yearly adjustments.

PERKINS LOANS

Private or alternative loans are available for students who find that federal loan programs don't meet their college-financing needs. For example, the Perkins Loan, a campus-based loan program, is available to students who can demonstrate exceptional financial need. Here's how the Perkins Loan works:

- The school acts as the lender using federal government funds.
- The loan is subsidized. The federal government pays the interest.
- The interest rate is 5% and there are no origination or guarantee fees.
- Students may repay the loan over ten years.

Perkins Loans are limited to a maximum of $3,000 per year for undergraduate students and $5,000 per year for graduate students, depending on fund availability at a particular college. Apply early for maximum consideration. There also are cumulative limits: $15,000 for undergraduate loans and $30,000 for undergraduate and graduate loans combined.

CHOOSING A COLLEGE

Now that you've figured out how to pay for college, why not take a look at which colleges are rated as the most military-friendly? Over the past year, GI Bill Express.com surveyed over 2,000 colleges nationwide to determine which colleges have special incentives set aside for current and former military members to help them with their education; 503 schools answered the call. Since military servicemen and servicewomen bring special skills and backgrounds to college campuses as compared to their civilian counterparts, GI Bill Express.com developed a formula to calculate how much a college recognizes military experiences. It's called the "Military Recognition Index."

The MRI, or Military Recognition Index, is a formula that takes into account four major categories:

- Tuition discounts
- Scholarships and fee waivers for military personnel
- Credit waivers for prior military training
- Job placement rates for graduates and special nonfinancial bonuses that are for military students or veterans only

The tuition discount category carries a 50% weight, the credit policy 30%, job placement 15%, and the special category is weighted at 5%. Scores are scaled from 0 to 100, with 50 representing the average score. So which colleges make the grade when it comes to extending special consideration to military personnel? Check out the tables beginning on the next page.

THE TOP 10 PUBLIC COLLEGES AND UNIVERSITIES FOR MILITARY PERSONNEL

RANK	SCHOOL	LOCATION	MRI	TUITION	INCENTIVES FOR MILITARY PERSONNEL AND VETERANS
1	Governors State University	University Park, IL	99.98	2,760	The Illinois Veterans Tuition Waiver*; military credit can be used for elective and required courses. 99% job placement rate for graduates.
2	The Evergreen State College	Olympia, WA	99.79	1,836	Evergreen has the Vietnam Tuition Waiver and the Persian Gulf Tuition Waiver and will transfer most military training for credit.
3	University of Wisconsin-Oshkosh	Oshkosh, WI	99.53	3,000	University of Wisconsin-Oshkosh gives two Roy VanderPutten Scholarships to veterans—$1,500 (nonrenewable).
4	Northern Illinois University	DeKalb, IL	99.43	4,238	The Illinois Veterans Tuition Waiver* and a 90% job placement rate.
5	Bloomsburg University	Bloomsburg, PA	99.10	4,278	Pennsylvania State Grants for Veterans; 64 credits can be transferred and applied toward graduation.
6	United States Coast Guard Academy	New London, CT	99.05	0	Military credit can be substituted for electives. 100% job placement. Zero tuition.
7	United States Air Force Academy	Colorado Springs, CO	99.05	0	Military credit can be substituted for electives. 100% job placement. Zero tuition
8	United States Military Academy	West Point, NY	99.05	0	Military credit can be substituted for electives. 100% job placement. Zero tuition
9	United States Naval Academy	Annapolis, MD	99.05	0	Military credit can be substituted for electives. 100% job placement. Zero tuition
10	West Texas A&M University	Canyon, TX	97.5	1,896	Admissions reports that school will go out of its way to apply military credit; Hazelwood Act for Texas Veterans*

Source: GI Bill Express.com

THE TOP 10 PRIVATE COLLEGES FOR MILITARY PERSONNEL

Rank	School	Location	MRI	Tuition	Incentives for Military Personnel and Veterans
1	College of the Ozarks	Point Lookout, MO	99.99	0	No tuition. The College of the Ozarks combines grants, work/study, and scholarships to defray the costs of your education. 98% job placement.
2	Ohio Dominican College	Columbus, OH	99.95	10,250	A $1,200 veterans' student scholarship, no application fee for veterans, and the Patriots program to assist veterans and spouses in transitioning from military life to college life.
3	Drexel University	Philadelphia, PA	99.90	17,500	Drexel offers a veterans' scholarship to those with an honorable discharge. Application fees are waived if you apply while visiting.
4	Xavier University of Louisiana	New Orleans, LA	98.70	8,900	Accepts and applies most military training for academic credit.
5	Park College	Parkville, MO	98.20	4,590	Accepts and applies most military training for academic credit.
6	Cardinal Stritch University	Milwaukee, WI	96.10	11,000	Cardinal Stritch University offers 25% off tuition for veterans.
7	Hampton University	Hampton, VA	95.00	9,596	Accepts and applies military training for academic credit.
8	Our Lady of the Lake University	San Antonio, TX	94.89	10,872	Accepts and applies most military training for academic credit.
9	Mount Aloysius College	Cresson, PA	94.88	13,620	Accepts and applies most military training for academic credit.
10	Regents College	Albany, NY	94.87	18,750	Will accept and apply almost all prior military training for academic credit.

Source: GI Bill Express.com

TOP 10 JUNIOR COLLEGES FOR MILITARY PERSONNEL

RANK	SCHOOL	LOCATION	MRI	IN STATE TUITION	INCENTIVES FOR MILITARY PERSONNEL AND VETERANS
1	Gateway Community Technical College	New Haven, CT	99.79	1,814	Gateway offers a tuition waiver for veterans with wartime service.**
2	Lincoln Land Community College	Springfield, IL	99.19	552	The Illinois Veterans Tuition* Waiver; applies and accepts most military training for credit.
3	Holyoke Community College	Holyoke, MA	99.19	2,452	Massachusetts has veterans tuition waivers for National Guard members and for certain veterans.
4	Central Texas College	Killeen, TX	98.41	20	Accepts and applies most military training for credit.
5	Blinn College	Brenham, TX	98.41	30	The James F. Dillon Post 7104/ Melvin Reddehase Scholarship provided by the Brenham VFW is awarded to the children of veterans.
6	Monroe Community College	Rochester, NY	97.06	2,700	Scholarships and tuition waivers for children of deceased veterans are available through HESC.
7	El Paso Community College	El Paso, TX	97.06	75	All credit is evaluated, even MOS, and if applicable will be applied toward graduation; Hazelwood Act. ***
8	Houston Community College System	Houston, TX	97.06	30	Texas veterans can apply for Hazelwood benefits if all benefits have been exhausted.
9	Palo Alto College	San Antonio, TX	97.06	24	Texas veterans can apply for Hazelwood benefits if all benefits have been exhausted.
10	Temple College	Temple, TX	97.06	930	The local Veterans of Foreign Wars (VFW) provides scholarships to deserving students. The Hazelwood Act is also available to eligible veterans.

Source: GI Bill Express.com

 * Tuition waivers/grants from public colleges in Illinois, Texas, Massachusetts, Wisconsin, and Pennsylvania are only available to veterans who are residents of those states. In addition, the state has to be your home of record.

 ** Connecticut tuition waivers are for Connecticut residents only. Must live in the state of Connecticut for 12 months to establish residency for tuition purposes.

 *** In Texas's Hazelwood Act, if you are a veteran and (1) you have used all of your GI Bill benefits or (2) have none, you can still go to college and have your tuition paid by the state. There are stipulations that apply. For more information, see the State Benefits section on GI Bill Express.com.

SUMMARY

In this chapter, you've learned about options for financing your college education. You've explored ways to pay for college while still serving on active duty: Tuition Assistance, scholarships, and the Montgomery GI Bill—though we don't recommend you use your GI Bill benefits while on active duty. You've also read about financing options you can use once you leave active duty: the Montgomery GI Bill and the Veterans Education Assistance Program, as well as scholarships, grants, and loans. Finally, you learned about the top ten public, private, and junior colleges for military veterans.

So far in this book, we've talked about the education and career advantages the military can offer you. Next, we'll look at ways you can locate civilian careers that capitalize on your military experience.

CHAPTER 6

Charting a Second Career

IDENTIFYING CAREERS THAT CAPITALIZE ON YOUR MILITARY EXPERIENCE

For many people, deciding when it's time to conclude their military career is easy. What's tough is identifying their next career. In fact, that's the spot where lots of people in career transition—not just servicemembers—get stuck. "If you've been involved in one career in one industry," says San Diego career counselor Dr. Judy Kaplan Baron, "it's common to feel like you have 'no idea of what's out there.'"

If that describes you, here's good news: No matter how unsure you are of your next career move, there is plenty of help available, most of it at no cost. In this chapter, you'll learn:

- How to identify your transferable skills.
- Methods and resources for pinpointing your ideal post-military career.
- How to transfer combat-oriented skills to the civilian job market.

WHAT DO YOU WANT TO BE WHEN YOU GROW UP?

If you're leaving the service for a civilian career field that is similar to your military specialty, your primary concern is probably locating and competing for job openings. But if you plan to change fields or are unsure of your career direction, you may be more worried about exactly what skills you have to offer in the private sector. If this describes you, it's time for an in-depth career assessment. While every job hunter would profit from a complete study of his or her values, environmental preferences, and personality type, let's focus for now on identifying potential career fields and assessing your transferable skills. Transferable skills are those vocational abilities you've acquired up to this point in your life that you can readily transfer to a new occupation. Did you know the average worker has more than 300 individual skills? Can you name your 300? If you're going to sell yourself to a civilian employer, you'll have to know what you're selling. Read on to learn one way to get to know yourself.

WHERE TO FROM HERE?

It's been said that if you don't know where you're going, you'll never get there. This is especially true in a job search. While you don't have to know exactly what kind of job you're looking for, you need to have some idea of what career fields interest you. Without this focus, you'll be traveling blind. Even the most general sense of direction will help you make a more effective assessment of your transferable skills.

Here are a few ways you can learn what types of jobs might interest you. The more research methods you try, the more rapidly you can begin to chart a career path that's right for you.

DAYDREAMING

Doesn't sound too scientific, does it? Well, it isn't. But daydreaming can be a useful tool in narrowing your hands-on research. Here's how it works: Try to imagine your ideal work environment . . .

- Are you indoors or out?
- Are you in an office? A warehouse? A shop?

- Broadly speaking, what kind of work are you doing? Typing at a PC? Fixing things? Talking to people?
- Are you wearing business attire or casual clothes?

The idea is to form a general picture of your preferred work environment. In this way, you can begin to crop out what you don't want in the picture and zoom in on more attractive possibilities. Start a list; write those possibilities down on paper. Are you outdoors? Think park ranger. Are you outdoors, but working with your hands? Narrow your picture to construction worker or landscape architect. At the end of this exercise, you will probably not leap out of your chair and yell, "Eureka! I've found my ideal career!" You will, however, have a better idea of what to leave in or rule out as you continue to narrow down your career possibilities.

ASSESSMENT TESTING

Career assessment testing can reveal areas of strength you may not have previously considered. You can try career self-assessment tests contained in reputable job search guides. A popular choice is Richard Nelson Bolles's *What Color Is Your Parachute*, an annually updated manual on how to mount an effective job campaign. Career testing options are also available through your service branch's transition assistance program or at community career development centers. I mentioned some commonly used assessment tests back in Chapter 4; let's take a closer look at them now:

The Holland Self-Directed Search (SDS) (www.self-directedsearch.com)—The SDS was developed by psychologist Dr. John Holland, whose theory of careers is the basis for many the career assessment tests in use today. This test or "inventory" is based on the theory that people are happier and more successful in jobs that match their interests, values, and skills.

The Kuder Occupational Interest Survey (www.kuder.com)—The Kuder™ Occupational Interest Survey—which pinpoints overlapping areas of interest or matches them with career "clusters"—is a valuable tool for people changing careers.

The Strong Interest Inventory—The Strong Interest Survey identifies your preferences in relation to six major career fields and groups your interests according to major themes. This survey also compares your responses with those of people who work in particular fields. For example, your results might show that your interests are comparable to people who also took the test and are employed as social science instructors, sociologists, ministers, counselors, or occupational therapists.

The idea is that these are careers that were chosen by people who indicated interests similar to your own.

The Myers-Briggs Type Indicator—The Myers-Briggs Type Indicator (MBTI) is a self-report personality inventory designed to yield information about your personality type. Isabel Briggs Myers and Katherine Cook Briggs began developing the MBTI in the early 1940s based on Jungian personality theory. The MBTI results indicate the respondent's likely preferences on four dimensions:

- Extroversion (E) or Introversion (I)
- Sensing (S) or Intuition (N)
- Thinking (T) or Feeling (F)
- Judging (J) or Perceiving (P)

There are 16 possible combinations of the eight qualities described above. For example, my own MBTI is "ESFJ"—I am extroverted; I rely on my five senses, rather than on intuition; I often base decisions on feelings rather than on straight thinking, or facts. I judge or weigh issues, rather than developing opinions based on perception. The "F" in my MBTI profile used to drive Linda, my business partner, crazy. Linda scored a "T" for thinking on the MBTI. So while I might feel sorry for a late-paying client and want to give them more time, she would think they ought to pay up and (rightly) ask for the cash. The MBTI is useful for determining what kinds of work teams you would mesh well with. (It can also explain why certain things about you drive your spouse nuts!)

If you decide to take an assessment test, add the career possibilities you come up with to the list you started when you were daydreaming. Keep the list . . . you'll be adding to it later.

HELPFUL HINT

Online Career Assessment

You can complete certain career assessment surveys right in your own home. Both Holland and Kuder offer assessment testing via their websites, and the cost is minimal. For example, you can take the Holland test for free, then receive a 12-page report and analysis of your test results for under $10. Visit www.self-directedsearch.com or www.kuder.com for details.

BRAINSTORMING

Use the information you gain from daydreaming and assessment testing to guide you in researching specific career fields. To easily research hundreds of occupational specialties online, check out the Occupational Profiles Data Base in the Gonyea Online Career Center (GOCC) on America Online (Keyword: Gonyea). Dr. Judy Kaplan Baron, a GOCC career advisor, put together the following list of career options to help her clients identify and brainstorm possible career alternatives. The lists are by no means exhaustive and mix together career fields and job titles in each category. The idea is to use these lists to spark your imagination.

Accounting/auditing—accountant; accounting clerk; budget analyst, credit specialist; inventory control auditor, public and private.

Advertising/public relations—advertising account executive; environmental public relations specialist; legal public relations specialist; corporate public affairs specialist; media relations; political media relations specialist; sales and promotion; advertising copywriter; social planner.

Architecture, planning and design—commercial, environmental, landscape, residential architect; urban and regional planner; city/county/state drafter; industrial designer; interior designer; investigative architect; space planner; tenant improvement; waste water planning.

Arts—arts administrator; cartoonist; commercial and graphic artist; illustrator; Web illustrator.

Banking, business and financial services—bank loan officer; credit unions; corporate financial analyst; economist; financial planner; governmental regulator for the FDIC, for example; investment banking; investment management; nonbank financial services firms; private banking; reorganization specialists; sales and marketing specialists; stockbroker. See also Accounting/auditing.

Computers and high tech—website designer/manager; artificial intelligence programming and development; computer design; software engineer; computer operator; computer programmer; computer security; computer service technician; computers systems engineers; LAN/WAN/networking; management information systems; research; software engineer; systems analysts (including managers).

Education/teaching—college, university, vocational or trade school instructor; preschool, elementary, and secondary public and private school teacher; corporate trainer; computer skills instructor; adult education instructor;

education administration; educational consultant; education technology; librarian (think about specializing in databases or computer information systems); reading specialist.

Energy—coal; solar; environmental concerns; natural gas; oil; nuclear.

Engineering—chemical; civil; computer systems; electrical and electronic; environmental; soils; mechanical; safety; materials; process.

Entertainment (see Television, broadcasting, entertainment, or Performing arts)

Government—local, regional, state, national, or international city management; legislative staff; state and/or federal departments of agriculture, communications, defense, Centers for Disease Control, education, energy, environmental protection, federal trade commission, food and safety, foreign affairs, general services administration, government printing office, health and human services, national institute of health, the interior, labor, bureau of land management, securities and exchange commission. (The government offers careers in almost every field imaginable and is the largest employer in the United States.)

Healthcare administration and management—clinics, eldercare/nursing home and long-term care facilities; home health care; HMOs/PPOs, hospitals; freestanding outpatient surgery and diagnostic centers; general administration; health services manager; industrial medicine; medical records administration; medical supplies; operations management; outpatient services; pharmaceutical manufacturers; physical rehabilitation.

Health assessment, treating, and diagnosing—alternative medicine specialties including aromatherapy, naturopathic physician, homeopathy; chiropractor; dentist, dental assistant, dental hygienist; nurse (registered, licensed practical, licensed vocational); nurse anesthetist; nutritionist and dietitian; occupational therapist; optometrist, optician; pharmacist; physician; physical therapist; podiatrist; respiratory therapist; speech-language pathologist and audiologist; veterinarian; women's medicine.

Healthcare technologists and technicians—dental hygienist; dispensing optician, EEG technologist, EKG technician; emergency medical technician; licensed practical nurse; medical record technician; nuclear medicine technologist; radiology technician; surgical technician.

Hospitality—chef/cook; community and food service for the elderly; director/manager; facilities management; food service; hotels, motels, casinos; restaurant service companies; meeting planner; transportation manager.

Human resources—benefits administration; employee assistance manager; employment interviewer; labor/industrial relations; management; organizational development; recruitment; training and development; wage and salary administration.

Insurance—claim examiner; estimator; salesperson; underwriter.

International careers—Department of State; international accounting, finance, health care executives, information systems; law; real estate; teaching; translators; U.S. Agency for International Development; U.S. Information Agency; Peace Corps; the United Nations; the World Bank.

Law—attorney (consider specialties in environmental, family, international, patent); court reporter; legal administration; paralegal.

Law enforcement/public safety—border patrol; CIA; city, county, state, national, and international; correction departments (officer/guard/jailer); Department of Justice; Department of Prisons; fire, police, probation, public safety, and sheriff departments; FBI, forest service; Occupational Safety and Health Administration (OSHA).

Marketing and sales—environmental; health care; financial services and insurance; franchise; personnel services; product manager; market research; real estate (commercial and residential); technically trained, e.g. pharmaceutical, engineer; telecommunications.

Medicine and medical specialists (see health categories).

Performing arts—actor/actress; arts management; dancer; musician.

Public relations (see Advertising/public relations).

Publishing/writing—book, magazine, or newspaper (including specialty); editor, copyeditor; technical writer; screenwriter, speech writer; script reader; story editor; copywriter; production; electronic media; self-publishing; specialized trade or professional; typesetter; printing; graphic design; writer, journalist.

Real estate—construction management; environmental services and waste management; real estate development; relocation specialist; sales (residential or commercial).

Retailing—direct-mail; international; specialty; technological; infomercials; home shopping television stations.

Science—agricultural; biologist, biotechnology, and environmental; chemist; food scientist; geologist and geophysicist; mathematician; meteorologist; physicist.

Teaching/training (see Education/teaching).

Technical/mechanical—aircraft technician; air traffic controller; automotive mechanic; appliance/power tool repairer; broadcast technician; telecommunications technician; computer-aided design (CAD) drafter; computer-aided manufacturing; computer repair; electrical and electronic technician; opthamologic laboratory technician; radiology equipment technician; robotics.

Telecommunications—equipment companies; fiber-optics engineers and technicians; local area network technician; network management; satellite technician; service companies; telecommunications engineer or technician.

Television, broadcasting, entertainment—actor, director, producer; cable, radio, television; cinematographer; engineering; management production staff; multimedia technician; radio/TV news reporter; sales or marketing; computer animation.

Travel—corporate travel manager; cruise lines; international business; local magazines; marketing and sales; meeting planning; tour manager; travel agent.

Transportation—airlines, barge lines, railroads, trucking; flight engineer; courier and messenger services; transportation manager; sales representative; port authorities; city transit systems.

There are a lot of possibilities in the list above. Did any of them appeal to you? If so, add them to your list.

RESEARCH

By now, you should have at least a few career possibilities on your running list. It's time to look deeper than job titles. One of the most widely used and respected sources of information about individual occupations is the Bureau of Labor Statistics (www.bls.gov), an agency of the U.S. Department of Labor. In recent years, the BLS has made nearly all of its most requested data available online. Much of the career assessment and analysis information you'll find at other sites and in other books—even this book—is derived from BLS research. Here are a few resources you'll find useful in doing your own research on possible post-military careers:

OCCUPATIONAL OUTLOOK HANDBOOK

The Occupational Outlook Handbook is a valuable resource to help you see what's happening in specific career fields and what developments you can expect over the next few years. Revised every two years, the handbook describes what workers do on the job, working conditions, the training and education needed, earnings, and expected job prospects in a wide range of occupations.

CAREER GUIDE TO INDUSTRIES

The *Career Guide to Industries* provides information on available careers by industry, including the nature of the industry, working conditions, employment, occupations in the industry, training and advancement, earnings and benefits, employment outlook, and lists of organizations that can provide additional information. The most current *Career Guide* (2000–2001) discusses more than 42 industries, accounting for over seven out of every ten wage and salary jobs. The *Career Guide* is a companion to the *Occupational Outlook Handbook*, which provides information on careers from an occupational, rather than an industrial, perspective.

THE NATIONAL COMPENSATION SURVEY PROGRAM

Maybe you're considering a career field, but would like to know what people who work in that field earn? The National Compensation Survey program (NCS) provides data on the average hourly earnings of occupational groups and individual occupations for about 80 metropolitan areas and 70 nonmetropolitan counties. The survey covers establishments employing 50 workers or more in goods-producing industries (mining, construction, or manufacturing); service-producing industries (transportation, communications, public utilities, wholesale and retail trade, finance, insurance and real estate); and state and local government. The NCS can be viewed online at www.bls.gov/opub/cwc.

EMPLOYMENT PROJECTIONS

The BLS regularly releases ten-year employment studies of the American workforce. Called "Employment Projections," these studies provide information on where future job growth is expected by industry and occupation and what the makeup of the workforce pursuing those jobs is likely to be. These projections of employment by industry, occupation, labor force, and economic growth are widely used in career guidance, in planning education and training programs, and in studying long-range employment trends.

Here are some examples of what you'll find in the BLS Employment Projections covering 1998–2008:

- Service-producing industries will account for virtually all of the job growth. Only construction will add jobs in the goods-producing sector, offsetting declines in manufacturing and mining.

- Manufacturing's share of total jobs is expected to decline, as a decrease of 89,000 manufacturing jobs is projected. Manufacturing is expected to maintain its share of total output, as productivity in this sector is projected to increase.

- Health services, business services, social services, and engineering, management, and related services are expected to account for almost one of every two non-farm wage and salary jobs added to the economy during the 1998–2008 period. The five fastest-growing industries all belong to one of these four industry groups.

- Professional specialty occupations are projected to increase the fastest and to add the most jobs—5.3 million . . . Other groups that are projected to grow faster than the average are executive, administrative, and managerial occupations; technicians and related support occupations; and marketing and sales occupations.

- Administrative support occupations including clerical are projected to grow slower than the average and slightly slower than in the past, reflecting the impact of office automation.

- Precision production, craft, and repair occupations and operators, fabricators, and laborers are projected to grow much more slowly than the average due to continuing advances in technology, changes in production methods, and the overall decline in manufacturing employment.

- The five fastest-growing occupations are computer-related occupations, commonly referred to as information technology occupations.

OTHER RESEARCH RESOURCES

The BLS isn't the only place to find information about careers. See the appendices for a list of great books covering career possibilities in a wide spectrum of industries.

HELPFUL HINT

Remember, if you don't have access to the Internet—and even if you do—be sure to visit your base or post transition center. Not only will your transition center carry many of the BLS resources in book form, it will also offer myriad other career exploration resources that can help you target a second career.

WHERE HAVE YOU BEEN ALL YOUR LIFE?

You should have quite a list of potential career fields going by now (if not, go back to the beginning of this chapter and start again). Now it's time to begin examining your own work experience. What skills and experience do you have that might be required by some of the jobs on your list? Notice I didn't say "What jobs have you done that could transfer to the civilian market?" Remember: The idea is to focus on transferable skills, not job titles. A job and the skills required to do a job are separate issues. More on that in a moment.

To identify some of your skills consider your collateral duties, or those extra jobs you were given in additional to your military specialty. You may find you have skill sets you hadn't thought about.

THE HAT TRICK

One amazing feat performed by military managers could rightly be called vocational magic. You might even call it "The Hat Trick." It goes something like this: You walk into work one day, get called in to see the boss, and suddenly you're a safety petty officer, or you're a computer security officer, or you're a HAZMAT NCO. Nothing up their sleeves, no advance notice required. They just hand you the associated paperwork, maybe a manual or two, and you've got a new "hat" to wear. Not only that, but you're expected to wear that hat well.

Although you may have felt a little like a chameleon at the time, those "extra" jobs you held can help you in your job search. Whether you gained a few transferable skills from those part-time responsibilities, or learned an entirely new vocation that could actually become a second career, the whole concept of collateral duties can strengthen your professional image in the eyes of potential employers.

Employers in general are looking to get the most bang for their buck. Collateral duties can demonstrate your ability to successfully handle diverse responsibilities, a trait that can save a firm money by reducing the need to hire more people. A statement like this one can be useful in a resume: "While working full-time in aviation electronics, I volunteered to manage a unit hazardous materials program. The program was a complete success, yielding 'no findings' scores on three consecutive audits." If you were indeed effective in handling multiple job descriptions simultaneously, that's a marketable skill. Write it down.

BEND AND LEARN

Another pair of positive traits demonstrated by collateral duties is flexibility and trainability. Many employers are attracted by a candidate who isn't afraid to tackle new and challenging assignments, especially when those tasks may stretch into an unfamiliar subject area. Again, it saves a company money when new projects can be assigned to existing staff. It's generally a lot cheaper to send a current employee for additional training than to bring on a fully trained new employee. Do you prefer to know exactly what needs to be done, or are you flexible? If you're flexible and adaptable, that's a marketable trait.

DETAILS, DETAILS

Don't overlook the record-keeping aspect of those extra hats you wore. Preparing and maintaining accurate records, inventories, correspondence, requisitions, and reports are a key part of most collateral duties, which is one reason the duties get farmed out in the first place! Your ability to perform administrative duties effectively can demonstrate accuracy, attention to detail, and follow-through to a potential employer. If you're a capable record keeper, add that to your list of skills.

IMPROVEMENTS

Collateral duties often provide you with an opportunity to shine. Regardless of the actual disciplines involved—safety, supply, human relations, or whatever—you probably had more autonomy and flexibility in your collateral job descriptions than you did in your primary assignments. For motivated individuals, this allows the freedom to improve on existing programs. Such improvements could be as simple as reorganizing the safety training records for easier access, or as complex as establishing an expanded tutoring program with a local elementary school.

Use these memory-jogging questions to help you unearth your collateral achievements: Did you ever . . .

- Reorganize a program? A procedure? A filing system? A communications pipeline?
- Find a way to reduce costs?
- Improve safety?
- Improve audit or inspection scores?
- Reduce personnel turnover?
- Improve staV knowledge or proficiency in a particular area?
- Repair something instead of replacing it?
- Win recognition for your command?
- Reduce time required to complete a task?
- Increase accountability or accuracy?
- Reduce an error rate?

Get the idea? The magnitude of any improvements you made isn't as important as the initiative you demonstrated in making them. Examine your own collateral duties for upgrades you initiated or even assisted in. Add these to your list.

BUT CIVILIANS DON'T DRIVE TANKS

So you've daydreamed, brainstormed, assessed, and researched. But you just can't seem to find a civilian job equivalent for submarine driver, tank gunner, cryptographer, or infantryman. That's a special challenge of combat-oriented military occupational specialties . . . not everyone who serves on active duty emerges with ready-made traditional job skills to take to the private sector market. But if you're serving in a military job with no apparent civilian equivalent, take heart. You can look in places other than your rating or MOS for skills to sell to employers.

WHERE TO LOOK

One great place to look for marketable vocational skills is in your collateral duties—those hats you wear in addition to your regular job title. From Training NCO to Supply Petty Officer, thousands of military veterans have successfully turned their collateral duties into full-time civilian careers. Take a close look at your service career, both past and present. Are there collateral duties in your military work history that can be translated into civilian employment?

And don't just look at actual collateral job titles. Collateral experience can be marketed, too. Take aviation ordnance technicians, for example. Dealing with hazardous materials isn't an extra hat they wear—it's just part of the job. But personnel with experience managing hazardous materials are in big demand among many private sector and government contract employers. Ordnance technicians may also have significant experience in supply management, including shipping and receiving, detailed inventories, storage facility layout, shelf-life considerations, and the like. These skills could also be marketed successfully to civilian companies.

The idea is to see your military job not as one big skill, but rather as a group of skills that can be broken up, mixed and matched, and sold in different packaging.

HAVE YOU WORN THESE HATS?

Here are a few of the more common collateral assignments to help spark your memory about extra hats you may have worn during your service career:

Administration

Career counseling

Classified materials

Computer security

Duty officer

EEO

Fire safety

Hazardous materials

Human relations

Legal services

Occupational safety

Physical security

Physical training

Police (cleanup)

Public relations

Publications

Repair parts

Security force

Substance abuse

Supply

Training

Remember, no job is too insignificant. Every collateral duty you held can be mined for job-search gold.

LEADERSHIP AND MANAGEMENT

Servicemembers in nontraditional fields can often successfully market leadership and management skills. Many law enforcement agencies look specifically for supervisory experience combined with heavy doses of interpersonal skills. Management opportunities also exist in the service, retail, and hospitality industries. But beware of the idea of "just getting some type of management job." In this age of corporate downsizing, the middle manager is headed rapidly toward extinction. To sell your management skills without experience in a specific industry may require additional training or certifications. That's okay though, as long as you begin your preparations early.

SECURITY CLEARANCES

A current, high-level security clearance can be a premium commodity in the private sector, especially among government contract employers who frequently work with classified military information and systems. Servicemembers with a bare minimum of transferable vocational skills may be able to land employment based almost entirely on a current (less than one year lapsed) clearance. Some employers are more willing to foot the bill for specific vocational training than expend time and money on a new employee whose clearance may not come through. To explore this avenue, try posting your resume (with appropriate clearance level and date) on the Internet and transition center databases. You may have employers contacting you, instead of the other way around.

SOFT SKILLS

In combination with other strengths, soft skills can be a hot seller for service-members seeking to market nontraditional skills. While some civilian employers can hold negative stereotypes of military employees, many recognize that positive traits like loyalty, self-discipline, and initiative are instilled by military service. In a job interview, it isn't always the person with the most experience who gets the job. Employers are equally, if not more, concerned about which candidate will be the best worker. If you're light on skills associated with a specific industry, you'll do well to play up your image as a model employee.

TALK IT OUT

Sometimes it can be difficult to step back and take an objective look at the broad range of your own skills. It's easy to see yourself only as a tank gunner or a fighter pilot. But talking to someone with experience in both military and civilian careers can help you clarify your view of what you have to offer in the private sector. Self-assessment and a meeting or two with a qualified career counselor may be just what you need to get you moving in the right direction.

START EARLY

There is one critical piece of advice for those preparing to transition into the real world after an ultramilitary tour: Start early. Transferable skills can go a long way toward launching your post-service career. But you'll wind up kicking yourself if you find out too late that there was additional training or volunteer work you could have completed in advance to shore up your strengths. Remember, it's never too early to start investigating the possibilities.

MIX AND MATCH

At this point in your research, you'll find yourself armed with a list of potential jobs and hopefully a list of your own skills, broken down by category (not job titles). You may not be qualified for every job on your list, but jobs are like gourmet dishes: Each has a recipe that calls for a certain number of specific ingredients (skills) that, when blended together, add up to more than the sum of the parts. With recipes, ingredients from a number of dishes can be mixed and matched to come up with new flavors. Jobs are no different. Take a few skills from this job and a few more from that and you may find yourself qualified for an entirely new position.

Here are the final three steps:

1. Choose a job—why not start with your favorite?—from the list you've created.
2. Identify the broad categories of skills a worker in that job might need.
3. Write out examples of how you've used those skills in your past work or nonwork experience.

Let's look at a real-life example. Joseph Karnes, a personnel clerk who had ascended to the rank of E-8, had considered the job of paralegal specialist as a second career option. He had experience investigating and adjudicating legal matters at one command, but without any civilian legal training, it appeared on the surface that Joe would never qualify for such a specialized position. Then he took a look at the major skill groups a paralegal specialist might need and came up with these:

- Administration and documentation
- Legal research and investigation
- Communication and interpersonal skills

Joe knew he had each of these skills. His next task was to write examples of how he had used them in his past work experience. Expanding on the examples he came up with, Joe prepared a successful federal job application and is now employed as a paralegal specialist with the U.S. Department of Immigration and Naturalization.

You can see from this example that it's important to identify target occupations before attempting to assess your skills. Without the context of the paralegal position, Joe could have drowned in his own 300 skills, not knowing which ones to identify first.

Joe's success story also demonstrates that by identifying and marketing transferable skills, you can make the transition from a specialized military occupational field to a seemingly unrelated civilian job.

Remember, as you conduct your occupational research, you may find jobs you're qualified for, partially qualified for, or not qualified for at all. You may choose to pursue a job you're ready for now. Or you may find something so appealing you decide to go back to school to complete the necessary credentials. Whatever the case, you'll be setting your course for a destination—and knowing where you're going is the first step to getting there.

SUMMARY

In this chapter, you've learned about methods and resources for settling on a second career. We've looked at imaginative, holistic methods like daydreaming and brainstorming, as well as more scientific paths like career assessment testing. You've also learned about valuable research tools like the studies and projections available through the Bureau of Labor Statistics. Finally, you learned where to look within the scope of your own military experience to unearth transferable skills that can translate into a brand-new civilian career. Next, we'll take a look at the transition assistance offered through the U.S. military.

CHAPTER 7

Transition Assistance

NO-COST CAREER SEARCH HELP FOR MILITARY MEMBERS EXITING THE SERVICE

In 1989, a major symbol of the Cold War, the Berlin Wall, was dismantled and the direction of the U.S. military forces underwent a shift. Three basic programs got underway to decrease the size of America's armed forces. Two offered servicemembers financial incentives to separate early from the military. Another simply downsized members whose services—whether because the members had not advanced quickly enough in rank or because their job specialties were overmanned—were no longer deemed necessary. To help exiting servicemembers cross the bridge to civilian employment, Congress passed legislation requiring all service branches to provide transition and job search assistance to every separating member. The program that is now called the Transition Assistance Management Program (TAMP) was born.

Since then, TAMP (the Army calls it ACAP; more on that below) has evolved to offer a variety of high-caliber career transition services. Below is an overview of the major resources you'll find at your base or post-military transition center.

JOB SEARCH RESOURCES

Most transition centers offer computerized job search assistance tools, including access to the Internet, America's Job Bank (AJB) and the Transition Bulletin Board (TBB). Though TBB has been around for nearly a decade and AJB even longer, Internet technology and advances in global connectivity have dramatically improved the usefulness of these tools over the past five years. Now, it really is a small world, after all: Coupled with communications advances, including e-mail and plummeting long distance telephone costs, this progress has nearly leveled the playing field for servicemembers who must search for stateside jobs while completing their final military tour at an overseas installation.

COMPUTER CENTERS

For servicemembers without personal Internet access, transition office computer centers are an extremely valuable perk. Some centers offer computer access by appointment; others observe a first-come-first-served policy, but impose a time limit on each user. Using transition center computers, you can jump-start your job searches by accessing Internet job search sites like The Destiny Group (www.destinygrp.com), the Monster Board (www.monster.com), and HotJobs.com. (This is a particularly convenient resource when you'd like to work on your career campaign during your lunch hour, but don't have time to go home and use your own computer.) You can also use center computers to work on resumes, cover letters, and federal job applications—just be sure to bring a 3.5" disk so you can save your work and take it with you. Transition centers usually do not afford hard drive storage space for the files of individual servicemembers.

AMERICA'S JOB BANK

America's Job Bank (AJB) is a computerized network that links state employment services offices. For job seekers, AJB boasts one of the largest available pools of active job opportunities. Most of AJB's job listings are full-time, private sector openings that span the career field spectrum, including blue collar, technical, and professional positions, as well as jobs in management and sales.

For employers, AJB provides national exposure for job openings and an easily accessible pool of job candidates. There is no charge to companies that list their openings with AJB. The service is funded through unemployment insurance taxes paid by employers. Corporate recruiters may search AJB using the Internet, but the AJB resume database is also available on computer systems in public libraries, colleges and universities, and even shopping malls.

Though individual states have cooperated through AJB since 1979, it wasn't until 1998 that the network added resume-posting services. Service members posting their resumes on AJB receive nationwide exposure.

TRANSITION BULLETIN BOARD

When the 1991 Defense Authorization Act required the Secretary of Defense to begin providing career transition services to departing servicemembers and their spouses, Operation Transition got underway—and so did the Transition Bulletin Board (TBB). Transition Bulletin Board is an automated service that links all five military branches with employers around the world. TBB lists help wanted and job wanted ads as well as other useful job search information, including available military job search support services, workshops, job fairs, education and training opportunities, and information on franchises and starting a business.

According to Operation Transition, 30,000 job seekers log on to TBB every month at transition centers around the world. More than 24,000 employers—from small businesses to Fortune 500 companies—have registered to use TBB to post job openings and look for candidates.

ARMY CAREER & ALUMNI PROGRAM

The Army's transition program provides the same services as do those of other service branches, but its program goes under a different name: the Army Career & Alumni Program (ACAP). Through ACAP, the Army helps its transitioning members (called "transitioners") succeed in moving from the federal environment to the next stage of their careers. To accomplish its mission, ACAP:

- Operates ACAP centers worldwide.
- Provides mobile transition services to selected installations where no ACAP center is located.
- Provides remote transition services where neither an ACAP center nor a mobile service is available.
- Develops and supports transition assistance classes, tools, and resources.

For soldiers, the ACAP process begins with a pre-separation briefing during which servicemembers learn about career options, transition benefits, and what services are available to assist them during their career transition. The ACAP center functions as a hub and provides some transition services, like counseling. Other services, like relocation assistance, are made available by other installation providers.

TRANSITION ASSISTANCE PROGRAM (TAP)

TRANSITION ASSISTANCE PROGRAM (TAP) COURSE

Most military transition centers offer a three- to four-day course called TAP, a program funded and supplied through the U.S. Department of Labor. By law, all servicemembers are eligible to attend TAP once they are within 180 days of separation. TAP classes are designed to introduce the transitioning servicemember to a variety of career transition and job search topics, like:

- Writing resumes and cover letters
- Succeeding in job interviews
- Locating job openings
- Researching companies
- Negotiating salary and benefits

Depending on programs offered at an individual base or post, TAP may also provide briefings on veterans' benefits like health and life insurance, as well as education and post-military vocational training. In addition to basic TAP classes that address the general transition needs of most servicemembers, larger transition centers may offer focused TAP courses for specific categories of transitioners who have specialized needs. Such categories include senior enlisted servicemembers and officers; servicemembers who are retiring (as opposed to separating at the end of an obligated service period); and members separating with service-connected disabilities. If you fall into one of these categories, check with your base or post transition center to learn whether it offers specialized TAP courses.

Transition doesn't begin when you separate from military service, but much earlier. The farther in advance you attend TAP, the more you'll be able to use what you learn there. Military transition specialist Bernard Marstall recommends that servicemembers attend TAP as early as six to nine months prior to separation. "By the time you get inside six months," he says, "you should already be researching companies and sending out inquiries. TAP will teach you to plan and execute an effective strategy."

By law, all servicemembers are eligible to attend TAP once they are within 180 days of separation. While most servicemembers are granted permission by their chains of command to attend TAP when they request it, some personnel may run into difficulties based on their unit's manpower needs—particularly if they request to attend the class well in advance of their separation date.

The Department of Defense has issued a directive requiring each service branch to provide TAP training for its members. Each service branch also has a directive governing TAP attendance and each directive is assigned a specific number. (Your TAP office can provide you with this number.) If your unit commander is reluctant to let you attend TAP as early as you'd like, transition specialist Bernard Marstall suggests you include on your written request to attend TAP the number of the directive governing TAP attendance for your service branch. This may help remind decision makers in your unit that attending TAP is a right, not a privilege.

TWO HEADS ARE BETTER

Husbands and wives can attend TAP together. Few do it, more should. Though transition centers promote the idea, it rarely happens. TAP facilitator Bernard Marstall estimates that fewer than one in ten servicemembers bring their spouses to TAP class. This is in spite of the fact that the spouse is in transition as much as the servicemember is. "Spouses need to know the same information as the servicemember," Marstall says, pointing out that the spouses of active members in transition will often also be seeking new employment.

While husbands and wives often have difficulty attending an entire TAP course together because of work conflicts or child-rearing obligations, even a day or two in class together can go a long way. "A spouse can contribute to research, help the servicemember avoid tunnel vision," says military transition expert Anne Stinson. A spouse can also function as a backup information filter, and may remember course material that the active duty member didn't catch.

Perhaps most importantly, attending TAP as a couple can help the member and spouse work as a team, providing support for one another when the going gets tough.

GETTING THE MOST FROM TAP

The TAP course itself, rather than use of transition center resources, is the primary source of job search expertise and assistance for many servicemembers. But there's a right way to approach TAP and a not-so-right way. Use the five tips below to help you get the most from TAP.

1. WRITE YOUR RESUME IN ADVANCE

While the specific structure and emphasis may vary from one TAP course to another, all courses include instruction on how to prepare your resume. In TAP classes designed for senior servicemembers, students who don't have a resume are required to write one during the duration of the course. But most TAP instructors say there's a better way: No matter how senior or junior you are, write your resume before attending TAP.

"The process is more important than the product," says military transition expert Anne Stinson. Stinson adds that necessary steps to writing a good resume, like self-evaluation and goal-setting, may take more time than is available during a three- or four-day course. Doing some of the difficult groundwork and writing up a draft before TAP can help students use TAP to advance beyond the basics.

Here's another reason to write your resume ahead of time: so you can leverage the TAP facilitator's experience to help you fine-tune your resume. While others in your class are being advised on beginning phases like format, you can use your TAP time to craft high-impact language and polish up achievement statements.

2. NETWORK WITH CLASS MEMBERS

Whether they're in the military or not, many job seekers are a little shy about networking. What better place to practice the process than in a class where everyone is in the same boat you are? "You must be able to tell people who you are and what you can do apart from your identity in the military," notes Stinson, adding that many servicemembers struggle with the second part of that equation. "TAP is a great place to practice talking about yourself without regard to your uniform."

Marstall notes a second advantage to networking with fellow TAP students: potential job leads. Think of each contact you make as a link to everyone that person knows and every job lead that person's learned of in his or her own job search. Many who attend TAP, Marstall explains, have already begun their own job searches. They may be willing to share information with you about people they've run across who are hiring in your field.

For the same reason, agree with your classmates to stay in touch after TAP is over. One easy way to do this: Have business cards made before you go. For less than 20 dollars, you can get a stack of 500 professionally printed cards—or you can buy laser-perforated business card paper and print them out on your home computer.

NETWORKING PAYS OFF BIG

Willard Jackson's "net" worked. The former Air Force master sergeant credits networking with his rapid transition from the military to a position as a senior systems engineer with Vanstar, a national computer network provider. Jackson landed his first civilian job when his wife mentioned Jackson's job search to a contact she had at her own job. And Jackson says that once he got himself established in the private sector, he assisted a number of his former Air Force colleagues in making contacts in the computer industry. He even helped a captain he'd worked with on active duty get hired at Vanstar as an enterprise engineer.

"Stay in touch with people who transitioned with you and before you," says New York–based career coach Terra Dourlain. "Send out a ton of holiday cards and don't lose contact!"

3. VOLUNTEER FOR EXERCISES AND ROLE-PLAYS

For the bold and determined, TAP can be the ultimate "learning by doing" experience. Most TAP curricula include role-plays and practice interviews designed to expose you to typical interview scenarios, as well as pitfalls and trap questions you may encounter on real interviews. Such exercises also help TAP attendees learn to verbalize work-related information like goals, strengths, and values. Some instructors even offer to videotape you so that you can critique your own performance at home.

Practicing for interviews can help you get your jitters under control before you attempt the real thing. "TAP is a safe place to practice," says Marstall. "Unless you participate in the role-plays, you won't get firsthand experience of what it feels like when the butterflies roll. Plus, you learn some things that aren't so obvious, like body language, and how it feels to ask the interviewer questions, instead of the other way around."

4. PARTICIPATE AND ASK QUESTIONS

Questions during role-plays aren't the only ones TAP attendees should ask. Students who ask questions tend to be the ones who gain the most from their TAP experience. Marstall says he's noticed that those who participate during class also tend to take more initiative in their job search than those who sit quietly through the course.

Asking questions and offering comments that are relevant and well timed also may help fellow students: "Someone else may benefit from your experience," Marstall says, "or they may also have needed to know the answer to the question you asked."

5. BRING YOUR SENSE OF ADVENTURE

Some TAP attendees, jaded from years of military training courses, arrive in transition courses with bad attitudes: "Another boring class," they think, or "I don't need this; I can read job search books instead." Such attitudes are a mistake, says Stinson. She suggests servicemembers leave their "'tudes" at home, and come to TAP instead with a sense of adventure.

"There's a lot of self-exploration involved in the class," she explains. "We look at values, goals, future plans. Bring your sense of adventure, because when you come, you never know what you're going to learn about yourself."

ADDITIONAL TRANSITION CENTER SERVICES

INDIVIDUAL COUNSELING

Military transition centers provide no-cost individual employment assistance counseling. Transition counselors are available to personally help servicemembers identify possible career options, develop a job objective, and track down job leads. Counselors may also critique resumes, cover letters, and federal job applications. In addition, transition center staffers can help servicemembers make optimal use of all available job search transition resources.

SPECIALIZED CLASSES

Full-length TAP courses offer training on topics like resume writing and job search techniques. But because there's a lot of ground to cover in a course that lasts less than a week, TAP may not provide as much in-depth training as some servicemembers need on certain subjects. Some larger transition centers offer specialized classes in addition to TAP. For example, Naval Station San Diego offers one- and two-day classes on topics like writing a resume and preparing a federal job application.

FEDERAL JOB APPLICATIONS

In addition to teaching separating servicemembers how to complete a federal job application, many transition centers also make available computer software to assist in that process. "Quick & Easy Federal Jobs" is a licensed software suite that partially automates completion of several federal job application forms including the main forms SF-171 and OF-612, and auxiliary forms called KSAs (Knowledge, Skills, and Abilities). Federal applications—even those that are supposed to be shorter and make the federal application process easier—are lengthy and detailed. Computerizing the process is about the only way to remain sane while applying for federal jobs. (Federal job applications will be discussed in detail in Chapter 10.)

SPOUSE EMPLOYMENT ASSISTANCE PROGRAM

Frequent relocation associated with the mobile military lifestyle creates career challenges for military spouses. The Spouse Employment Assistance Program (SEAP) addresses those challenges through one-on-one counseling and, when necessary, by referring spouses to guidance counselors of educational institutions. At many larger installations SEAP is specially managed by a designated counselor who devotes most of his or her time to attending to the special needs of military spouses.

SEAP's goals are to:

- Assist spouses in choosing a career.
- Assist spouses in finding employment.
- Develop successful job search strategies.
- Provide information on education and volunteer opportunities.

Spouses may also use transition center resources like computer centers and America's Job Bank. There is no cost to the spouses of active duty members to use these services.

VMET

There is one key service that the transition assistance programs provide to all service branches: helping servicemembers obtain their VMET. The VMET, or Verification of Military Experience and Training (DD Form 2586), is like an enhanced resume. Prepared by the central personnel offices of the various service branches, the VMET is created from a servicemember's computerized service record files. It lists a generic description of a member's military job specialty and training history, recommended college credit information, and civilian equivalent job titles. To put it in another way, the VMET is an extended compilation of information from the ACE guide (discussed in Chapter 4), the *Dictionary of Occupational Titles* (discussed in Chapter 8), and an individual member's service record.

The VMET is designed to help servicemembers recall specific technical details of their military work experience and training. It has proven helpful for members filling out resumes and job applications. But, because it is extremely long and generic, it is not designed to be used as a resume.

Each branch of the military is required to provide this document to a servicemember at least 120 days prior to separation. If you are within 120 days of separation and do not yet have a copy of your VMET (DD Form 2586), your unit career counselor or base military transition office can assist you in getting one.

SUMMARY

In this chapter, you learned what resources are available for you at your base or post-military transition office. From four-day job search courses to specialized classes that meet specific needs, the training you'll need to launch a successful post-military career is available at no cost. In addition, your service branch will provide spouse employment assistance, help with resumes and federal job applications, and access to high-end electronic job-hunting resources like America's Job Bank and the Transition Bulletin Board. Stay tuned: In the next chapter, you'll learn how to market your military experience.

CHAPTER 8

Marketing Your Military Experience

HOW TO CREATE A RESUME THAT LANDS INTERVIEWS

In the race to build the resume you'll use to launch your civilian career, it's likely you'll run into a pair of ugly hurdles. The first one is the problem of Milspeak (that is, military language that civilians are unlikely to understand). Left lurking, Milspeak could trip up your resume before you get out of the starting blocks. The second hurdle is that of selecting a proper format for your resume. On the surface, it may seem like a minor decision. But jammed into the wrong resume format, even the most stellar career history can be about as exciting to read as the Navy Personnel Transfer Manual. Add the fact that the chronology of a military career seldom resembles that of a civilian work history and the choice becomes doubly difficult. But like its Milspeak twin, the format hurdle can also be cleared. In this chapter, you'll learn how to:

- Choose just the right format in which to market your military skills to civilian employers.
- Write an achievement-based resume that sparkles.
- Snuff out Milspeak before it snuffs out job opportunities.

CHOOSING A RESUME FORMAT

As I hinted earlier, choosing the right format for your resume is a decision that can either open doors to interview rooms or shut them. But while it's important to make the right choice, you do live in the computer age—you can always change your mind with a series of keystrokes. Meanwhile, let's look at a few basic considerations.

Not too many decisions in life can be boiled down to strict Dos and Don'ts, but here's one: Don't choose a resume format because it looks nice. Yes, your resume is a career-marketing brochure and marketing brochures should look nice. But a pretty brochure filled with irrelevant, poorly organized text will sell nothing. In your resume, it's the order, organization, and relevance of information that will sell you—not a fancy layout. That said, there's no excuse for a sloppy-looking resume. Whatever format you choose, the finished product should be neatly typed or laser printed with generous margins and an easy-to-follow layout. The point is, looks shouldn't dictate your choice of format.

Remember: You control what employers see on your resume. You choose what to include, what to leave out, and how the information is presented. But because some formats require that you include certain types of information, you may give up control if you try to fit your career into the format that your buddy used, or one you found in a book. But by choosing wisely from the three basic formats, and worrying about page layout later, you can display your strengths in a way that benefits you most.

BACK TO BASICS

You may already know the basic three resume formats. You'll find examples of each type of resume, discussed below, in Appendix C. Following the definitions of the three types of resumes is a discussion of how to choose which is best for you.

- *Chronological.* A chronological resume organizes your experience by date. It lists and describes each job you've held, beginning with the present and working backwards.
- *Functional.* A functional resume groups your skills into headings or categories without regard to date. For example, a hospital corpsman's resume might include three headings: Patient Care, Medical Equipment Knowledge, and Tests and Procedures.

- *Chronofunctional.* As its name suggests, a chronofunctional resume combines features of both resume types. This resume type is sometimes called a "combination" resume.

CHOOSING CHRONOLOGICAL

A Navy electronics technician wanted to go into private sector electronics research and development. He had advanced steadily from communications technician to shop supervisor to engineering technician. Since his service pattern showed steady career growth with variation in assignments, and directly supported his civilian job objective, a chronological resume format worked well for him.

Consider yourself a good candidate for a chronological resume if you too can show a history of upward mobility and increased responsibility in the same general field at each of your last three or four assignments. In addition, this history must support your current objective. If you veered off and spent a tour recruiting, or in some other field unrelated to your current objective, this format is probably not your best choice. If you are changing career fields (for example, you were in electronics and now you want to go into finance), the chronological resume is definitely not for you.

Only a very small percentage of military career seekers can use the chronological resume successfully. Most candidates can use the space more effectively by choosing one of the alternatives below. Before you decide to use a chronological resume, be sure you fit all the prerequisites.

CHOOSING FUNCTIONAL

A functional resume breaks your experience into skill groups that describe different functions you've performed, or even categories of knowledge (like Equipment Knowledge) you've gained. The functional resume groups your experience under these headings, regardless of when in your career the experience was gained. Put another way, a chronological resume describes your history job by job, but a functional resume describes it skill area by skill area. For example, the headings on a functional resume for an E-5 personnel clerk might read Records Management, Planning and Organizing, and Personnel Supervision.

Use the functional resume when you've held several unrelated positions in your last three or four assignments, or when your most recent career experience does not support your post-military job objective. You can also use the functional format effectively when marketing collateral experience not related to your primary occupational specialty.

For example, a retiring Army helicopter pilot wanted to pursue a second career in sales. Using a functional resume, he emphasized his experience in marketing, sales techniques, and public relations gained during a successful mid-career tour as a recruiter. Although this experience was more than ten years old, the functional resume did not reveal that, and was therefore an effective format choice for marketing this former pilot's potential as a sales professional. The functional resume is an excellent alternative when you're changing career fields. It enables you to mix and match your skills to present those that will give you the best chance of meeting your objective.

CHOOSING CHRONOFUNCTIONAL

In a chronofunctional, or combination, resume, individual assignments are listed chronologically, but functional skill headings are also included under one or more job descriptions. A combination resume works well when your service experience over the past ten years relates to your job objective, but you would like to emphasize specific skills that add to your value as an employee. This format is especially effective for technicians and mechanics who have often acquired valuable collateral experience in fields like quality assurance, hazardous materials, or planning and estimating.

In addition, the combination format can expand a short military career by providing a natural place to list related duties or previous civilian experience. It can also be an effective way to synopsize and condense a longer career. (See examples in Appendix C.)

ANOTHER CHOICE

Here's another concern for separating servicemembers, especially senior personnel, preparing their second career resumes: They're qualified to work in more than one career field, and aren't sure how to cram it all onto one or two pages. The answer is simple: don't.

Instead, prepare a targeted resume for each career field in which you're interested. Properly written, a targeted resume is tightly focused and easy to read. It catches an employer's eye because of its unrelenting relevance—there's no wasted space, no unnecessary information. When preparing targeted resumes, include only experience that's absolutely relevant to that particular job objective. And no matter how dear to your heart certain pet achievements are, leave them off the resumes where they don't support the objective. Save your space for the information that will land you the interview.

Preparing multiple resumes may seem like a lot of work, but it's worth the time and effort invested at the outset to reap the rewards at the end.

RESUME BUILDING BLOCKS

No matter which format you choose, your transition resume will include certain information blocks that add to or round out the actual work experience section. Here are a few tips to help you build your resume. For varied, specific examples of each of the blocks described below, see Appendix C.

Summary—Also called *Career Summary* or *Highlights*, this block is like a commercial for the rest of your resume. It should catch the reader and hold on. The summary also bears the distinction of being the only area in your resume where you can be subjective. Adjectives like "mature," "reliable," and "dedicated" can be effectively used here to describe your work ethic. Who's going to argue? This is also a good place to include facts you'd really like an employer to notice, like a high-level security clearance or a second language.

Licenses and Certifications—It's useful to break these out in a separate heading so that they stand out and catch the eye. For separating servicemembers with civilian certifications, this can be especially effective when placed high in the resume. Remember, this technique is useful only when you hold licenses or certifications that support your resume objective. If you are transitioning into a sales career and hold a certification in heating systems repair, leave it off. (Unless of course, you're transitioning into the sale of environmental control systems.)

Education—Since the word "education" may seem a little out of context when listing vocational-type schools, I like to title this information block *Education and Training*. Later in this chapter, you'll learn how to list your schools so that a civilian employer can understand them.

Honors and Awards—Use this section to list military awards that don't pertain directly to an achievement in your career field. Meritorious Service Medals, Humanitarian Service Medals, and General Commendations fit well here. Awards related to achievements in your career field should be listed in your work experience section.

Additional Experience—Include a heading like this if you have civilian, preservice, or nonvocational experience you think will strengthen your case. Example: You're an off-duty computer whiz and would like employers to know you have significant computer skills.

HELPFUL HINT

Don't try to write your resume in one day. Instead, take it one section at a time: Summary, Education and Training, Honors and Awards, and Work Experience. The Work Experience section should be broken down further depending on which resume format you choose, chronological or functional. Complete a description of one job or one skill group each day. Take as many days to complete your resume as there are sections to complete. Your transition resume is one of the most important documents you'll ever prepare—don't procrastinate, and don't do a rush job.

KILLING MILSPEAK

Try to remember a time when you weren't associated with the military and you can probably recall a time when you thought of the armed forces in a "GI Joe" kind of way: guns, tanks, cammies, dog tags, marching back and forth to the mess hall. Many employers still think of the armed forces that way. It's not that they aren't aware of the advanced technology and training that power military operations. It's mostly that they've never considered the military as a source for employees.

While many private sector employers will not immediately understand the value of your military training and experience, you can bridge the gap—if you learn to communicate in language they can relate to. If your resume reads like a battle plan, they'll walk away scratching their heads. But if you convert your experience into private industry terminology and use current buzzwords to demonstrate your transferable expertise, you'll be well on your way to the interview.

THE LANGUAGE BARRIER

Most employers don't speak Military, so you'll have to learn to speak Civilian. Your first mission is to learn to recognize Milspeak when it rears its camouflaged head. Here's an example. A Marine Corps major's resume that recently made the rounds at a job fair read this way: "As Commanding Officer of a 400-man unit, was responsible for the health, morale, and welfare of all personnel."

Health, morale, and welfare? Just think of the incredible range of skills and experience buried helplessly in that Milspeak phrase. When the military publishes a job description, it often resembles one of those dehydrated sponges that inflates to ten times its original size when dropped into water. Broad-ranging, important responsibilities are reduced to clipped, stiff phrases that bear no resemblance to descriptions of similar real-world jobs. But drop the Milspeak sponge into real-world water and "health, morale, and welfare" becomes policy development, human resource management, budget planning and administration, risk management, process improvement, operations management, staff development, and more.

Translating Milspeak into civilianese isn't difficult, but it does require a time investment. First, you'll need to mount a search-and-destroy mission. Closely examine job titles, responsibilities, training course names, and technical systems nomenclature to identify and eradicate all Milspeak lurking in your resume. Then, thoroughly research those items to identify civilian counterpart terms you can substitute instead.

Let's look at the most common places Milspeak turns up in a resume.

JOB TITLES

Many military job titles are ambiguous; some are downright misleading. For example, a Navy Fire Control Technician does not put out fires. Instead he or she operates and maintains electronic weapons targeting systems. There are a couple of ways to avoid confusing a potential employer.

First, if there is a simple way to translate your job title without misleading a reader, do so:

- Fire Control Technician = Electronic Weapons Systems Technician
- Mess Cook = Food Service Specialist
- Unit Diary Clerk = Administrative Specialist
- Embarkation NCO = Logistics Coordinator

When applying for jobs where your specific work experience doesn't apply to the position you're seeking, but your management experience does, you can list your organizational position instead of your job title. For example, an E-6 air traffic controller applying for a management position in the hotel industry listed her job title as "Facility Supervisor." She then added the details of her experience within the body of her resume. This drew readers further into her resume. Had she listed her title as "Air Traffic Control Supervisor," she might have lost readers who formed an immediate prejudice that her supervisory skills were limited in scope.

Another type of problem job title, unless you're applying for law enforcement positions, is the straight combat Military Occupational Specialty (MOS): infantry, tank gunner, reconnaissance marine, and the like. There are a number of ways to handle these. One, you can choose a functional resume format that emphasizes skills first and lists work history (and job titles) last. Two, you can list your relative position in an organization. For example, a platoon sergeant might list his job title as "Unit Supervisor." Three, if you spent significant time in collateral duties, and that work experience is what you're selling, you can mine that for an appropriate job title. For example, a tank commander seeking a position in staff development and training based on his collateral duty as a training officer, could list "Training Officer" as his title. Just be sure any dates you list in conjunction accurately reflect the amount of time you spent in a particular position.

The word "officer" is used in real-world employment and is a term human resources professionals understand. But when listing enlisted job titles, leave off references to rank or grade like NCO, petty officer, and sergeant. Unless an employer has military experience, these terms won't communicate your relative position within an organization. Instead, list civilianized equivalents:

- Safety Petty Officer = Safety Coordinator
- Training NCO = Training Supervisor
- Barracks Sergeant = Barracks Manager

When using this method, be sure to choose a term appropriate to your level of authority.

RESPONSIBILITIES

Once you've translated your job titles into civilianese, you'll be faced with actually describing what you did in those jobs. When you present your qualifications, never assume an employer will be able to infer your range of expertise from your job titles alone. To alert civilian employers to your value as their potential new hire, it's important that you provide specifics. But military members often have trouble breaking the daily grind down into specifics. One way to overcome this problem is to answer a series of questions.

Let's say you're a technician:

- What types of general technologies are you familiar with and what specific systems have you worked on?
- Are you an operator performing first-echelon maintenance, or are you proficient in component-level fault analysis and repair?
- Do you troubleshoot and repair only, or have you installed modifications and design changes?
- At what organizational level have you worked? Production? Fabrication? Technical supervision? Quality control?
- Do you read blueprints, schematics, or technical drawings?

Or, perhaps you're a manager. Typical management responsibilities include budget management, policy development, staff training, long-range planning, facility management, operations management, process improvement, resource management, logistics, and more.

- How many people did you supervise and what did those people do?
- Did you also manage money? How much and for what purposes?
- What other resources did you oversee? Materials? Equipment? Supplies?
- What types of planning did you do? Operations planning? Events planning? Future staffing needs?
- What other organizations did you work with?

Your objective in describing your duties is not to provide an exhausting, detailed description, but to hit high points that will let an employer know exactly how much training he would not have to provide if he hired you. These "mountaintops" will be accompanied by high-impact achievement statements. (More on achievement-based resumes later in this chapter.)

REAL PEOPLE

Ron Joy didn't just civilianize the language in his resume—he actually went out and got civilian work experience while on active duty in the Air Force. Now a civilian and the public affairs chief at Ft. Carson, Colorado, Joy served as an Air Force public affairs officer from 1982 to 1994. Along the way, he sought out opportunities to work with local television broadcasters as a way to network in the industry and broaden his knowledge of civilian broadcast communications. To further develop his industry intelligence, Joy joined the Colorado Springs Media Assocation and other trade associations.

"Absolutely seek out civilian work experience and contacts," advises Mary Jane Range, an executive recruiter based in New York City. "You can overcome a big hurdle when employers see that a private sector firm has already taken a chance on you."

FILLING IN THE BLANKS

For many people, asking a series of questions won't be enough to write a good overview of their job responsibilities. Though it may seem a little odd that you might have to do research in order to figure out exactly what it is you did in the service, for many people, research is exactly what it takes. That's when a good reference book or website can come in handy. The *Occupational Outlook Handbook* is both. As discussed in Chapter 6, the *Occupational Outlook Handbook* is a nationally recognized source of career information, designed to provide valuable assistance to individuals making decisions about their future work lives. The handbook's descriptions of what civilian workers do on the job can help you match your military responsibilities with civilian equivalents. You can access this valuable reference tool at www.bls.gov.

The *Dictionary of Occupational Titles* (D.O.T.), which describes information about worker skills, working conditions, and training requirements for more than 12,000 occupations, is another valuable resource. Unfortunately, it costs $50 to order the D.O.T. from the U.S. Department of Labor (DOL). If you don't mind spending the money, call 202-512-1800 to order the book from the Government Printing Office. If you don't want to invest in your own copy, try your military transition center. Many make the D.O.T. available at no cost. Soon it will be even easier to access information contained in the D.O.T. The Employment and Training Administration (also a DOL entity) will soon post a searchable Internet database that will eventually replace the D.O.T. entirely.

Together, the D.O.T. and the *Occupational Outlook Handbook* can provide you with the basic duties associated with thousands of private sector and government positions. Use these references to be sure you include all the necessary "nuts-and-bolts" terminology relating to your specialty.

A WORD ON BUZZWORDS

Describing your military skills using buzzwords—that is, terms and phrases that are current in your target industry—can help you in two important ways:

1. Human resources managers reading your resume will sit up and take notice.

2. When your resume—written using appropriate buzzwords—is scanned into a database, it is more likely to be hit on when hiring managers search the database for candidates.

Here are three great sources for current industry buzzwords:

• *Print and online help wanted ads*: Compare several requests for professionals in your field to learn common requirements. (The *National Business Employment Weekly* compiles ads from regional editions of *The Wall Street Journal* and is a great source for management buzzwords.)

• *Trade journals*: Read trade journals that serve workers in your target industry to learn the current industry-specific terms and phrases.

• *Professional associations*: Check the websites of professional associations for job listings containing current industry terminology.

• *People*: Call department managers at companies in your target industry. Ask what they look for in new hires in your particular specialty. While you're at it, be sure to request company literature, especially brochures and pamphlets pertaining directly to hiring programs.

All this research and translation may sound like a big job, but for your resume, it can mean the difference between a trip to the "no" pile and a trip to the interview room.

EDUCATION AND TRAINING

Okay, you've civilianized your job titles and descriptions. The hardest part is already done. Just a couple more language repairs to go. First, let's look at eradicating Milspeak from your list of training and education. The United States military offers some of the best training available on the planet. But the names of many courses and schools would leave even the most experienced personnel professional wondering what exactly you're trained to do. It's critical to list your training in a way that will provide immediately apparent support for your job objective.

If the name of a school or course doesn't communicate what was taught there, change it. Don't be shy about this. The purpose of your resume is to inform, not mystify. If it makes you feel more comfortable, you can always inform interviewers that you demilitarized course names to make clear the nature of your education and training.

Common problem areas include MOS or rating schools, technical systems courses, and general management and human relations courses. Let's look at a few examples:

- SNAP II Maintenance School = Honeywell Mainframe Computer Maintenance School
- NALCOMIS Training = Automated Maintenance and Material Control System Training
- Mess Management School = Food Service Management School
- NCO Leadership Training = Leadership and Management Training

Get the idea? To help reviewers understand the depth of your training, list the number of classroom hours involved. To determine the number of hours, multiply the number of course days by eight, or the number of weeks by 40. If you completed the course within the last ten years, list the completion date. If the course is older, leave off the date:

Leadership and Management Training, 3/95 (160 hours).
or
Leadership and Management Training (160 hours).

Don't underestimate the significance of shorter courses. Consider this: A college course that meets three times a week for a semester includes about 48 classroom hours. A one-week military course includes about 40. That's a significant amount of time. Even one-day seminars and annual refresher training in subjects like occupational safety or human relations can help mold your image as a well-trained prospect.

EASING THE TRANSITION

Look at it this way: If you were planning to spend a few years in Spain, you'd probably take the time to learn to speak some Spanish. Since you'll probably spend the rest of your life in private sector companies, take the time now to learn to speak like a civilian. The time and effort will pay off in an easier transition.

So far, so good. You know how to choose a resume format, what information blocks to include, and how to kill any lurking Milspeak. Next we'll discuss the single technique that will set your resume apart: building it on achievements.

It's your job to make your military transition resume stand out in the herd of applicants. To do this, tell prospective employers not only what you did in past jobs, but also how well you did it.

Wendy Enelow, a career expert and employment writer in Lynchburg, Virginia, believes showing employers how you can benefit their companies is critical. "Provide detailed information," she says, "to substantiate not only your qualifications, but also your ability to contribute to the corporation and effect positive change."

The "career obituary" resume that lists dates tombstone-style, along with responsibilities, has been replaced with the achievement-based resume. This winning resume contains high-impact achievement statements that demonstrate your value as an employee.

"Employers don't need a job description; they need to know what you *accomplished*," said Yana Parker, the author of *Damn Good Resume Guide* (Ten Speed Press, 1998). "In recounting past experience, be sure to describe the value or benefit to the organization from your activity. In other words, answer the implied question, 'So what?'"

DISCOVERING YOUR ACHIEVEMENTS

To communicate your value to hiring managers, you must first decide what you've achieved above and beyond simply describing your assigned duties. While that sounds like a cinch, lots of folks find it difficult to distinguish between achievements, awards, and just doing their jobs. How can you tell the difference?

First, a military award is not an achievement. The achievement is what you did to get the award. A medal, ribbon, or award letter is simply a tangible pat on the back. (More on awards later.) Second, the idea that any positive contributions you made should be dismissed as "just doing your job" is a self-defeating form of modesty that has no place in your job search.

"Don't be modest about saying you're good at what you do," said Parker. "You may have been 'just doing your job,' but if you did it with pride and professionalism and got excellent results, that does matter. Don't take your accomplishments for granted."

So, with misplaced modesty and awards out of the way, only achievements remain. How do you figure out what you've achieved? In preparing her clients's resumes, one California-based career coach used to ask her clients a rapid-fire question: "What have you done better-faster-stronger-safer-cheaper?" In other words, what improvements or contributions had they made to their military units above and beyond duty's call? How about you? Did you ever improve or streamline a formerly cumbersome procedure? Did you ever troubleshoot and repair a system that had been "hard down" for a long period? Did you increase training effectiveness? Cut unnecessary paperwork? Save money on supplies? Any improvement you've made that's relevant to your objective should be listed on your resume as an achievement.

WRITING ACHIEVEMENT STATEMENTS

Every achievement is built from three basic bricks: situation, action, and results. That is, the situation that confronted you, what action you took, and the results of your actions.

Here's an example.

> *Situation*: After a month as his unit's new Training NCO, Sergeant Smith found that training records for personnel in his division were poorly organized and badly out of date.
>
> *Action*: Consulting current manuals, he streamlined and updated the records, aligning them with his unit's regulations.
>
> *Result*: Personnel whose qualifications had expired received immediate refresher training. The reorganized records received a grade of outstanding on a subsequent administrative inspection.

Now, that's a fairly long tale to include on a resume. A more simple, direct version of Sergeant Smith's achievement statement might look like this:

"Reorganized and updated division training records. Improved currency of employee qualifications and received outstanding scores on a subsequent records audit." (Notice two things here: the tightly written achievement statement, *and* the simultaneous eradication of Milspeak. "Personnel" became "employees"; "grade" became "scores"; and "inspection" became "audit.")

A PLACE FOR EVERYTHING

After you've distilled your successes into punchy phrases, you're ready to decide where to place them on your resume. Achievements tacked on to the end may be missed by HR personnel who will toss your resume in the "no" pile if you don't grab their interest quickly. On the other hand, a resume that begins with an extended description of how great you are can lack context and seem inflated. One effective way to present your achievements is to link them with brief summaries of general responsibilities. This method results in a series of satisfying snapshots of your experience, showing a) the responsibilities of each position and b) your success in handling those responsibilities.

Here's an example:

Network Systems Administrator
9/96–4/98
Naval Training Systems Center, San Diego, CA
Provided professional and consistent maintenance and repair of desktop systems, LAN, and wide area network. Administered and supported multiple VAX and PC, DEC Open VMS 6.1, NT 3.51–4.0, Windows 95. Communications experience includes varied hardware and protocols, such as NDLC and X.25, frame relay, TCP/IP, and ISDN.

+ Analyzed and modified desktop systems and VAX cluster, optimizing integration of all information systems resources.
+ Played key role in design and installation of a 100-node Novell network.
+ Improved work center communication and efficiency.
+ Established hardware and software inventory, increasing effective use of available resources and eliminating unnecessary expenditures.

This candidate's resume demonstrates initiative, organizational skills, and concern for efficiency. It also covers a broad range of technical knowledge and skill without boring the reader with obvious details (like test equipment knowledge, which is implicit in the text).

ABOUT AWARDS

Private sector employers are interested in what you can do for them, not how many medals jingle on your dress uniform. To add even more punch to your achievement-based resume, translate your awards into achievements. But be sure of two things: one, that each award you list is relevant to your objective and two, that you explain why you received it.

For example, an administrative specialist might list her Army Achievement Medal this way: "Identified alternate source of office supplies, saving more than $1,000 annually. Received the Army Achievement Medal."

Another way to include awards is by listing them in a separate heading called "Honors and Awards." This works well for high-ranking awards, general awards, and combat honors. Remember, many civilian employers wouldn't know a Good Conduct Medal from a Silver Cross, so when you use a separate heading, be sure to list the achievement associated with each award.

DON'T EMBELLISH

One final warning: When you write an achievement-based resume, don't exaggerate. One recent study showed that more than 50% of all resumes screened contain lies or embellishments—and it is HR personnel who discover them. Avoid the temptation to land more interviews by revving up your resume with inflated accomplishments—like elevating the importance of low-level projects or taking full credit for a team effort. An experienced interviewer will probe your resume's claims in detail. If he or she catches even a hint of a lie or embellishment, the interview will be over. Stick with the truth—it will pay off in the long run.

QUALITY CONTROL CHECK

Run your resume through this quick test to ensure it's ready for "inspection."

- Have you translated all Milspeak into clear civilian language? Have you eliminated all acronyms?
- Have you listed systems and equipment in a way that a civilian technician would recognize the technology?

- Do all school names communicate what was taught? Have you included leadership training?
- Did you include current buzzwords and phrases appropriate to your target industry?
- Have you appended awards to the achievements that earned them? If you've included a separate section for awards, have you explained the significance of each honor?
- Have you stressed personal traits instilled by your military service like reliability, integrity, loyalty, and motivation to excel?

If you answered "affirmative" to each of these questions, your military transition resume is mission-ready. Start practicing for those interviews!

An additional note for officers: If you intend to use an employment recruiter, check with two or three to determine their resume format preferences. Many will want a description of your responsibilities by job title, almost like a chronological format, but without the years spent at individual posts. Incidentally, this format can work well for any officer selling management experience, because it highlights important assignments and allows you to select only the assignments that support your objective.

SUMMARY

In this chapter you learned how to successfully market the skills and abilities you gained in the military to civilian employers. By keeping up with events and trends in your industry of choice, learning how to discuss your military background in the civilian language of the business world, identifying the methods that best suit the needs of your job search, and capitalizing on the practical value contained in your military experience, you'll be well on your way to getting called in for the interviews you want. In the next chapter, you'll learn important interview strategies so you can succeed at this vital part of the civilian job search process.

CHAPTER 9

Interviewing Like a Pro

PREPPING AND PERFORMING FOR JOB INTERVIEW SUCCESS

Consider this . . .

- If you were scheduled to make an important presentation, you would probably research and rehearse.
- If you had to take a big test, you would probably study and prepare.
- If you were about to meet with a person of some importance, you would probably make a list of important issues to address.

A job interview is all of these things—with a potential payoff that's usually greater than that offered by any of the scenarios above. Yet most job hunters spend zero time preparing for this important event and arrive in the interview room imagining they will somehow improvise. The problem is, most of us do not improvise well under pressure. Instead we fumble, falter, or even choke.

To impress an interviewer, you must prepare in advance. And while this holds true for every job seeker, the military candidate must work even harder.

In addition to researching the company and the job being offered, the military job seeker faces another challenge: battling stereotypes.

Many civilian hiring managers harbor stereotypes about military personnel that can work against you in an interview. Company recruiters may be wary of hiring a candidate whose work experience was gained in an environment so different from their own. Employers may also be concerned about work ethic and personality differences instilled by military service.

"I couldn't believe how many interviewers thought that because I was in the military, I couldn't think for myself," said Dave Felcher, 38, who served as a Navy Combat Information Center (CIC) officer before leaving the service in 1992. Felcher now heads a nonprofit environmental rehabilitation agency, but his post-military job search was an uphill climb made steeper by employer stereotyping.

Stereotyping like that faced by Felcher can spawn interview questions intended to confirm, or dispel, the interviewer's preconceived notions. By becoming aware of this barrier now, you can prepare to answer questions that arise from military stereotypes when you encounter them during your job search. You can determine whether you're battling a stereotype through careful listening. Before answering, take a moment to peer beneath the surface of each question: What is it that the interviewer really wants to know?

Here are several interview questions designed by recruiters to probe the more common military stereotypes. Each set of questions is followed by a statement of the stereotype with which it is associated. Each is also accompanied by tips on answering questions in ways that will shatter stereotypes and display your skills and experience in a positive light.

QUESTIONS:

- What are some of your outside activities?
- What involvement have you had in the local community?
- What social activities do you enjoy?

Stereotype: Military personnel don't know how to fit in with the civilian community.

Honestly examine your own ability to fit into civilian society. Prepare examples from your work and social history that demonstrate you're not a soldier, sailor, airman, or marine 24 hours a day. These may include community service, work with outside contractors, or a part-time job.

QUESTIONS:

- How would you feel if you were given the freedom to handle a project however you chose?
- How have you been innovative in solving a problem at work? Give me an example.
- Can you tell me about a time when you had to be flexible?

Stereotype: Military personnel are rigid and lack creativity.

Prepare detailed examples of projects that required adjustments in planning and scheduling. Try to show how you've responded to change in a positive way. Rehearse an example of a time when you employed creativity to get the job done.

QUESTIONS:

- How do you handle being told what to do?
- How would you handle a difficult employee?
- Have you ever disagreed with your boss? How did you handle it?

Stereotype: Military personnel will try to "run things" and use their rank to get things done.

You can dispel this stereotype by showing an interviewer that the military chain of command required you to be both an effective supervisor and a cooperative subordinate. Talk about formal management training you've completed, and show how "pulling rank" is normally the military management method of last resort.

QUESTIONS:

- Have you ever managed a budget?
- Have you ever found a way to reduce operating costs?
- What things do you consider to be top priorities for a business?

Stereotype: Military personnel don't understand budgets or the profit mentality.

Specific examples involving money, budgets, and profit work well here. If you have no experience in these areas, you can cite improvements in efficiency or reductions in man-hours. For private companies, these achievements translate into a healthier bottom line. But don't count on an interviewer to draw that parallel. If, for example, you reduced the number of man-hours required to keep a certain batch of records up to date, be sure to point out to the interviewer that such a time savings in the military would equal cost savings in corporate America.

QUESTIONS:

- What kinds of pressures have you had to face in your past positions?
- What do you consider the "ideal job"?
- How do you handle stress?

Stereotype: Military life is easier than civilian life.

You're probably laughing out loud right now, and that's good because this is no time for a sob story. If you detect that an interviewer doesn't feel your military experience counts as a "real job," it's not the time to whine about long deployments and all the MREs you choked down. Instead, cite specific examples of successful performance *despite* the stresses of deployments, family separation, and long working hours to show you've had a "real-world" existence.

REAL PEOPLE

Mike Williams knows what it's like to be in the job interview "hot seat"—literally. In 1995, the retiring Navy lieutenant commander applied for a staff position with the San Diego City Council. When he arrived for an interview, council staffers directed Williams to sit in a single chair facing a panel of four interviewers. The conference room was sweltering—at least 85 degrees, remembers Williams—and he was wearing a wool suit. The interviewers sipped cool drinks, but offered him nothing.

"They peppered me with questions, one right after the other," Williams says. "I was getting more and more uncomfortable from the heat, but I just tried to remain calm and collected and reel off the best answers I could."

He later learned that the whole interview—the wilting heat, the single chair, the imposing panel of inquisitors—had been staged to see how he'd react under pressure, which is an ever-present part of politics. But Williams had already worked under more pressure than the city council could manufacture—as a military intelligence officer. Based partly on his ability to remain cool under fire, Williams got the job.

QUESTIONS:

- Can you give me an example of a time you used initiative?
- If your boss dumped a job in your lap without instructions, what would you do?
- What kind of experience have you had planning and managing projects?

Stereotype: Military personnel are used to being told exactly what to do, and how.

Many civilians have the idea that servicemembers spend their days responding to orders barked out by a drill sergeant. Your job here is to portray yourself as an individual, with the ability to initiate, evaluate, plan, and decide. You might gently point out that, beyond boot camp, military service is all about initiative. Then back that up with examples of how you used initiative on the job.

While job hunting laws are certainly not written in stone, here's one you can count on: The time you invest in preparing for interviews will increase your chances of being hired sooner rather than later.

One great reference for learning how to prepare for and handle tough interview questions is *Interviewing* (John Wiley & Sons, 1994), a volume in the Premiere Guides series produced by the *National Business Employment Weekly*. This book addresses a broad range of issues including research and preparation, typical and not-so-typical questions, dealing with the unexpected, and what employers look for (it isn't always what you think!). Another useful source is *Great Interview*, published by LearningExpress. The "success story" strategy emphasized in this book can prove very helpful in highlighting your military experience to civilian interviewers.

FIVE SALES SECRETS

A job interview isn't a casual discussion with a friendly mentor who wants to help you out. It's a classic sales encounter. You're the salesperson and the corporate interviewer is the buyer's agent. The product? Your skills, experience, and what you can do for the company. During this sales encounter, the buyer's agent must be convinced that what you have to sell is worth purchasing.

While military job candidates may find time to practice for interviews, most are unprepared to sell their product to prospective employers. But by learning and practicing the five sales secrets below, you can win over interviewers and land a great job offer.

1. KNOW YOUR MARKET

Among military units engaged in the same "business" (aviation, for example), the same set of standard regulations, coupled with some locally written requirements, generally govern operations. The biggest adjustment military personnel usually face when changing units is the fresh batch of personalities whose quirks must be learned and mastered. Thus, a pilot or aviation mechanic transferring to a new aircraft squadron can expect a new set of faces—but an *organization* that's doing business in the same general way as the squadron he or she just came from.

In the civilian world, things aren't so simple. Sure, the personality maze still exists (after all, people are everywhere). But even among firms operating in the same industry, there are vast differences in corporate identity, rules, culture, and hiring needs. According to David Green, manager in San Diego of Dale Carnegie Centers for Excellence, an international sales training firm, researching those differences is the key to targeting your sales pitch to each company that interviews you for a job.

Think about the last time you shopped for a car. Did the salesperson charge up to you and blurt, "Hey, here's a great little model and here's why you should buy it!" Probably not. More likely he introduced himself first, then asked you a series of questions: "What are you looking for today? Oh, a truck? Two-wheel or four-wheel drive? Will it just be you and a passenger, or do you think you'll need an extended cab?"

No salesman worth his salt makes a pitch without knowing a little about the buyer. Why spend time trying to sell a sedan to someone who wants to buy a truck? Similarly, you too should know *your* buyers, that is, each company you plan to interview with.

"Research helps an applicant see issues from the company's point of view," says Green, who also is a hiring manager for Carnegie. Green says it's "impressive" when a candidate asks informed questions about the company. That shows that he or she is "genuinely interested in the company and isn't just going on as many interviews as possible."

Here are a few things you should learn about each company to which you apply:

- Culture: What is the company's mission and management style? How do employees dress?
- Structure: What is the organizational structure like? Who are the firm's chief executives?

- Lines of business: What services, technologies, or products does the company sell?
- Crossover: What technologies used or sold by the company are similar to military technologies with which you're familiar?

You can find management and financial information about publicly held companies in *Standard & Poor's, Dun & Bradstreet, Hoover's,* and other corporate directories. Such reference books are available in your base or post transition center and in local libraries. Limited versions are also available online. To learn more about culture, products and services, and company mission, try calling customer service or public relations departments and requesting product literature or annual reports. Recent media coverage can also give you a good handle on company trends. Check Internet search engines to see if your target firm has recently been featured in any newspapers or magazines. Many companies have a corporate website that can provide a wealth of information about personnel, products and services, and recent developments at the company. The look and feel of the site can also tell you a lot about the corporate culture.

2. KNOW YOUR PRODUCT

So you know the company, but do you know yourself? Recognizing your own worth is essential to selling your skills effectively. Know and be able to communicate the value of your military skills and experience to civilian employers. Before heading for an interview, complete the exercises in Chapter 6 to make sure you have a comprehensive grasp on how you can use your military background to bring value to post-military employers.

3. SHOW BENEFITS

In sales, there's a saying that goes like this: "People don't buy drill bits; they buy holes." In many cases, it's not that buyers are eager to own a particular product. Instead, they want whatever benefits that product can deliver. Similarly, while interviewers may be interested in your background, their bottom-line interest is in the benefits your background will provide to the company and its customers.

"When an interviewer asks, 'Tell me what you're good at,' don't just say, 'Well, I'm very good at keeping accurate records,'" says Florida-based vocational counselor Joseph Land. "Provide examples of how your record-keeping ability translated into time saved or efficiency improved. There are lots of good record keepers. How will your record keeping benefit your target company?"

Go back to the achievement statements you prepared for your resume. Sit down at your computer and expand on those accomplishments a bit. Practice telling a brief story (one minute or less) about each. Rehearse until you can tell each story in an unrehearsed fashion. But don't rely on your resume alone. Instead consider that document a "first date" with the interviewer, and be prepared to tell interviewers about benefits they don't already know. Write up a couple of situation-action-results (see Chapter 8) stories that aren't on your resume. "Wow" the interviewer with new examples of how you added value in the workplace.

4. COUNTER OBJECTIONS

You may not be the perfect candidate for every job for which you apply. For this reason, it's a good idea to identify potential objections to your candidacy before you go into an interview, then be ready to discuss them. As noted earlier in this chapter, you may face objections, some based on stereotyping, related to the fact that you gained your experience in the military.

"Some employers feel military veterans don't understand civilian culture and may be too structured and inflexible to fit in with their companies," says Anne Stundahl, former chief of transition services at Naval Station San Diego. Other concerns involve power struggles. As discussed earlier in this chapter, some employers believe senior military personnel, having been used to being in charge, may come in and try to "take over."

Handle such objections by telling interviewers that you're aware of the differences between military and civilian work environments. Provide examples that show how you've managed to be successful both as a subordinate and, if applicable, as a supervisor. Here are a few examples of other potential objections and examples of how to handle them.

Objection: The military receives unlimited supplies from the government. You've never worked in a real, budget-driven work environment.

Counter: True, the military receives some supplies from government sources. But we still operated under quarterly budgets and maintained strict accounting over our inventories. In fact, when I was inventory control supervisor, I developed a stock rotation system that decreased waste by 15%.

Objection: You don't have a college degree. We prefer degreed candidates.

Counter: True, I don't have my degree yet. But I'm enrolled in school now and will finish in less than two years. Meanwhile, I've been working hands-on for four years with technology exactly like that which your company sells. I'm confident I can do a great job as a sales representative for you because I am very familiar with how your equipment works. Then when I finish school two years from now, you'll have an experienced rep with a degree *and* hands-on technical experience.

Objection: You have management experience, but not in this industry.

Counter: I can see why you'd be concerned about that. But in the military, I learned to use effective leadership and management skills in a variety of different work environments. Motivating people to excel, holding them accountable, and rewarding them for good performance is a formula that works no matter where you go.

If you've ever spent time on the phone with a telemarketer, you know countering objections is a key to making sales. But be forewarned: Good salespeople anticipate specific objections and practice navigating around them. Don't imagine you can counter objections in a job interview without putting in a little practice yourself.

5. ALWAYS BE CLOSING

In sales, there are salespeople and there are closers. A closer is a salesperson who has the guts to make the moves and ask the questions that seal the deal. Let it be said that as a job applicant, you have to be careful of "closing" so much that you appear pushy. But you can still make moves toward closing that will help you check your progress and steer the interview in the right direction.

Many top sales training firms teach their salespeople to use a technique called the trial close. A trial close helps a salesperson know how close the buyer is to buying and what obstacles might stand in the way of a decision to buy.

Here's how to do it: When the moment seems right, choose one of your strongest qualifications and ask the interviewer a question designed to see where you stand. For example:

You: Ms. Johnson, I understand this position requires experience in supervising work teams of 10 to 15 people. Is my Army experience as a personnel office supervisor along the lines of what you were looking for?

Interviewer: Yes, your office supervision experience would seem to fit well here. We have a lot of young workers just out of college who could use firm guidance.

By using this trial close, you've learned that the interviewer views your military supervisory experience favorably. At this point, you might offer a short example of how you promoted efficiency in a work environment where a younger workforce was involved.

By now you may be thinking, "Great, but what if I try the trial close and the interviewer gives me a negative response?" No worries: the trial close works great then, too. For example:

> *You*: Ms. Johnson, I understand this position requires experience in supervising work teams of 10 to 15 people. Is my Army experience as a personnel office supervisor along the lines of what you were looking for?
>
> *Interviewer*: Well, your supervisory experience is helpful, but we're in transition and are more interested in a candidate who can set up new administrative systems.

Now, instead of continuing to talk about your experience managing people, you can concentrate on giving the interviewer examples of your skills in an area the buyer really needs—experience in administrative management. The trial close worked to get you on track with the buyer's needs.

At the end of the interview, use closing techniques to come to an understanding with the interviewer: "Ms. Johnson, after learning more about this position and how I might fit in at Tech Corp., I'm very interested in the job. From your questions, it sounded like you're also interested in pursuing this with me. Is that right?"

This close achieves two ends. First, if the interviewer has additional objections, she'll likely bring them up then, affording you an opportunity to counter. Second, if the interviewer confirms her interest in you, you can ask about the next step in the hiring process.

By recognizing a job interview as a sales situation, you can understand and prepare for your role as seller. Then, like any salesperson worth his or her salt, you'll be prepared to close the deal on your first post-military job.

CIVILIAN UNIFORM REGULATIONS

While you're honing your interview skills, you also need to figure out how to dress yourself. To some, that may seem like a subject that needs no discussion, but let's face it: Beyond choosing between a working uniform and a dress uniform, many military veterans have never had to make decisions regarding what clothes to wear to work, much less a job interview. Whether you're among the fashion-savvy or the "clothing-challenged," here are a few tips to help you make the best possible impression on a potential employer.

ATTITUDE ADJUSTMENT

You've heard it said, "Clothes make the man." Now we might say, "Clothes make the person." Old or new, what the saying means, of course, is that your appearance communicates a message about you. Like it or not, nearly everyone you'll meet will make a snap judgment about you based solely on your appearance. It's a fact of human nature—and an unbreakable law of human resources management. With mere minutes to decide whether you'll fit into the company, an interviewer will take your appearance into serious account.

It's important to realize that during your job search, dressing well isn't about the clothes you wear; it's about what the clothes you wear say about you. The failure to recognize that your appearance is another way of communicating your potential to an employer can significantly lengthen your job search.

The best universal advice for interview dressing is to strive for an impression of understated professionalism. That is to say, your appearance should be strictly professional in every detail, but that individual details should not draw attention to themselves.

Here's a head-to-toe checklist to help you dress and groom for interview success.

HAIR

Men: A short haircut is usually safest for an interview. Of course, this won't be a problem if you're just getting out of the service. But if you've been out for awhile, you may need a trim.

Women: A short, professional-looking cut works well with suit dressing. If your hair is of medium length, wearing it down and styled is also appropriate. But if you normally wear your hair longer and unstyled, you should definitely pull it back when going for an interview. After years of adhering to military regulations on women's hairstyles, you may have to resist the temptation to let your hair down—literally.

Everyone: Avoid excessive gel, mousse, and hair spray. If you can see what's holding your hairstyle together, it's probably too much.

CLOTHES

Military professionals leaving the service often have only two kinds of clothes in their closets: casual and uniforms. If this describes you, you may need to plan ahead and actually budget for a job search wardrobe. You'll need at least two suits (you don't want to show up for successive interviews wearing the same thing), and enough accessories to vary your look from day to day.

Men: A darker color, like charcoal or blue, is usually more powerful, especially when paired with a crisply pressed, ultra-white dress shirt. At this writing, the perfect tie begins with a small, tight knot, and is very narrow at the top, widening considerably from knot to tip. Avoid holiday ties and "statement" ties that feature your favorite NFL team or environmental cause. Also be careful of loud prints or cutesy ties such as those featuring cartoon characters. Instead, choose sedate prints or stick with a solid.

Women: A tailored skirt and jacket, rather than a dress, imparts the most professional impression. If your suit is in a brighter color, choose stockings in a natural shade. With a more conservative suit color (i.e., blue, or gray) natural stockings also work, but you could opt for a sheer color that matches your skirt and shoes.

HELPFUL HINT

One question often asked by military job hunters is, "Should I dress for the interview as I would dress for the job?" In other words, should I dress blue-collar for a blue-collar position, and wear a suit for a professional opening? The short answer is a qualified "no." Dress for the interview, not for the job. A job interview isn't the job itself; it's a business meeting between buyer and seller. So wearing jeans and a workshirt, even for a job as a mechanic, wouldn't be appropriate. However, some experts feel that wearing a suit may give the impression you're overqualified for a blue-collar position, or that you might be afraid to get your hands dirty. Other job search professionals argue that a suit is always the right prescription for interview success—that the more professional you look, the better.

You'll have to decide for yourself which advice sounds the most reasonable. But, if you decide wearing a suit for a blue-collar interview might indeed be overkill, there is an in-between. Consider wearing slacks with a dress shirt and tie. This is a standard "uniform" for service technicians in many fields that is also appropriate for a business meeting.

If you're a woman applying for hands-on technical openings, a similar approach works well—minus the tie, of course. Choose a simple blouse and low-heeled shoes to create the impression that while you know what's appropriate for the interview, if you're hired, you won't be afraid to get your hands dirty.

JEWELRY

Women: Choosing the right jewelry can complete a look that says "professional." For interviews, be conservative and selective.

Men: While men won't have as many decisions to make in this area, there are some important considerations about jewelry. What kind of watch to wear is a big one. Many military personnel wear large, multipurpose watches on the job—diving watches, aviation watches, or sports watches. And while you may feel the need to check your heart rate during an interview, your watch shouldn't reflect that. Choose a classic watch with a metallic band and medium-sized face to create the best impression. If you wear a tie pin or cuff links, keep them simple and understated.

HELPFUL HINT

While every job applicant should make sure his or her hands and nails are clean and groomed, hands are especially important for women. Why? Because studies have shown that many people subconsciously judge a woman's maturity and professional status based on the appearance of her hands. Manicures are inexpensive and getting one can help you make the best impression at an interview. Choose a clear polish or a light (but not bright) shade.

SHOES

Everyone: When budgeting for clothing, be sure you don't stop at your ankles. An old, worn, or inappropriate pair of shoes can completely ruin the overall appearance you've worked hard to create.

Men: Choose conservative, laced dress shoes of a single color that matches your belt. Penny loafers and other slip-ons may be too casual for suit dressing. Your socks should match your belt and shoes.

Women: While sandals or other, more casual, open-toe styles may be appropriate on the job, remember that an interview is a business meeting, and closed-toe shoes say "business." Medium-heeled pumps that coordinate with the dominant color in your outfit are appropriate, for example.

A FINAL WORD

For separating servicemembers, jumping into business attire can be an uncertain leap. Just remember, the idea is to make an impression that says "professional." Stick with conservative choices and pay close attention to details like jewelry, socks, and creases. Pretend you're going to be inspected, because in reality, you will be. And remember that other old saying about appearances: "You never get a second chance to make a first impression."

SAYING THANK YOU

There's one final note on interviews: the thank you note. Taking the time to thank the interviewer, particularly in today's fast-paced it's-all-about-me world, communicates thoughtfulness and professionalism. During your job hunt, keep a pack of professional-quality thank you notes (you can find these at office supply stores), along with a book of stamps, in your bag or briefcase. As soon as you get back from your interview, write out a note thanking the interviewer for his or her time, and mail it right away. Many jobs, when the hiring decision comes down to a two candidate toss-up, fall to the candidate who has the good manners to send a thank you note.

SUMMARY

In this chapter, you learned to view job interviews as sales encounters. You read about five sales secrets that can help you succeed in interviews, and also how to counter stereotypes recruiters may hold about military job candidates. In addition, you learned how to select interview attire that will create an impression of understated professionalism. Next we'll explore the career possibilities for those who want to serve their country outside of the military—Chapter 10 looks into the civil service option.

The Civil Service Option

WORKING FOR UNCLE SAM—WITHOUT THE UNIFORM

Who's the nation's largest employer? If you answered Microsoft, General Motors, or AT&T, guess again. America's largest employer is the federal government. The U.S. government employed more than 3.3 million civilian workers in 1999. Of those, more than 2.2 million, or about 70%, were full-time permanent employees. Another million or so worked in part-time or full-time temporary federal jobs. According to the U.S. Office of Personnel Management (the federal government's human resources agency):

- Almost half of federal workers held managerial or professional jobs, a rate twice as high as the workforce as a whole.
- The vast majority of federal employees work full-time, often on flexible or "flextime" schedules.
- The average salary of federal employees was over $46,000 in 1998.
- About four out of five federal employees work outside the Washington, D.C. metropolitan area.

Federal employment is projected to decline slightly due to budgetary constraints, the growing use of private contractors, and the transfer of some functions to state and local governments, but Uncle Sam still hires an average of more than 300,000 new employees each year to replace workers who retire, transfer to other federal positions, or leave the civil service.

"If you're looking for good pay with excellent benefits, pursue the federal job market," says Dennis V. Damp, the Pennsylvania-based author of *The Book of U.S. Government Jobs* (Bookhaven Press, 7th Edition). "Excellent job opportunities are available for those who know how to tap this lucrative market."

More on tapping the market in a moment. But first, what kinds of workers are these federal employees and what kinds of jobs do they hold?

Americans are probably most aware of the influence of the federal government in their lives right around April 15th—the day they pay their taxes. But the U.S. government touches the citizens of this country in more places than just their wallets. The U.S. Constitution divides the government into three branches: executive, legislative, and judicial. Collectively, these branches:

- Operate and maintain a national defense to combat or deter foreign aggression.
- Represent American interests abroad through diplomacy and international commerce.
- Protect the health and well-being of citizens by passing and enforcing laws.
- Administer a variety of programs and agencies that help make the country a clean, safe place to live.

Federal employees are the workers who carry out these functions. Such workers hold jobs in all three branches of government, and also in the U.S. Postal Service, which is itself a distinct federal agency. The legislative branch employs only about one percent of federal workers, nearly all of whom work in the Washington, D.C., area. The judicial branch employs about the same number of people as the legislative branch, but its offices and employees are dispersed throughout the country.

The executive branch, however, is a different story. In 1998, it employed about 98% of all federal civilian employees (excluding postal workers). The executive branch is composed of the Executive Office of the President, 14 executive cabinet departments, and over 90 independent agencies, each of which has clearly defined duties. The Executive Office of the President is composed of several offices and councils that aid the president in policy decisions. These include the Office of Management and

Budget, which oversees the administration of the federal budget; the National Security Council, which advises the president on matters of national defense; and the Council of Economic Advisers, which makes economic policy recommendations.

Why is all this important? Because each of the 14 executive cabinet departments administers programs that oversee an element of American life. Together, the departments described below represent more than more than two million full-time permanent jobs, plus another million part-time, temporary, and intermittent positions:

- *Defense:* Manages the military forces that protect our country and its interests, including the Departments of the Army, Navy, Air Force, and a number of smaller agencies. The civilian workforce employed by the Department of Defense performs various support activities, such as payroll and public relations.
- *Veterans Affairs:* Administers programs to aid U.S. veterans and their families, runs the veterans' hospital system, and operates our national cemeteries.
- *Treasury:* Regulates banks and other financial institutions, administers the public debt, prints currency, and carries out law enforcement in a wide range of areas, including counterfeiting, tax, and customs violations.
- *Agriculture:* Promotes U.S. agriculture domestically and internationally and sets standards governing quality, quantity, and labeling of food sold in the United States.
- *Justice:* Enforces federal laws, prosecutes cases in federal courts, and runs federal prisons.
- *Interior:* Manages federal lands including the national parks and forests, runs hydroelectric power systems, and promotes conservation of natural resources.
- *Transportation:* Sets national transportation policy, runs the Coast Guard except in time of war, plans and funds the construction of highways and mass transit systems, and regulates railroad, aviation, and maritime operations.
- *Health and Human Services:* Sponsors medical research, approves use of new drugs and medical devices, runs the Public Health Service, and administers the Social Security and Medicaid programs.
- *Commerce:* Forecasts the weather, charts the oceans, regulates patents and trademarks, conducts the census, compiles statistics, and promotes U.S. economic growth by encouraging international trade.

- *State:* Oversees the nation's embassies and consulates, issues passports, monitors U.S. interests abroad, and represents the United States before international organizations.
- *Energy:* Coordinates the national use and provision of energy, oversees the production and disposal of nuclear weapons, and plans for future energy needs.
- *Labor:* Enforces laws guaranteeing fair pay, workplace safety, and equal job opportunity, administers unemployment insurance, regulates pension funds, and collects economic data in the Bureau of Labor Statistics.
- *Housing and Urban Development:* Funds public housing projects, enforces equal housing laws, and insures and finances mortgages.
- *Education:* Provides scholarships, student loans, and aid to schools.

So how does all that shake out into individual jobs? Take a look at the following table. It will give you a better idea of what kinds of positions can be found with the federal government.

EMPLOYMENT IN THE FEDERAL GOVERNMENT, EXCLUDING THE POSTAL SERVICE, BY OCCUPATION, 1998 AND PROJECTED CHANGE, 1998–2008
(Employment in thousands)

OCCUPATION	1998 EMPLOYMENT		1998–2008
	NUMBER	PERCENT	PERCENT CHANGE
All occupations	1,819	100.0	−9.0
Professional specialty	561	30.8	−0.4
Engineers	90	5.0	−12.2
Systems analysts	54	3.0	31.8
Registered nurses	46	2.5	−1.8
Physicians	45	2.5	−3.4
Life scientists	38	2.1	5.8
Teachers, librarians, and counselors	32	1.8	12.2
Physical scientists	31	1.7	−4.1
Judges, magistrates, and other judicial workers	31	1.7	0.9
Lawyers	26	1.4	24.3
Social scientists	25	1.4	−7.5
Administrative support, including clerical	410	22.5	−16.2
Other clerical and administrative support workers	180	9.9	−4.4
Secretaries	63	3.5	−25.0
Office clerks, general	54	3.0	−7.6

Bookkeeping, accounting, and auditing clerks	36	2.0	−9.8
Office and administrative support supervisors and managers	30	1.7	−6.0
Stock clerks and order fillers	25	1.4	−29.7
Welfare eligibility workers and interviewers	23	1.3	−26.3
Computer operators	21	1.2	−42.9
Executive, administrative, and managerial	321	17.7	−5.3
Inspectors and compliance officers, except construction	53	2.9	3.8
Accountants and auditors	51	2.8	−26.6
Management analysts	37	2.1	13.8
Buyers and purchasing agents	33	1.8	−3.4
Tax examiners, collectors, and revenue agents	27	1.5	−0.2
Human resources, training, and labor relations specialists	25	1.3	4.5
Precision production, craft, and repair	168	9.2	−17.2
Mechanics, installers, and repairers	89	4.9	−13.4
Construction trades	32	1.8	−16.8
Blue-collar worker supervisors	25	1.4	−29.7
Technicians and related support	151	8.3	−13.0
Health technicians and technologists	41	2.3	−11.5
Engineering technicians	39	2.1	−20.9
Air traffic controllers and airplane dispatchers	25	1.4	−3.4
Service	125	6.8	7.1
Police and detectives	42	2.3	9.7
Health service occupations	22	1.2	−12.1
Operators, fabricators, and laborers	58	3.2	2.3
Helpers, laborers, and material movers, hand	26	1.4	−50.2
Transportation and material moving machine and vehicle operators	18	1.0	−25.0
All other occupations	26	1.4	−12.3

Source: *Career Guide to Industries*, 2000–2001, Bureau of Labor Statistics

WHAT IT'S LIKE TO WORK FOR UNCLE SAM

Basically, working for the federal government is a lot like working in the private sector. Since nearly every job found in private industry is also found in government, it includes a diverse set of work environments. Federal employees work full-time, flextime, and rotating schedules. Some travel and some telecommute. Whether it's a white-collar, eight-hour day in an office building, a part-time blue-collar job on a construction site, or a lab-coated graveyard shift on a hospital ward, the range of ways and places you can earn a living as a federal employee is as varied as the private sector.

Pay and Advancement

In federal employment, advancement is based on a system of occupational pay levels called "grades." Here are the basic facts:

- Workers enter the federal system at the starting grade for a particular position. In most cases, these grades are known by the abbreviation GS (which stands for "General Schedule"), plus a number. The exact pay grades associated with a job's career track depend upon the occupation. For example, an accountant's job might be a GS-5, 6, 7 position. A new worker meeting the minimum job requirements of that position would be classified as a GS-5.

- Workers then are awarded a series of noncompetitive promotions (which usually occur at regular intervals if the worker's performance is satisfactory) until they reach the full-performance grade for that occupation. In the case of the accountant, the full-performance grade would be GS-7.

- Once workers reach the full-performance level of a career track, they must compete for subsequent promotions, and advancement becomes more difficult. At this point, promotions occur as vacancies arise, and they are based solely on merit.

Though other pay systems exist in civil service, most federal workers are paid under the "General Schedule," or GS, system. Here's a GS pay breakdown for 2000:

GS-1	$13,870	GS-6	$23,820	GS-11	$39,178
GS-2	15,594	GS-7	26,470	GS-12	46,955
GS-3	17,015	GS-8	29,315	GS-13	55,837
GS-4	19,100	GS-9	32,380	GS-14	65,983
GS-5	21,370	GS-10	35,658	GS-15	77,614

Source: U.S. Office of Personnel Management

GS pay is adjusted geographically and the majority of jobs pay a higher salary at each grade—6.78% to 15.01% higher in the continental United States—than the basic rate shown here. Also, certain hard-to-fill jobs, usually in the scientific, technical, or medical fields, may have higher starting salaries. In 1999, the average full-time GS worker earned $46,600; the average full-time federal worker in a white-collar, professional field earned $61,600.

Here's a sampling of average annual salaries in selected federal jobs.

AVERAGE ANNUAL SALARIES IN THE FEDERAL GOVERNMENT IN SELECTED OCCUPATIONS, 1999

OCCUPATION	SALARY
All occupations	$46,580
Patent administrator	98,900
Astronomer	81,310
Attorney	77,740
Financial manager	73,350
Economist	67,790
Computer scientist	66,510
Chemist	64,230
Electrical engineer	63,590
Statistician	62,840
Microbiologist	62,570
Architect	62,180
Podiatrist	61,960
Personnel manager	59,060
Accountant	58,190
Chaplain	57,330
Ecologist	57,130
Librarian	56,370
Intelligence agent	54,210
Physical therapist	51,370
Forester	51,010
Social worker	50,230
Botanist	48,770
Nurse	46,950
Engineering technician	46,230
Law clerk	41,810
Border patrol agent	40,200
Computer operator	34,220
Secretary	30,230
Police officer	29,990
Medical technician	27,820
Nursing assistant	24,990
Mail and file clerk	23,740
Telephone operator	23,560

Source: U.S. Office of Personnel Management

TRAINING AND EDUCATION

In federal service, there are no shortcuts to professional success. Training and educational requirements in civil service are virtually the same as those in the private sector for major occupational groups. Doctors, engineers, and scientists still need the requisite degrees and practical training. Journeyman craftsmen must still be experts in their trades. Accounting clerks must still have practical number-crunching experience.

Beyond initial training requirements, each federal department or agency determines its own training requirements and offers workers opportunities to improve job skills or become qualified to advance to other jobs. These may include technical or skills training, tuition assistance or reimbursement, fellowship programs, and executive leadership and management training programs, seminars, and workshops. This training may be offered on the job, by another agency, or at local colleges and universities.

As in the private sector, pay and education are linked in federal employment. Here's how it works:

- Typically, workers without a high school diploma who are hired as a clerks start at GS-1, and high school graduates with no additional training hired at the same job start at GS-2 or 3.
- Entrants with some technical training or experience who are hired as technicians may start at GS-4.
- Those with a bachelor's degree are generally hired in professional occupations, such as economist, with a career ladder that starts at GS-5 or 7, depending on academic achievement.
- Entrants with a master's degree or Ph.D. may start at GS-9. Individuals with professional degrees may be hired at the GS-11 or 12 level.

THE MILITARY ADVANTAGE: VETERANS' PREFERENCE

Good news: Military servicemembers do have an edge in landing federal jobs. Since the time of the Civil War, armed forces veterans have been given some degree of preference in appointments to federal positions. Congress passed laws that recognized the sacrifices made by military members, and prevented veterans seeking federal employment from being penalized because of the time spent in military service. The resulting "perk," called "Veterans' Preference," gives hiring preference over nonveterans to former servicemembers who fall into certain categories:

- Disabled veterans.
- Veterans who served on active duty in the armed forces during certain specified time periods.
- Veterans who served on active duty in military campaigns.

These categories of veterans are entitled to preference over nonveterans both in federal hiring from competitive lists of eligible workers and in retention during reduction-in-force, or downsizing efforts.

The goal of preference is not to fill every vacant federal job with a military veteran. Such a practice would be incompatible with the merit principle of public employment. Nor does it apply to promotions or other personnel actions occurring within civil service. But preference does provide a way that former service members seeking federal jobs can be given special consideration.

PREFERENCE IN EXAMINATION

Civil service job applicants must take a written examination or undergo an evaluation of their experience and education. Veterans who meet preference criteria, and who score 70 or higher, have either 5 or 10 points added to their numerical ratings depending on the nature of their preference. This can help veterans leapfrog over competing federal job candidates in these ways:

- For scientific and professional positions in grade GS-9 or higher, names of all eligible candidates are listed in order of ratings, augmented by veteran preference, if any.
- For all other positions, the names of 10-point preference applicants, who have a compensable, service-connected disability of 10 percent or more, are placed ahead of the names of all other eligible candidates on a given register.
- The names of other 10- and 5-point preference applicants, and non-veterans, are listed in order of their numerical ratings.

Entitlement to veterans' preference does not guarantee a job. But veterans' preference in federal hiring is another "Military Advantage."

GENERAL REQUIREMENTS FOR PREFERENCE

To be entitled to preference, a veteran must meet the eligibility requirements in section 2108 of title 5, United States Code. The following eligibility conditions apply:

- To qualify for preference, veterans must be honorably discharged from military service.
- National Guard or Armed Forces Reserve active-duty-for-training time does not qualify for preference.
- When applying for federal jobs, eligible veterans should claim preference on their application or resume. Applicants claiming a 10-point preference must complete form SF-15, Application for 10-Point Veteran Preference. This form is available through OPM, and at base or post civilian personnel offices (CPO). It is also included in the Quick & Easy Federal Jobs Kit.
- Unless they are disabled, military retirees at the rank of major, lieutenant commander, or higher are not eligible for preference.

TYPES OF VETERANS' PREFERENCE

5-POINT PREFERENCE
Five points are added to the passing examination score of a veteran who served:

- During the period December 7, 1941, to July 1, 1955
- For more than 180 consecutive days, any part of which occurred after January 31, 1955, and before October 15, 1976
- During the Gulf War from August 2, 1990, through January 2, 1992; or
- In a campaign or expedition for which a campaign medal has been authorized, including El Salvador, Grenada, Haiti, Lebanon, Panama, Somalia, Southwest Asia, and Bosnia.

Medal holders and Gulf War veterans who enlisted after September 7, 1980, or entered on active duty on or after October 14, 1982, must have served continuously for 24 months or the full period called or ordered to active duty. The service requirement does not apply to veterans with compensable service-connected disabilities, or to veterans separated for disability in the line of duty, or for hardship.

10-POINT PREFERENCE
Ten points are added to the passing examination score of:

- A veteran who served at any time and who has a present service-connected disability or is receiving compensation, disability retirement benefits, or pension from the military or the Department of Veterans Affairs. Individuals who received a Purple Heart qualify as disabled veterans.
- An unmarried spouse of certain deceased veterans, a spouse of a veteran unable to work because of a service-connected disability, and
- A mother of a veteran who died in service or who is permanently and totally disabled.

ANOTHER ADVANTAGE

There's another "Military Advantage" in federal hiring practices. In 1998, Congress passed the Veterans' Employment Opportunities Act (VEOA). Increasingly, federal agencies were limiting announcements just to "status" candidates, meaning those who were already civil service employees. The VEOA was designed to open more federal job opportunities to veterans. Under the VEOA, an agency that is willing to accept applications from federal employees working for different departments or agencies must also allow eligible veterans to apply.

"Veterans," for this purpose, are servicemembers who have been separated under honorable conditions from the armed forces with three or more years of continuous active service. Veterans' preference, as described in the preceding section of this chapter, does not apply to selections made under this procedure. But VEOA opens up job opportunities that formerly were closed to non-civil service veterans.

CIVIL SERVICE EXAMS

According to the *Book of U.S. Government Jobs*, about eight in ten civil service jobs are filled through a competitive examination of a candidate's background, work experience, and education—not through a written exam. Still, some agencies have the option to screen federal applicants through testing. Here are some broad categories in which candidates for specific occupations may be tested:

- Health, safety, and environmental
- Writing and public information
- Business, finance, and management
- Personnel, administrative and computer benefits review, and tax and legal occupations
- Law enforcement and investigation

In addition, positions with "positive education requirements" may also be tested. Examples include jobs dealing with economics, foreign affairs, manpower research and analysis, and international relations.

The OPM and individual agencies announce job openings and specific application requirements, including testing. To learn whether testing is required for a job in which you're interested, check requirements listed on job announcements or contact the individual agency doing the hiring for that job.

FINDING AND APPLYING FOR FEDERAL JOBS

Applying for a federal job used to be about as efficient as counting grains of sand on the beach—and about as much fun. Civil service application forms were lengthy and laborious. Fortunately for you, all that's changed.

"There have been significant improvements in federal hiring," notes Dennis Damp. "The federal sector has taken advantage of the many new communication tools now available to job seekers. The Internet offers instant access to job vacancy announcements, pay scales, and special recruitment programs."

The Federal Government's Employment Information System is a network of easily accessible automated information. One very useful resource is USAJOBS (www.usajobs.opm.gov). Developed by OPM, USAJOBS provides worldwide job vacancy information, employment information fact sheets, job applications and forms, and has online resume development and electronic transmission capabilities. USAJOBS is updated every business day from a database of more than 7,500 worldwide job opportunities.

There are three main ways to access USAJOBS:

1. *Website access*: On the USAJOBS website, job seekers can access worldwide current job vacancies, employment information fact sheets, applications and forms, and in some instances, apply for jobs online. Complete job announcements can be retrieved from the website. The USAJOBS website also has an Online Resume Builder feature. Using the resume builder, job seekers can create online resumes specifically designed for applying for federal jobs. Resumes created on the USAJOBS resume builder can be printed for faxing or mailing to employers and saved and edited for future use. For many of the vacancies listed on the site, job seekers can submit resumes created through USAJOBS directly to hiring agencies through an electronic submission process.

2. *Kiosk access*: USAJOBS is also available through a kiosk network of self-service information providers located in OPM offices and many federal buildings nationwide. Using touch-screen technology, job seekers can access worldwide current job vacancies, employment information fact sheets, and applications and forms. Complete job announcements can be retrieved from each kiosk.

3. *Telephone access*: USAJOBS is also accessible by telephone. An interactive voice response telephone system can be reached at 912-757-3000 or TDD 912-744-2299 or at 17 OPM Service Centers located throughout the country. By telephone, job seekers can access worldwide current job vacancies, employment information fact sheets, and applications and forms. In some instances, you can apply for jobs by phone. Federal agencies list job opportunities on the Federal Employment Information System. You can find the location nearest you using the government blue pages in the front of your local telephone book.

VACANCY ANNOUNCEMENTS

You can use USAJOBS to find federal opportunities that interest you. But that's only the first step. Next, you'll need more information on specific opportunities and appropriate application forms. USAJOBS features automated access to specific "vacancy announcements." Each vacancy announcement is an important source of information. Each lists vital details about individual openings, like:

- Specific duties of the position
- Whether or not a written test is required
- Educational requirements
- Duty location
- Salary and grade/step structure of the job
- Application deadline or closing dates for applications

OTHER SOURCES OF FEDERAL JOB OPENINGS

USAJOBS is one source, but there are other Internet sites as well. Various periodicals, digests, and job hotlines are also valuable sources of civil service openings. For a listing of these resources see Appendix E of this book.

APPLYING FOR THE JOB

Whether you use USAJOBS or some other resource to find openings and announcements, you may apply for most jobs with a resume, or the Optional Application for Federal Employment (OF-612). For jobs that are unique or filled through automated procedures, you may be given special forms and/or instructions in the job announcement. Although the federal government does not require a standard application form for most jobs, certain information is needed to evaluate your qualifications. If you decide to submit a format other than the OF-612, (i.e., a resume), the following information must be included:

- **Job Information**—Announcement number, title, and grade.
- **Personal Information**—Full name, mailing address (with zip code), day and evening phone numbers (with area code), social security number, country of citizenship, veterans' preference, reinstatement eligibility, and highest federal civilian grade held.
- **Education**—High school name, city, and state, the name, city, and state of the colleges or universities you attended, and majors and year of any degrees received (if no degree, show total credits earned and indicate whether semester or quarter hours).
- **Work Experience**—Job title, duties and accomplishments, employer's name and address, supervisor's name and phone number, starting and

ending dates (month and year), hours per week, salary, and indicate whether or not your current supervisor may be contacted. Prepare a separate entry for each job.

- **Other Qualifications**—Job-related training courses (title and year), job-related skills, job-related certificates and licenses, job-related honors, awards, and special accomplishments.

HELPFUL HINT

During your federal job search, you may run across a job announcement that says you can apply for the opening using "any written form you choose." Technically, that's correct. OPM regulations say job candidates may use "any written form" to apply for most federal positions. But it's to your advantage to stick to one of the standard application formats. First, by doing so you'll ensure you've provided all relevant information that's normally required by civil service hiring managers. Second, such managers are only human: It's easier for them to compare apples to apples (or OF-612 to OF-612) than it is to compare competing candidates' apples to your lonely orange. If you're the right person for the job, that fact will probably be more apparent to hiring managers when you highlight it using an application form they're used to dealing with.

FEDERAL APPLICATION SECRETS

The first three categories of information required on a federal job application—job information, personal information, and education—are fairly straightforward. The tricky parts of the OF-612 are Block 8, Work Experience, and Block 13, Other Qualifications.

BLOCK 8: WORK EXPERIENCE

According to OPM literature, your work experience section must include the following data for each position you've held:

- Job title
- Duties and accomplishments
- Employer's name and address

- Supervisor's name and phone number
- Starting and ending dates (month and year)
- Hours worked per week
- Salary

The above information, particularly the duties and accomplishments portion, should relate to the duties of the position you're applying for. But how do you know what those duties are? That's where the OPM Qualification Standards come in. These standards provide you with detailed information about the duties and responsibilities of each federal position.

Take a few moments to read through the sample qualification standard below. You'll quickly see how it can help you tailor a federal application to fit the job you're applying for:

Correctional Officer Series GS 007

Education or Experience Requirements

EDUCATION

Undergraduate Education: Successful completion of a full four-year course of study in any field leading to a bachelor's degree, in an accredited college or university, is qualifying for GS-5 level positions.

Graduate Education: One full academic year of graduate education with major study in criminal justice or one of the social sciences is qualifying for GS-7. Graduate education may be prorated according to the grade level of the position to be filled; however, it is not qualifying for positions above GS-7.

OR

EXPERIENCE

General Experience (for GS-5 positions): Three years of general experience, one year of which was equivalent to at least GS-4, are qualifying for positions at the GS-5 level. This experience must have demonstrated the aptitude for acquiring knowledge, skills, and abilities required for correctional work, and, in addition, demonstrate the possession of personal attributes important to the effectiveness of correctional officers, such as:

- Ability to meet and deal with people of differing backgrounds and behavioral patterns
- Ability to be persuasive in selling and influencing ideas
- Ability to lead, supervise, and instruct others

- Sympathetic attitude toward the welfare of others
- Ability to reason soundly and to think out practical solutions to problems
- Ability to make decisions and act quickly, particularly under stress
- Poise and self-confidence, and ability to remain calm during emergency situations

Qualifying general experience may have been gained in work such as:

- Social case work in a welfare agency or counseling in other types of organizations
- Classroom teaching or instructing
- Responsible rehabilitation work, for instance, in an alcoholic rehabilitation program
- Supervising planned recreational activities or active participation in community action programs
- Management or supervisory work in a business or other organization that included directing the work flow and/or direct supervision of others
- Sales work, other than taking and filling orders as in over-the-counter sales

Specialized Experience (for positions above GS-5): One year of specialized experience equivalent to at least the next lower level in the normal line of progression is qualifying for positions at grade GS-6 and above. Specialized experience must have equipped the applicant with the particular knowledge, skills, and abilities to perform successfully the duties of the position to be filled. Experience may have been gained in work such as police officer, mental health counselor in a residential facility, or detention officer.

EMPLOYMENT INTERVIEW
The personal qualities and characteristics of the applicant are the most critical of all the requirements for Correctional Officer positions. The applicant must be willing to perform arduous and prolonged duties on any of three shifts. In addition, the applicant must possess certain personal qualities in order to relate to inmates effectively in a correctional setting. These include empathy, objectivity, perceptiveness, resourcefulness, adaptability and flexibility, stability, and maturity.

As you can see, a specific qualification standard like the one above helps you accomplish at least two things: (1) complete a winning civil service application, and

(2) help you see how you may be qualified for a job even though you don't have the traditional kinds of education and experience that job may seem to require. For example, a person with a bachelor's degree and experience in social work would be qualified for the position of GS-7 Correctional Officer. But so would a military instructor who had spent significant time in a counseling role.

You can't overestimate the value of obtaining the qualification standards for federal jobs you'd like to apply for. You can find a comprehensive listing of qualification standards at www.federaljobs.net.

Now, back to the "work experience" section of the application: Here are a few tips to help you complete that section:

- Break descriptions of past work experience into three sections: Summary, Duties, and Accomplishments.
- Wherever possible, describe your work experience using keywords found in the job vacancy announcement and OPM qualification standards for your target job.
- Use bullets to capture reviewers' attention. Large blocks of text can bury the highlights of your qualifications and are difficult for reviewers to wade through.
- Don't scrimp on job descriptions. Many federal applicants try to squeeze their job descriptions into the small amount of space available on the preprinted OF-612 form. This is a mistake. Use Continuation Page forms (available on the automated OF-612), or create a continuation page of your own. (See the sample OF-612 below.)
- As in resume writing, avoid military acronyms. Spell out any equipment or program names and, whenever possible, use civilianized language.
- Be sure to include any volunteer and nonpaid work experience that relates to the target job opening.

BLOCK 13: OTHER QUALIFICATIONS

Block 13 is the place on your OF-612 to list all items that don't fall readily into the Work Experience section of your application. This could include awards you've earned, licenses and certifications, job-related training courses, recent reading, and outside interests. In addition, you can list specific skills you've acquired that may not necessarily have been learned on the job. Whatever you list in Block 13 should be related to your target civil service job. For an excellent example of a properly completed Block 13, see the sample OF-612 below.

Form Approved
OMB No. 3206-0219

OPTIONAL APPLICATION FOR FEDERAL EMPLOYMENT - OF 612

You may apply for most jobs with a resume, this form, or other written format. If your resume or application does not provide all the information requested on this form and in the job vacancy announcement, you may lose consideration for a job.

1 Job title in announcement	2 Grade(s) applying for	3 Announcement number
Management Analyst, GS-0343-07	GS-07	99-0916 LV

4 Last name	First and middle names	5 Social Security Number
SMITH	John Q.	123-45-6789

6 Mailing address		7 Phone numbers (include area code)
3401 Main Street		Daytime 202-123-2456

City	State	ZIP Code	
Hyattsville	MD	20782	Evening 301-234-5678

WORK EXPERIENCE

8 Describe your paid and nonpaid work experience related to the job for which you are applying. Do **not** attach job descriptions.

1) Job title (if Federal, include series and grade)

Computer Analyst

From (MM/YY)	To (MM/YY)	Salary	per	Hours per week
04-23-96	Present	$27,958	year	40

Employer's name and address	Supervisor's name and phone number
Hendricks Inc	Gene Porter
435, Smithfield Drive, Smithfield, MD 20782	202-123-2456, Ext. 410

Describe your duties and accomplishments

Summary

Currently serve as the lead automation analyst for a large wholesaler that distributes products to retail outlets and services a four state area. Hendricks' employs 797 workers that are located at 7 offices in Maryland, Virginia, Pennsylvania and Delaware. Position includes providing a full range of continuing automation technical and advisory services to our operating offices, system users, company officials and warehouse managers, as well as technical expertise, Novell System Certified and LAN/WAN management.

Continued on a Separate Page

2) Job title (if Federal, include series and grade)

Computer Specialist

From (MM/YY)	To (MM/YY)	Salary	per	Hours per week
04-12-94	04-22-96	$17,547	year	40

Employer's name and address	Supervisor's name and phone number
National Rental Corp	Charles Massie
101 Fifth Street, Silver Spring, MD 20901	202-234-2345

Describe your duties and accomplishments

Summary

As a computer specialist I was responsible for user terminal maintenance and new software training at their branch office in Silver Spring Maryland There were 47 specialist and 5 managers stationed at this facility. I maintained and serviced over 67 desk top and lap top terminals for the organization. Worked closely with the department managers to insure systems were functional and that specialists were able to perform needed automation functions. I had several collateral responsibilities including researching the potential for LAN deployment at our branch office and new system integration vendor training. I attended a number of strategy sessions with vendors and managers to explore the feasibility of expanding our automation system capabilities.

Continued on a Separate Page

9 May we contact your current supervisor?

        YES [X]   NO [   ] ▶ If we need to contact your current supervisor before making an offer, we will contact you first.

EDUCATION

10 Mark highest level completed. **Some HS** [   ] **HS/GED** [X] **Associate** [   ] **Bachelor** [   ] **Master** [   ] **Doctoral** [   ]

11 Last high school (HS) or GED school. Give the school's name, city, State, ZIP Code (if known), and year diploma or GED received.

Northwestern S.H., Baltimore MD

12 Colleges and universities attended. Do **not** attach a copy of your transcript unless requested.

Name	Total Credits Earned		Major(s)	Degree - Year
	Semester	Quarter		(if any) Received
1) Community College of Baltimore Maryland			IRM Automation	
City: Baltimore State: MD ZIP Code: 16652				A.A. 1991
2)				
3)				

OTHER QUALIFICATIONS

13 **Job-related** training courses (give title and year). **Job-related** skills (other languages, computer software/hardware, tools, machinery, typing speed, etc.). **Job-related** certificates and licenses (current only). **Job-related** honors, awards, and special accomplishments (publications, memberships in professional/honor societies, leadership activities, public speaking, and performance awards). Give dates, but do **not** send documents unless requested

Awards

In 1989, I was selected for an award by the U.S. Army for developing a communication deployment strategy that was accepted by the DOD for worldwide implementation. Received the Dickens Award for Outstanding Achievement.

In 1998, I developed the Frederick Company's internet web site. I received a substantial cash bonus for developing this site.

Licenses/Certifications

FCC Radio Telephone Communications License with Ship Radar Endorsement (Current)
NOVEL Certified

Recent Reading

"The Seven Habits of Highly Effective People" by Stephen R. Covey
"Lincoln on Leadership"
"Networking in the 21st Century? by Bill Gates

Additional Training (job related)

Continued on a Separate Page

GENERAL

14 Are you a U.S. citizen?   YES [X]   NO [   ] ▶ Give the country of your citizenship.

15 Do you claim veterans' preference? NO [   ] YES [X] ▶ Mark your claim of 5 or 10 points below.

    5 points [X] ▶ Attach your DD 214 or other proof. **10 points** [   ] ▶ Attach an *Application for 10-Point Veterans' Preference* (SF 15) and proof required.

16 Were you ever a Federal civilian employee?

        NO [   ] YES [X] ▶ For highest civilian grade give:

	Series	Grade	From (MM/YY)	To (MM/YY)
	0050	GS-02	09/93	03/94

17 Are you eligible for reinstatement based on career or career-conditional Federal status?

        NO [X] YES [   ] ▶ If requested, attach SF 50 proof.

APPLICANT CERTIFICATION

18 I certify that, to the best of my knowledge and belief, all of the information on and attached to this application is true, correct, complete and made in good faith. I understand that false or fraudulent information on or attached to this application may be grounds for not hiring me or for firing me after I begin work, and may be punishable by fine or imprisonment. I understand that any information I give may be investigated.

SIGNATURE   **DATE SIGNED**

ADDITIONAL WORK EXPERIENCES

SMITH, John Q.   123-45-6789
Management Analyst, GS-0343-07   99-0916 LV   GS-07

3) Job title (if Federal, include series and grade)

Computer Specialist Intern, GS-02

From (MM/YY)	To (MM/YY)	Salary	per	Hours per week
9/1/93	3/15/94	$ 14,021	year	40

Employer's name and address	Supervisor's name and phone number
Internal Revenue Service	Eric Savage
Office of TPS & Compliance, Baltimore MD 20910	301-222-2222

Describe your duties and accomplishments

Summary

Worked with the IRS as a Computer Specialist Intern to satisfy the internship requirement for my Computer Specialist Associate Degree from the Community College of Baltimore Maryland. I worked on various IRS terminals and individual computer systems to resolve problems and to return the terminals to service. Worked with Microsoft Office desktop software applications used by the IRS. Performed data entry tasks in Excel and Access for operational managers. Worked with the IRM staff to restore systems and assisted with day-today automation tasks such as system backup, resetting the LAN, configuration control, and administrative functions.

Towards the end of the internship I was able to maintain the specialist's desktop units unassisted and had full responsibility for the office's daily system backup, email account management, coordination with automation vendors, and IRM parts ordering for the office.

Continued on a Separate Page

4) Job title (if Federal, include series and grade)

Communications System Repairman U.S.ARMY

From (MM/YY)	To (MM/YY)	Salary	per	Hours per week
05/30/89	06/01/91	$ 9,789	year	40

Employer's name and address	Supervisor's name and phone number
United Stated Army (Active Duty) National Training Center	Msgt Don Riley
11th Armored Cavalry Regiment, Operations Group, Fort Irwin, CA 92310-5067	760-999-9999

Describe your duties and accomplishments

Summary

Attained the rank of Sargent and was responsible for maintained and servicing the training center's field communications systems such as FM handsets, VHF and UHF transmitters and receivers used to communicate with air support and armored cavalry command units. I was assigned collateral duties to maintain field computers used to direct and coordinate troop movements with headquarters command.

Duties

- ➢ Repair and service FM hand held transceivers
- ➢ Repair VHF/UHF Transceivers
- ➢ Program field computers used for troop movement
- ➢ Work with computer specialists to repair field computers
- ➢ Order supplies to insure sufficient stock of parts on hand
- ➢ Troubleshoot telephone systems and switching equipment

Continued on a Separate Page

OF 612 Continuation Page

SMITH, John Q.   Page 1   123-45-6789
Management Analyst, GS-0343-07   99-0916 LV   GS-07

Question 13 - Other Qualifications

4/93 Microsoft Word
5/93 Microsoft Excel
2/94 Quality Worklife & Team Work (1 week)
7/94 Work Station Integration & LAN Connectivity (1 week)
7/95 NOVEL Certification Course (2 weeks)
6/96 Microsoft Office Professional (1 week)
9/97 LAN/WAN Office Configuration management Course (6 weeks) Sponsored by employer

In addition to the courses I have taken to acquire further knowledge for the positions I have held, I also have experience and expertise in the following areas:

Interpersonal Relations
I deal effectively and professionally with all people. I am a team player as evidenced by my military background and success at Frederick Corp to integrate and consolidate branch offices. I enjoy working in groups and have been trained in Quality Worklife and Partnership initiatives.

Communications Skills
I am experienced in dealing successfully with all types of people at all educational levels.I am a member of Toastmaster's **International** and have achieved the level of *"Competent Toastmaster."*

Writing Skills
I have an excellent grasp of the English language and have experience in a variety of different writing styles including reports, grants, informational material, speeches, brochures and promotional materials.I have authored several automation software articles that have been published in major journals and national magazines.

Training Skills
I have demonstrated my abilities in the area of training by developing and conducting classes for office software for over 200 employees. I have taught in a class room environment and provided on-the-job training to individual users on an as needed basis. I use the *Job Centered Training* methods that were used by the IRS when I was an intern their in 1991.

Computer Skills
Since 1985 my interest in computers has led to experience with all types of personal computers, and I have expertise in word processing, database management, spreadsheets, desk top publishing, form design and BASIC programming. I have an Associates degree in IRM Automation and have taken numerous evening courses in all facets of automation. During my tenure with Fredrick's I designed and was their web master for the corporation's internet web site. I also develop internet web sites in the evenings for small companies.

Office Skills
I am knowledgeable in all aspects of office operations and am proficient in operating a wide variety of office machinery including calculators, word processors, copiers, postage meters, telephone systems (including PBX), fax machines, electronic mail and computer modems as well as all types of audiovisual equipment such as slide and film projectors, tape recorders, and video recorders and cameras. I have an in depth knowledge of Powerpoint and have developed and fielded 5 major presentations for upper management in this format.

Work Experience Continuation

SMITH, John Q.   1) Computer Analyst - Page 1   123-45-6789
Management Analyst, GS-0343-07   99-0916 LV   GS-07

I am **Novell Certified** and proficient in most Microsoft software applications including but not limited to: **Word, Excel, Powerpoint, Scheduler, Project, Frontpage 98 and Access.** I have trained over 127 users in these applications over the past two years. I also develop web sites at home for small companies and my sites have won several internet design awards. Over the past two years I have had 3 articles published in major national magazines on NOVELL upgrades and system integration issues.

DUTIES

- Technical automation expert for our Leesburg Virginia headquarters Novell LAN operation
- Analyze and advise management on all aspects of LAN operations and WAN integration
- Train detached staff office warehouse managers on system integration and LAN applications
- Perform feasibility studies concerning support staff automation needs at field facilities
- Maintain IBM NT computer work stations at headquarters for 127 employees
- Maintained company lotus ccmail for the entire organization. Updated address databases and worked with vendors concerning major problems and software failures
- Train 127 users on new system functions and software applications
- Maintain the company's internet web site
- Performed cost/benefit evaluation for work station NT Upgrade.
- Recommended field system upgrade and LAN integration through Wynnframe deployment
- Develops the company's annual (IRM) Information *Resource Management* budget
- Site automation administrator maintaining all user data, access levels, and system security passwords and documentation.
- Initiate daily backups for LAN data
- Maintain a comprehensive technical and software application library for users
- Debug, repair and service operating systems and software/hardware throughout the organization

ACCOMPLISHMENTS

- Developed written automation configuration reports to upper management to consolidate three field offices and personnel into a central hub facility at Baltimore Maryland.
- Management accepted my Wynnframe LAN field integration recommendation after I performed a cost/benefit analysis and feasibility study for the upgrade. I developed Gant and Milestone charts to accomplish upgrade, then provided training and integration after field installations were completed.
- Developed the company's internet web site on my own time. Management accepted first proposal after viewing an interactive Powerpoint presentation that I developed and viewing a live online demonstration that featured the web site's functionality. I received a substantial cash bonus for developing this site.
- A member of the company's strategic planning committee. I researched and performed a cost/benefits analysis for our automation needs through 2005 and developed Y2K strategies for the year 2000. All systems are now Y2K compliant and we have a long term IRM plan developed for major new system integration for 2003.This is coincident with a major expansion to two additional states scheduled for 2004.

Work Experience Continuation

SMITH, John Q.	2) Computer Specialist - Page 1	123-45-6789
Management Analyst, GS-0343-07	99-0916 LV	GS-07

DUTIES

- ➤ Coordinate and maintain terminal repair for all employees and managers
- ➤ Performed daily backup of critical branch office databases
- ➤ Provided one-on-one training to staff and managers for Microsoft desk top applications
- ➤ Maintain and monitor special projects involving automation software deployment within the organization.
- ➤ Researched and developed email internet accounts for all employees
- ➤ Assigned site administrator duties that included terminal and database security, database and pass word user definitions, and virus protection upgrade deployment for all users
- ➤ Upgraded systems as new replacement equipment was purchased
- ➤ Coordinated internet accounts for all system users

Accomplishments

- ➤ Analyzed the upgrade of our server to the latest NOVELL version and lead the upgrade initiative. The upgrade went smoothly with minimal down time and impact to our users and customers.
- ➤ Wrote numerous reports on various IRM issues including NOVELL upgrade, user system upgrades, and Oracle database deployment to all branch offices.
- ➤ Developed a new IRM security directive/regulation that was accepted by headquarters for use throughout the organization.
- ➤ Required to investigate the feasibility of implementing a paperless administrative corporate office. Developed a plan that included researching options, deployment strategies, and cost/benefit analysis. Initiated plan which included OCR scanners for all incoming documents and electronic daily files for all incoming and outgoing correspondence. LAN directories were assigned to all major program areas and hourly automatic file backup procedures were initiated.

Work Experience Continuation

SMITH, John Q.   3) Computer Specialist Intern, GS-02 - Page 1   123-45-6789
Management Analyst, GS-0343-07   99-0916 LV   GS-07

Contacted taxpayer account processors to:

- Coordinate computer system restoration.
- Perform Virus computer scans.
- Initiate corrective actions based upon user complaints under supervision of a senior computer specialist.

My duties and responsibilities also included:

- IRM parts ordering and supply stock.
- System daily backup
- Assisting specialists with software familiarization
- Verified account passwords for users
- Data entry for various spreadsheets and databases
- CPU repair including hard drive replacement, SIMMs upgrade, Modem installations, Keyboard replacement, and system configuration integrity checks.

Work Experience Continuation

SMITH, John Q.   4) Communications System Repairman U.S.ARMY - Page 1   123-45-6789
Management Analyst, GS-0343-07   99-0916 LV   GS-07

- Top Secrete clearance for Crypto communications and maintenance

Accomplishments

- Coordinated the utilization of limited communication resources for field deployment at the training center for over 2,000 active duty and reserve troops. Prioritized order of delivery and level of communications needed for deployments of various types.
- Crypto trained for Top Secrete scrambled communications between command centers and senior field command officers. Responsible for safeguarding equipment and destroying it at all costs if enemy infiltration discovered.
- Prioritized critical communications with limited resources determining who or which field command unit would receive support and when.
- Evaluated and developed a communications deployment scheme with automation support that was implemented throughout the Department of Defense.

.

MORE APPLICATION HELP

There's really a lot more to filling out a federal application than can be covered here. To learn more about the process—and the secrets—of completing a winning OF-612, visit www.federaljobs.net. This site includes free tips and examples on how to fill out a federal application that will get you hired. Also included: free access to OPM Qualification Standards. These standards are comprehensive descriptions of federal jobs that civil service hiring supervisors use to evaluate applicants. By keying your OF-612 to these standards, you can make sure your application highlights the parts of your background that are most relevant to the job you're applying for.

While you're online, also visit www.quickandeasy.com to learn more about the automated version of the OF-612. No, it's not free—but if you've ever tried to fill out a federal job application manually, you'll agree that it's worth paying for software that automates the process. But remember that you may be able to access OF-612 software at your transition center at no charge.

SUMMARY

In this chapter, you've explored the world of federal employment. You've learned what civil service is, what kinds of jobs are available, and what some of them pay. You've also learned how to find federal job openings, how to use Office of Personnel Management resources online, and how to complete a civil service job application.

In the next chapter, we'll put everything together and help you develop your transition plan for success.

CHAPTER 11

Making the Transition

WHO TO CALL FOR HELP, PLUS A THREE-YEAR PLAN FOR SUCCESS

In the last five chapters, you've learned how to pinpoint post-military career options, how to market your military skills, and what military resources are available to help. But as good as military career transition programs can be, there also are off-base resources you can use to speed your search. Read on for an overview of career services—and rip-offs—you'll find online and in the civilian community.

CAREER COUNSELORS

There is no test you can take that will tell you instantly what you're supposed to do in your next life. So for some servicemembers seeking new career directions, career assessment services offered by base or post transition centers may not be enough. While transition centers offer assessment tools such as testing and interest surveys, many do not employ certified career counselors who can help you interpret and cross-reference results. That's why professional counseling—counseling that combines test and survey indicators with such factors as available time for education, money, desire, family situation, and willingness to relocate—is important for some servicemembers in transition. In general, you may be a candidate for professional career counseling if you want to transition to an entirely new career field but aren't sure what you want to do for a living. You should still start at your military transition center. But if, after having used its resources to the fullest, you're still unsure of your new career path, consider a professional civilian career counselor. You can find a directory of reputable counselors through the National Board for Certified Counselors (www.nbcc.org).

CAREER COUNSELOR DOS AND DON'TS

- **Don't sign up for any package deals (some cost thousands) that promise bells and whistles like access to resources, contact lists of hiring managers, and the like. Most such deals include a fine print escape clause that legally nullifies all promises.**
- **Do find a career counselor who charges an hourly fee. That way you're assured of specific services for a specific price. Expect to pay between $50 and $250 per hour.**
- **Don't use a career counselor who promises to find you a job.**
- **Do find a Nationally Certified Career Counselor (NCCC). You may pay a little extra, but you'll be assured of quality services.**

HEADHUNTERS

Headhunters have a mixed reputation. Also known as executive recruiters, personnel recruiters, and recruiting managers, they work for companies, not for job-seekers, and they do it for large fees. For this reason, some people see them as the career-services equivalent of ambulance-chasing lawyers. Corporations hire headhunters to find candidates who are exactly right for specific openings, fit into a corporation's culture, who want to work for that particular company, and who won't quit immediately after starting. Employers reward headhunters handsomely (an amount equivalent to 25% to 30% of the new hire's annual salary) for finding such plum candidates. Thus, if a candidate's qualifications are not perfect for an opening the headhunter is trying to fill, he or she will not be considered. "Never use a headhunter," some career counselors advise: "They don't care about you. They're only in it for the money."

To which I say, "So what?" If a headhunter finds you your dream job, do you really care about his motivation? A recruiter's services are of no cost to you, so, as long as the job he or she is promoting is one you want, you have nothing to lose. However, a recruiter will only present you as a candidate for positions that are closely related to your experience. If you are interested in looking for a position that represents a change of direction, then a recruiter may not be the best choice for you.

"Use every available job search method in the proportion to which it has proven successful," writes job search guru Richard Bolles in his perennial classic *What Color Is Your Parachute?* Makes sense, doesn't it? Therefore, if you're seeking a high-tech, professional (such as health care or law), or management job with a salary above $50,000, get your resume into the hands of a headhunter with a proven track record in your field. But don't wait by the phone—get on with other job search methods. If the recruiter finds an opening for you that's a perfect fit—great! If not, they won't waste their time—or yours—by sending you on interviews that won't be likely to land you a job.

"Use every available job search method in the proportion to which it has proven successful." Richard Bolles, author, *What Color Is Your Parachute?*

JMO RECRUITERS

Some headhunters specialize in placing former military servicemembers. Known as Junior Military Officer or JMO recruiters, these search firms work with companies who are specifically seeking the skills and knowledge imparted by military service. As the name implies, most JMO recruiters work to place commissioned officers below the rank of O-5 in specific management, professional, or technical positions. But the increasingly technical nature of America's employment landscape has spun off headhunters who hunt military technical heads.

For example, Lucas Group (www.lucascareers.com), an Atlanta-based full-service search firm with offices nationwide, offers both JMO and Military Technician recruitment services. The firm holds 24 recruitment conferences each year in cities across the country. Each event includes 40 to 80 hiring companies, enabling candidates to interview with four to nine potential employers (on average). To find JMO recruiters in your area, check the World Wide Web, or consult your area Yellow Pages under "Placement," "Executive placement," or "Career."

HEADHUNTER DOS AND DON'TS

- **Research a headhunter's reputation. What companies has he or she worked with? Get proof. How many placements has he or she made in the past six months? Once again, get proof.**
- **Get references. If a headhunter won't give you any, find another recruiter.**
- **Find out how long a recruiter has been in business. Recruiting is a tough profession with a high turnover. Simply put, headhunters who don't place candidates in jobs don't eat. Longevity is a good indicator of success.**
- **Don't sign a contract giving a recruiter the exclusive right to represent you. In your job search you need to have as many resources working for you as possible.**
- **Don't sign a contract that states that you will repay the recruiter's placement fee should you leave a job he finds for you before some specified period of time has elapsed. Read every word—especially fine print.**
- **Don't treat a recruiter as your best friend and confidante. Remember: she is essentially an employer's agent. When a recruiter interviews you, treat it like a job interview and put your best foot forward.**
- **Don't pay a recruiter any kind of consulting fee. Remember, he will be paid by an employer should he find you a job.**

RESUME WRITING SERVICES

When it comes to having a resume prepared, military members often are discouraged from hiring a civilian resume service. Such counsel, offered sometimes by transition program personnel and other times by friends, goes something like this: "Don't pay someone to write your resume; you can get that done on base for free," or "Civilian resume writers don't understand how the military works, so how can they write you an effective resume?"

Each of these advisories is partially true; each also is a bit shortsighted. Let's take a look at each one.

"DON'T PAY SOMEONE TO WRITE YOUR RESUME . . ."

Yes, no-cost assistance is available at your base or post transition center. But in most cases, it's just that—assistance. Military transition counselors will not write your resume for you. They simply don't have the time. One Navy transition counselor who worked at a large West Coast base told me that her office consulted on about 100 servicemembers' resumes per day. "Even spread out among the transition counselors we had, we couldn't write the resume for the members," she said. "We were only able to give them about 10 or 15 minutes worth of suggestions. They had to write the resumes on their own."

Here's the problem: For many people, writing a coherent letter is intimidating, not to mention writing a resume, one of the most important documents of their lives. I like to make this comparison: I'm a writer, not a mechanic. If I wanted to rebuild the engine in my Ford Explorer, I suppose I could have a professional mechanic coach me through it. But no matter how much advice a professional mechanic gave me on how to rebuild the engine in my Ford Explorer, I still wouldn't feel comfortable doing it. I'd much rather hire a professional who can build an engine I'm confident will work.

Should every servicemember who's not a writer by trade run out and hire a professional resume writer? Absolutely not. If you're even moderately comfortable with writing, you can—aided by examples, counselors, and transition classes—put together a resume that will get you interviews. But if you're completely uncomfortable with writing, you might consider paying a professional resume writer to do the job for you.

But there are very few civilian resume writers who can write an effective military transition resume. That gets back to that second piece of well-meaning advice:

"CIVILIAN RESUME WRITERS DON'T UNDERSTAND HOW THE MILITARY WORKS, SO HOW CAN THEY WRITE YOU AN EFFECTIVE RESUME?"

Unfortunately, that statement is often true. Every day, military members across the country pay hundreds of dollars to civilian resume writers who wouldn't know a mess-treasurer from a unit diary clerk. The resumes these "professionals" write are severely limited by the writer's knowledge of military language and systems. They are either woefully generic, just skimming the surface of the member's military career, or omitting truly meaningful skills and accomplishments. Or they are full of untranslated military-speak that the writer has lifted from the member's service record, but will actually hurt the member's chances with HR people who also don't understand the military. Often, servicemembers are duped into believing such substandard resumes are good ones, because they are professionally formatted, laser-printed on linen paper, and because the resume writer is a "professional." Thus, good money is wasted on a lousy product.

So, how do you hire a professional who will both write your resume for you and do an outstanding job? Follow these simple guidelines:

- Be sure the resume writer is a military veteran. The nuances of military service—as well as military language, systems, and infrastructure—cannot be learned; they must be experienced.

- Interview potential resume writers over the telephone. Ask questions to find out whether they've worked with military servicemembers in your field before. Don't say, "Have you worked with anyone in my field before?" Instead ask something like, "Tell me what civilian language you would use to describe my experience working with FPN-63 radar."

- If you will be crossing into a new career field, ask potential resume writers how they would "sell" you on paper. For example, if you are an avionics technician who is planning to look for a job in occupational safety and health, ask resume writers how they would handle that in your resume.

  Here's a sample bad answer: "Have you had any courses in occupational safety and health?" the resume writer asks. "If so, I would list those up top. I would also write about your management and organizational skills, and include your avionics skills just to keep your options open." Here's a sample good answer: "I would stress the skills and experience you've had that are related to occupational safety and health," the resume writer tells you, "and list all related training you've completed. I would mention your avionics experience, but not take up a lot of space with it since that's not your job objective right now."

- Is the resume writer willing to spend 10 or 15 minutes with you on the telephone? If a resume service you phone seems in a hurry to set an appointment and get you off the line, find someone else. If they're not willing to invest the time in making a good first impression on you, chances are they will not be overly concerned with the first impression made by your resume.
- Do not hire a resume writer who plans to have you fill out a form, but does not plan to personally interview you.
- Before hiring a resume writer, ask to see samples of military transition resumes he or she has written. Compare these with the resume "quality control checklist" in Chapter 8.
- Finally, will the resume writer you call quote you a price over the telephone? If not, again, move on to someone else. Some large chain services base the price of your resume not on how much work it will take to get the job done, but on how much they think you'll pay. To find that out, they have to get you in the door first. Look for a service that bases the cost of your resume on a combination of your paygrade and time-in-service. Why does this make sense? It's a simple matter of paperwork. An O-3 with six years in will have a skinny service record; the resume writer can read it in a flash. An O-5 with 20 years in will have a mountain of fitreps and awards to wade through; it may take hours for the resume writer to read.

RESUME PRICE MYTHS

Myth: A one-page resume should cost less than a two-page resume.
Reality: A one-page resume often requires more time and skill to write, since it involves culling out only the most relevant information and writing it concisely.

Myth: It's worth paying more to a resume service that offers perks like resume presentation folders and fancy paper stock.
Reality: Neatness counts, but employers are more interested in your skills and education than in your taste in resume paper. In the information age, most resumes are faxed, e-mailed, or posted electronically anyway.

Myth: It's worth paying more to a resume service that offers job search resources, electronic resume posting, and lifetime free updating and storage.

Reality: Between your military transition center, the Internet, and this book, you've already got all the job search resources you need. And if you or anyone you know has a computer, you can handle your own lifetime updates and storage.

Bottom line: As the Internet and other technology (like high-resolution inkjet printing) render most resume "perks" obsolete, many resume-writers try to trot out window-dressing services that add cost but not value. Don't bite.

"CAREER MANAGEMENT" FIRMS

Career management firms seem to have a lot to offer: career assessment testing, resume development services, job search coaching, job search seminars, job interview training, even "exclusive" lists of the phone numbers of corporate hiring managers. Some even afford their clients plush private offices—complete with Web-enabled computers, telephones, and private voice mailboxes—from which clients can conduct their job searches. Sound good? At prices of $2,000 to $8,000, they're actually too good to be true. Jack Riley, a Navy technician-turned-warrant officer, paid such a firm in San Diego $4,500 to help him launch his post-military career. Their offer sounded fabulous: All the services mentioned above, plus a money-back guarantee if he didn't find a job. Turned out the guarantee included fine print. Despite the perks and training, Jack would still be doing all the legwork for his own search. And the firm would return Jack's money all right—if he hadn't found a suitable job in *three years.*

Let me be clear: All firms doing business under the heading "career management firm" are not the same. Some offer genuine outplacement services, but beware of any firm that wants to charge you thousands of dollars to help you find a job. Especially if there are no licensed career counselors on staff, but plenty of "career coaches" supposedly available at your beck and call. There is no service such a firm can offer you that you can't find for less money—or even free—elsewhere.

START YOUR ENGINES

You've learned it all: how to assess yourself for a second career, how to market your military skills, and who can help you on-base and off. Now it's time for the lowdown on where and how to actually look for a job.

BE A 75-PERCENTER

According to job search expert Richard Bolles, about 75% of all jobs are found through informal contacts. What does that mean? It means that most jobs aren't found through personnel agencies or classified ads, but through good, old-fashioned pavement pounding. While agencies yield about 9% of permanent job placements, and ads another 10%, more than seven out of ten job-seekers lands a new job through one of the following avenues:

- Networking
- Career fairs
- Conventions
- Professional associations
- Temporary work
- Volunteer work
- Internships
- Externships

These avenues are your connection with the hidden job market. That's the 80% of available job openings that experts say are never made public. If 75% of job seekers succeed in landing one of these hidden openings, wouldn't it make sense to invest three-quarters of your job search effort in developing these contacts? Not surprisingly, most people don't. Why? Because most people prefer to use methods that take the least effort, like sitting at a computer and clicking through online classifieds. Don't be one of them. Be a 75-percenter. Remember, people prefer to hire job candidates that they know or who were referred to them. You can't get to know people sitting at a computer. Get out of the house and attend functions, join organizations, and volunteer your time. Not only will you get to know those who are qualified to hire you, you'll gain valuable experience in the process.

THE OTHER 25 PERCENT

Though 75% of jobs are landed through informal contacts, 25% are landed through classified ads and employment agencies. So don't write them off entirely. Spend about a quarter of your job search time responding to ads or checking with placement services about available openings. Temp agencies aren't the only kind. You can also contact:

- Personnel agencies (who deal in permanent placement)
- Federal hiring offices
- State unemployment offices
- Recruiters

When it comes to classified ads, the newspaper and the Internet aren't the only sources. To expand your options, also look for ads in:

- Company newsletters
- Magazines and journals
- Radio and television
- Association newsletters
- Flyers
- Personnel office listings

But consider each ad carefully before you apply. Is there a company name listed, or does the ad read "growing sales organization"? Are specific qualifications requested, or does the ad ask for "energetic people who want an upwardly mobile career"? Send or fax a resume and cover letter only in response to ads that list a company name, a specific job title, and requested qualifications. Remember: You only have 15 minutes of every hour to spend on ads. Don't waste your time on dead ends.

TRANSITION TIMELINE: A THREE-YEAR PLAN

As the time approaches for you to separate from military service, time will begin to play tricks on you. Here's how it works: When you have about two years left to serve, that magic future date on which you will turn in your green ID card and, for the last time, walk out the front gate, will glisten on life's horizon like a tantalizing mirage. It will beckon, but not urgently. It will inspire daydreaming, but will not inspire you so much that you get your butt off the couch and do something about it. The next thing you know, you'll have one year left. The day after that you'll officially become a "short-timer," and you can begin to count down in months.

Right about then, you'll hit a time warp: months will flash by like weeks, weeks like days. You'll begin to worry that you won't find a job and wish that you'd gotten that college degree. You'll wish you hadn't leased that expensive sport utility vehicle and that you'd spent that reenlistment bonus to pay off your bills. You may even start to think about extending or reenlisting.

All this will happen, *if* you don't plan your separation or retirement well ahead of time. The following information—based on a military-to-civilian transition course offered by Navy Family Service Center San Diego—will help you plan a smooth transition from military service to a new civilian career.

THREE YEARS TO ONE YEAR PRIOR

SELF-ASSESSMENT

Now—not six months prior to getting out—is the time to assess your skills and interests with an eye toward your next career. Your base or post transition center probably offers free tools you can use to assess your interests, aptitudes, knowledge, and skills. Many such tools even offer likely matches between test results and possible careers. A thorough, early examination of your skills and interests can help you begin preparing for a post-military career that fits—instead of one that just pays the rent.

RESEARCH CAREERS, COMPANIES AND SALARIES

Begin exploring possible career paths. What kinds of companies use people in those career fields? What salaries can you expect? Is the number of job openings in those fields rising or falling? The Internet is a great place to undertake this research. A stroll through online job boards (monster.com; hotjobs.com) can give you an idea who's hiring whom. Surprisingly, investment research sites are also helpful. Sites like *The Motley Fool*, where investors snoop for corporate data, can also yield valuable information for job-seekers. The Bureau of Labor Statistics website (www.bls.gov) is a treasure of occupational data, like average salaries for specific jobs, and which career fields are growing or shrinking. You can also investigate career fields and salaries by using print references. Try *The Dictionary of Occupational Titles* or *The Occupational Outlook Handbook*, both published by the U.S. Department of Labor, and both available at libraries and transition centers. To research specific companies, try hoovers.com or Standard & Poor's Industry Surveys (available at most libraries).

This is also the time to start networking with people in your chosen industry. Check the Web for professional associations related to your career field. Join one and get to know players in your field. The old adage still holds true: "It's who you know."

DEVELOP A PLAN TO GAIN NECESSARY SKILLS, EDUCATION, AND EXPERIENCE

Once you've decided on a career field, create a plan to get the education, training, and experience that potential employers will want to see in a job candidate. Will you need a college degree or will a professional certification do the job? How about practical work experience? If you're planning on a complete change of career fields, might you need to work part-time or volunteer in your future full-time occupation?

Visit your base or post education office to find out what degree or certification program might help your cause. Again, professional organizations can also point you in the right direction.

DEVELOP A JOB SEARCH ORGANIZING SYSTEM

Identify a space in your home that you'll use exclusively for managing your transition. It could be as elaborate as a spare bedroom converted into an office, or as spare as a rolling file cabinet positioned near the kitchen table. Use this timeline to create a transition action plan (with deadlines!), then post your plan where you can see it every day. Establish a filing system for career field and company research.

RESEARCH TARGET RELOCATION AREAS

Some servicemembers are willing to move wherever a hiring company wants them to. Others would prefer to relocate based on housing prices, state tax structure, or whether or not they'd have to shovel their car out of the snow every morning. To learn more about a city or state, try visiting the websites of specific cities or chambers of commerce. For a handy print reference, try the Economic Research Institute's *Geographical Reference Report Book*, available at base transition and relocation offices.

DEVELOP AND IMPLEMENT A FINANCIAL PLAN

Calculate the salary and benefits you'll need to achieve your desired post-military standard of living. If you want to match or exceed your military pay and benefits, be sure to figure in housing costs you may not be currently paying (like utilities, if you live in military housing). If you are not retiring, be sure to calculate the price of non-commissary groceries and civilian health care plans. Remember, as a civilian all your pay will be taxed, and you may need to deduct additional retirement savings from your future civilian pay. For help with these issues, visit your base or post financial planning office.

Two other issues to consider: (1) What bills you would like to have paid off by the time you separate and (2) How much you'll need to save to cover living expenses during your transition in the event that you don't land the right job right away. Experts recommend a six-month emergency cushion.

TWELVE MONTHS TO SIX MONTHS PRIOR

RECHECK SELF-ASSESSMENT AND CONTINUE PURSUIT OF SKILLS AND EDUCATION

As you enter the home stretch, pause for a progress check. Have you met the goals you established in your action plan? Have your interests changed? Did you ever get around to joining that professional association? Take time now to catch up what you've missed, and make any necessary adjustments to your transition action plan.

If you never made an action plan, create one now and fold in the items you've already missed from the list above. You'll really have your work cut out for you, but better to do your career planning now than find yourself in a panic six months from now.

RECHECK YOUR FINANCIAL PLAN TO SEE IF IT'S ON TRACK; MAKE NECESSARY ADJUSTMENTS

Are you proceeding "on plan" financially, or have you had major life changes or setbacks? Will your current post-military career plan finance needs that have developed since you first began your transition planning? How's your savings plan going? Do you need to increase the amount you save to meet your emergency cushion goal? Again, help with these issues is available at your base or post financial planning office.

CONTINUE RESEARCHING COMPANIES AND SALARIES

Begin researching specific companies to develop profiles on corporate culture, career ladders, and hiring trends. Catalog key company facts like locations, earnings, current projects, products, and services. Great resources for company research: *Moody's Fact Sheets: Industry Review*; various business directories published by Dunns, and *Standard and Poor's Register of Corporations, Directors and Executives.*

BEGIN LEARNING JOB SEARCH SKILLS

As early as possible before your separation or retirement date, arrange to attend the appropriate career transition course offered by your service branch. Transition classes feature in-depth job search training on resumes, federal applications, job interviews, company research, developing job leads, and networking. Many transition classes require students to prepare a working resume, so begin gathering these materials to prepare yours: copies of fitness reports or performance evaluations, records of military and off-duty education, and the citation portion of any military awards you've earned.

CONTINUE RESEARCHING TARGET RELOCATION AREAS; NARROW DOWN TARGET AREAS

If you can swing it, visit a town or two to see how it suits you. If you've already pinpointed your final destination and will be buying a home, consider making contact with a real estate agent.

SIX MONTHS TO THREE MONTHS PRIOR

INTENSIFY NETWORKING: TOUCH BASE WITH ESTABLISHED CONTACTS AND ADD NEW ONES

Continue informational interviewing and professional association liaisons.

PREPARE RESUMES AND COVER LETTERS

Now's the time to write your resume and cover letters or, if you've already prepared these items in a transition class, fine-tune them for actual use. (If you're planning to market yourself in more than one career field, write a customized resume for each one.) Many people find resume writing intimidating. But don't put it off or you may find yourself having to let attractive job openings slip by because you don't have your resume prepared.

RESEARCH ACTUAL JOB OPENINGS

Begin in earnest looking for job openings that match your qualifications. Surf career websites and make regular visits to your transition center to see what openings are advertised there. Subscribe to newspapers in your target relocation areas and scan their classifieds—or see if those publications post their classifieds online. During this period, servicemembers seeking professional or management positions may elect to apply for specific openings. Generally, for highly placed openings within an organization, it is acceptable to apply with some lead time before you would start working. Usually, the higher the position, the longer the lead time.

OBTAIN LETTERS OF RECOMMENDATION AND REFERENCES

Write a couple of sample reference and recommendation letters (you can find these in most resume-writing books). When you approach contacts to ask them for a recommendation, offer your samples as a guide to give them a "running start" on the task.

PRACTICE INTERVIEWING

Most people spend more time studying for their drivers' license exam than practicing for what could wind up being one of the most important meetings of their life. For most people, answering probing questions about themselves is not natural. So practicing for job interviews cannot be overemphasized. Rehearse with your spouse, friends, and professional contacts. If possible, arrange to videotape a practice session or two. Seeing yourself on tape can help you polish your delivery and eliminate any nervous habits.

THREE MONTHS TO SEPARATION DATE

REGISTER WITH THE EMPLOYMENT DEPARTMENT IN THE STATE WHERE YOU RELOCATE

If you haven't found any promising job leads yet, and would like to receive unemployment benefits, now's the time to contact your state employment department to find out what your state requires. State employment offices also feature job listings, job search classes, and, in many cases, specific help for military veterans. Benefits vary by state. Check the Government Blue Pages, an Internet search engine, or your transition center for state-specific contact information.

CONTINUE NETWORKING

Touch base with people you haven't spoken with in two months or more. Don't be shy about letting contacts know exactly what kind of work you're looking for and when you'll be available. Continue networking via professional organizations and informational interviewing.

APPLY FOR JOBS; GO ON ACTUAL INTERVIEWS

Now that you're close to separating, it's time to begin applying for actual openings. Create a binder for tracking applications. For every resume or application submitted, note the date, company name, contact information, person contacted, scheduled follow-up date, and the actual follow-up date and results.

Immediately after interviews, make notes of your impressions. What did you do well? What could you have done better? How will you improve next time? File these sheets in your application binder.

If you faithfully follow the steps outlined above, one of these sheets will include the note: "Got the job!"

Afterword

You've done it! You conducted a savvy job search campaign and have landed that first post-military job. Now how do you impress your first post-military boss? Punctuality and a polished appearance still score points with employers, but read on to learn what four civilian managers say fresh-from-the-base military veterans can do to shine in their post-military jobs.

1. Positive Attitude

"A lot of military people have learned a can-do, 'take that hill' mentality," says Kitty Egger, regional director of business development for the Eastridge Group, a San Diego-based staffing firm. "In the civilian world, employers are looking for people who will take that hill, who want to be there, and have a positive attitude and a passion about what they do."

A positive attitude can translate to professional success, says Egger, adding that such an attitude is portable: It can go with you into any work environment to help forge a successful relationship with employers.

"You can be positive and passionate on a production line, developing software, or anything in between," Egger notes.

2. A WINNING SMILE

After less than a year at her new job, Shannon Hough smiled her way to a merit-based pay raise. Hough is a former Navy cryptologic technician who was hired as a desktop publishing technician at Publisher's Printing Factory in Mililani, Hawaii. "It didn't matter what kind of mood I was in—I always tried to go in with a smile," said Hough. She says it was her cheerful approach to the job, at least in part, that earned her a higher-than-normal first-year pay raise.

In certain industries, smiling faces are especially important. Sixto Aspeitia, director of Peterson Hotel Properties in San Diego, said his firm actually offers customer service training in which new employees are taught to smile.

"In (the hotel) industry, good customer service is really important," said Aspeitia. "Smiling faces keep customers coming back."

3. SELF-STARTER

Shannon Hough didn't count too much on her smile. Her new supervisors quickly came to know her as a self-starter. Hough took the initiative to venture beyond her desktop publishing job description to learn other printing factory functions, including quality assurance and book bindery.

Magazine editor Janet Bernstel ranks initiative at the top of her new employee wish list: "I'm impressed by a new employee who comes up with his or her own solution to a problem, then comes to me to see what I think of their idea." Bernstel, who in 1998 added seven new hires to her staff in a six-month period, said a self-starting employee saves her time and hassle. She said she would appreciate a new employee who, for example, took the initiative to secure benefits forms that might have been overlooked by a supervisor during the hiring process.

"I would be really impressed if (a new hire) came to me and said, 'I asked such-and-such in the HR department for those forms because I thought I might have to fill them out this week—is that okay?' " Bernstel said. "That saves me time and shows me they can function somewhat autonomously."

4. LISTEN AND LEARN

Take care, though, when exercising initiative, not to exercise so much of it that you cut other people out of their own realms of authority. This can be perceived as pushy, and may serve to confirm the stereotype that ex-military workers can't fit in in the civilian world.

"Some new employees feel they have to come in with guns blazing to show everyone the depth of their knowledge," Bernstel said. "But I am most impressed by a person who can keep quiet and observe. The first few months are about the employee fitting into the new environment, and to do that, they have to listen."

5. INGENUITY

But there does come a time to speak up—after you've forged what Egger calls a "reciprocal trust" with your supervisor. Sometimes, a company's departments or divisions can get into a rut. It often takes a fresh eye to identify tasks that could be done in a better way.

"The worker bee mentality—where you go in, learn the job and do it the same old way it's always been done—is alive and well," Egger said. "But after you and your supervisor develop an atmosphere of trust, let your ingenuity shine through."

If you've figured out a way to trim costs or improve on a procedure, Egger said, don't be afraid to make thoughtful suggestions.

6. HIGH-TECH SOLUTIONS

Your ability to make suggestions and add value to the company is probably one reason you were hired in the first place. Innovative ways of doing business developed through "breakthrough thinking" can sometimes mean seven-digit savings, according to Bruce Hatz, corporate staffing manager for Hewlett-Packard, the San Mateo, California-based high-tech giant. Hatz said he's most impressed by new staffers who can use technology to improve his company's performance.

"I want someone who can use technology to solve real business problems," Hatz says, noting one employee who wrote a simple software program to automate a formerly time-consuming task. "It's the concept of working hard versus working smart."

7. HARD WORK

That's not to say that working hard is out of fashion. Former Air Force sergeant Dino Elkins learned that when he hired on at Questar Gas in Clearfield, Utah, as a security alarm technician. His first post-military employers told him hard work would be the key to his success with the firm.

"In my job, hard work means getting the job done as quickly as possible and doing it right the first time," said Elkins, adding that his "quality first" attitude is a direct carryover from his military experience.

Egger agrees: "Employers notice that kind of loyalty and commitment," she says, "And they'll reward it with incentives like bonus pay or extra time off."

8. CAREER SELF-RELIANCE

Hewlett-Packard's Bruce Hatz says it's not only what you put into your job that counts—it's also what you put into your career. At Hewlett-Packard, employees quickly learn a mindset the company calls "career self-reliance."

"Nobody is in charge of your career but you," said Hatz. "That means you're not a pawn being moved around in your career by someone behind the scenes." Instead, he says, a worker who is career self-reliant:

- Takes the initiative to keep up with developing career field trends.
- Stays late researching new developments.
- Takes occasional professional development classes at night.

"That's the kind of thing I like to see," Hatz says. "People who continue adding to their skill sets are the ones who will make it in the long term."

Appendix A

EDUCATION RESOURCES

www.voled.doded.mil
Department of Defense Voluntary Education site. Your absolute, #1 stop for learning about voluntary, off-duty education. Military regulations, programs, financing, testing—this site has it all.

www.gibillexpress.com
Complete information on active-duty and post-military college financing.

www.finaid.org
Financial aid information, including grants, loans, and scholarships.

www.fastweb.com
Free scholarship search.

www.collegenet.com
CollegeNET is the #1 portal for applying to college over the Web. Also boasts college search and financial-aid search features.

www.campusregistry.com
An online campus community for college students and alumni. Articles, chats, and boards.

www.supercollege.com
Comprehensive site featuring college search, financial aid search, admissions, testing tips, and more.

www.financialaid.about.com
Advice page with current education-
related news, articles, advice, and financial
aid search tools.

www.cash4students.com
Financial aid search and advice site.

www.collegeboard.com
Lots of information about entrance exams
like SAT, PSAT, and CLEP, plus test-prep
help. College search feature.

www.back2college.com
A great site for "reentry" students—those
returning to college after a layoff. Distance
learning, college profiles, adult education,
curriculum descriptions, internships, and
more.

CERTIFICATION PROGRAMS

DANTES has agreements with over 30
nationally recognized certification associations. Certification examinations
document a person's level of competency
and achievement in a particular area.
Military personnel may already have the
experience and knowledge required to gain

certification in their occupational specialty.
On the following pages is a sampling of
available certification programs. To learn
how to pursue one of the programs below,
visit www.voled.doded.mil/dantes/cert/
index.htm.

NAVY CERTIFICATION MATRIX

CERTIFICATION AGENCY	TYPES OF CERTIFICATION	NER/NEC	EXAM?	COURSES/ TRAINING	OTHER
Association of Boards of Certification (ABC) Environmental Occupations 515-232-3623	Water Treatment, Distribution, Wastewater Treatment, Collection, Analysis, Industrial Wastewater, etc.	HM	YES, Class I, II, III, and IV	College courses, 1-4 yrs site experience	DEPH Chpt 9
American Board of Industrial Hygiene (ABIH) Board of Certified Safety Professionals (BCSP) Joint Committee for Certification of Occupational Health and Safety Technologists www.bcsp.com/jointcomm_fr.html 217-359-9263	Occupational Health and Safety Technologist	HM	YES	Associate's degree in safety and health or a bachelor's degree in any field	DEPH Chpt 3
American Council on Exercise (ACE) www.acefitness.org 619-535-8227	Aerobic Instructors, Personal Trainers, Lifestyle and Weight Management Consultant	HM	YES, Overseas only	Valid adult CPR	DEPH Chpt 4
American Medical Technologist (AMT) www.amt1.com 847-823-5169 ext 213	Registered Medical/Dental Asst., Med Technologists, Medical Lab Technician, Registered Phlebotomy Technician	HM,DT	YES	Minimum associate's degree, graduate of medical program	DEPH Chpt 5
American Nurses Credentialing Center (ANCC) www.nursingworld.org 1-800-284-2378	Registered Nurse, Certified Registered Nurse, Certified Specialist	HM	YES	Education beyond basic nursing course	DEPH Chpt 6

CERTIFICATION AGENCY	TYPES OF CERTIFICATION	NER/NEC	EXAM?	COURSES/ TRAINING	OTHER
National Institute for Automotive Service Excellence (ASE) www.asecert.org 703-713-3800	Master/Auto Tech, Master/ Medium/Heavy Truck Tech, Master/Auto/ Body Tech, Master/Engine Machinist Tech, School Bus Tech	CM, MM, GS, BT, EN, AS	YES, Dantes funded	Minimum of 2 yrs experience	DEPH Chpt 28
American Speech-Language-Hearing Association (ASHA) www.asha.org 301-897-5700	Certificate of Clinical Competence	HM	YES	Master's degree and field experience	DEPH Chpt 8
Association of State and Provincial Psychology Boards (ASPPB) www.asppb.org/roster.htm 334-832-4580	Psychologist	9519, 951, HM, HC, 9588	YES	Make application to the state or provincial psychology licensing board. Doctorate degree, 2 yrs experience	DEPH Chpt 10
American Society for Quality Control www.hanson-dodge.com/ web/sites/asqc/default.html 414-272-8575	Quality Manager, Technician, Reliability Engineer, Mechanical Inspector, Quality Engineer, Quality Asst.	BT, MM, 1588	YES	Minimum of 2 yrs experience, up to 10 yrs experience	DEPH Chpt 7
Board of Certified Safety Professionals (BCSP) www.Bcsp.com 217-359-9263	Certified Safety Professional	DC, MM, HT	YES	Associate's degree in safety or bachelor's in any field, 4 yrs experience	DEPH Chpt 11
American Board of General Dentistry (ABGD) 312-440-4306	Certified General Dentist	DT	YES	Minimum 2 yrs experience or 1 yr with 600 hours	DEPH Chpt 2
Cardiovascular Credentialing International (CCI) www.cci-online.org 1-800-258-4914	Certified Cardiographic Technician, Registered Cardiovascular Technologist, Registry Exams	HM	YES	Minimum 2 yrs experience with associate's degree or bachelor's degree	DEPH Chpt 12

CERTIFICATION AGENCY	TYPES OF CERTIFICATION	NER/NEC	EXAM?	COURSES/ TRAINING	OTHER
Certified Technical Trainer (CTT) www.chauncey.com/survey 1-800-258-4914	Certified Technical Trainer	9502, 2186, MOST TRNG SPEC, NC, 9588, 9589	YES, Computer delivered, video	Minimum 2 yrs field experience	DEPH Chpt 13
Dental Assisting National Board (DANB) www.dentalassisting.com 312-642-3368	Certified Dental Asst., Oral and Maxilloficial Surgery, Dental Practice Management Asst., Orthodontic Asst.	DT	YES	Graduate of dental program, 2 yrs experience or 3500 hrs in 2-yr period. Adult CPR	DEPH Chpt 14
The Education Institute of the American Hotel/Motel Association (EIAH&MA) www.ahma.com/index.htm 1-888-575-8726	Certified Hotel Administrator, Food/Beverage Exec., Hospitality Housekeeping Exec., Human Resources Exec., etc.	SH, SK, AK, MS	YES	Hospitality associate's degree or 3 yrs experience	DEPH Chpt 15
The National Registry of Emergency Medical Technicians (EMT) www.nremt.org 614-888-4484	Emergency Medical Technician— Basic, Intermediate, and Paramedic	HM	YES	State license and C level CPR	DEPH Chpt 32
Electronics Technicians Association International (ETA-I) www.eta-sda.com 765-653-8262	Associate Electronic Tech, Electronics Journeyman Tech, Senior/Master Electronics Tech, Fiber Optic Installer, (FCC) Commercial Operator License Exam	AT, AE, ET, EM, EN, MT, GM, OTM, ST, CT	YES	Minimum 2 yrs full-time experience	DEPH Chpt 16
Food Protection Certification Program (FPCP) www.voled.doded.mil/dantes/ cert/DEPH-PT3/FPCP 609-720-6535	Food Protection Certification	HM, MS	YES, Dantes funded	2 yrs experience	DEPH Chpt 17

CERTIFICATION AGENCY	TYPES OF CERTIFICATION	NER/NEC	EXAM?	COURSES/ TRAINING	OTHER
Institute for Certification of Computing Professionals (ICCP) www.ICCP.org 847-299-4227	Certified Computing Professional, Associate Computing Professional	DP, DS, YN, AZ, PN, CTR, RM	YES	4 yrs experience or master's degree for certified professional	DEPH Chpt 18
Institute of Certified Professional Managers (ICPM) http://cob.jmu.edu/icmp	Certified Manager	AK, PN, RP, CTA, AZ, BM, DK, LN, NC, SH, SK	YES, 3 parts	4 yrs experience as a manager	DEPH Chpt 20
Institute for Personal Finance (IPF) www.hec.ohio-state.edu/hanna/ afcpe/index.htm 602-912-5331	Accredited Financial Counselor, Certified Housing Counselor	DK	YES	Minimum 2 yrs as a financial counselor and full-time experience	DEPH Chpt 19
American Association of Bioanalysts (AAB) Board of Registry (formerly the Credentialing Commission of the International Society for Clinical Laboratory Technology (ISCLT)) www.aab.org 314-241-1445	Registered Medical Technologists, Laboratory Tech, Physicians Office Laboratory Tech	HM	YES	Minimum associate's degree with 3 yrs full-time experience	DEPH Chpt 1
The Liaison Council on Certification for the Surgical Technologist (LCC-ST) www.lcc-st.org 1-800-707-0057 x225	Certified Surgical Technologist, Certified First Assistant	HM	YES	Graduate of accredited program	DEPH Chpt 23
The National Association of Radio and Telecommunications Engineers, Inc. (NARTE) www.kmxnet.com/narte 508-533-8333	Telecommunication Class I-IV, EMC-Engineering Tech, ESD-EngineeringTech, FCC-All elements (commercial) Entry-level tech/engineers	RM,CTR	YES	Education and minimum 2 yrs experience	DEPH Chpt 24
National Association of Social Workers (NASW) www.socialworkers.org 202-408-8600	Academy of Certified Social Workers	9519, HM, NC	YES	Membership, master's degree with 2 yrs full-time experience	DEPH Chpt 25

CERTIFICATION AGENCY	TYPES OF CERTIFICATION	NER/NEC	EXAM?	COURSES/ TRAINING	OTHER
National Board for the Certification of Orthopaedic Technologists (NBCOT) www.nbcot.org 301-990-7979 ext 3131	Certified Orthopaedic Technologist	HM	YES	Occupational therapy degree and fieldwork	DEPH Chpt 26
National Board for Respiratory Care (NBRC) www.nbrc.org 913-599-4200	Certified/Registered Respiratory Therapy Tech, Certified/ Registered Pulmonary Function Tech, Perinatal/ Pediatric Respiratory Care Specialist	HM	YES	Graduate from respiratory therapy education program	DEPH Chpt 27
National Institute for Certification in Engineering Technology (NICET) www.nicet.org 1-888-426-4238	Associate Engineering Tech, Engineering Tech, Senior Engineering Tech	AT, AE, ET, EM, EW, FC, IC, MT, GM, OTM, ST, BB, CE, EA, EO, EQ, SW, CT	YES	Bachelor's degree	DEPH Chpt 30
The National Institute for the Certification of Healthcare Sterile Processing and Distribution Personnel (NICHSPDP) www.sterileprocessing.org/ nichspdp.htm 1-800-555-9765	Certified Sterile Processing and Distribution Tech, Supervisor, and Manager	HM	YES	Associate's degree	DEPH Chpt 31
International Association of Administrative Professionals (IAAP) (Formerly Professional Secretaries International (PSI)) www.iaap-hq.org 816-891-6600	Certified Professional Secretary	DK, YN, PL, AZ, CTA	YES, 3 part	No degree then 4 yrs experience, associate's with 3 yrs experience, bachelor's with 2 yrs experience	DEPH Chpt 21
Society of Broadcast Engineers (SBE) www.sbe.org 317-253-1640	Broadcast Technologist, Broadcast Engineer, Senior Broadcast Engineer, Professional Brodcast Engineer	AT, GSE, AE, ET, EM, EW, FC, IC, CTM	YES	Academic degree or professional field experience	DEPH Chpt 33

ARMY NATIONAL GUARD CERTIFICATION MATRIX

Certification Agency	Types of Certification	NER/NEC	Exam?	Courses/ Training	Other
Association of Boards of Certification (ABC) Environmental Occupations 515-232-3623	Water Treatment, Distribution, Wastewater Treatment, Collection, Analysis, Industrial Wastewater, etc.	91 series, 77W	YES, Class I, II, III, and IV	College courses, 1-4 yrs site experience	DEPH Chpt 2
American Board of Industrial Hygiene (ABIH) Board of Certified Safety Professionals (BCSP) Joint Committee for Certification of Occupational Health and Safety Technologists www.bcsp.com/joint.htm 217-359-9263	Occupational Health and Safety Technologist	91 series, 77W	YES	Associate's degree in safety and health or a bachelor's degree in any field	DEPH Chpt 3
American Council on Exercise (ACE) www.acefitness.org 619-535-8227	Aerobic Instructors, Personal Trainers, Lifestyle and Weight Management Consultant	Related training/additional skill identifier	YES, Overseas only	Valid adult CPR	DEPH Chpt 4
American Medical Technologist (AMT) www.amt1.com 847-823-5169 ext 213	Registered Medical/Dental Asst., Med Technologists, Medical Lab Technician, Registered Phlebotomy Technician	91E, 91K, 91	YES	Minimum associate's degree, graduate of medical program	DEPH Chpt 6
American Nurses Credentialing Center (ANCC) www.nursingworld.org 1-800-284-2378	Registered Nurse, Certified registered nurse, Certified Specialist	91C	YES	Education beyond basic nursing course	DEPH Chpt 7
National Institute for Automotive Service Excellence (ASE) www.asecert.org 703-713-3800	Master/Auto Tech, Master/ Medium/Heavy Truck Tech, Master/Auto/ Body Tech, Master/Engine Machinist Tech, School Bus Tech	63 series, 44 series, 45 series, 52 series, 62 series	YES, Dantes funded	Minimum of 2 yrs experience	DEPH Chpt 8

CERTIFICATION AGENCY	TYPES OF CERTIFICATION	NER/NEC	EXAM?	COURSES/ TRAINING	OTHER
American Speech-Language-Hearing Association (ASHA) www.asha.org 301-897-5700	Certificate of Clinical Competence	Related training	YES	Master's degree and field experience	DEPH Chpt 9
Association of State and Provincial Psychology Boards (ASPPB) www.nationalregister.com/ asppros.htm 334-832-4580	Psychologist		YES	Make application to the state or provincial psychology licensing board	DEPH Chpt 10
American Society for Quality Control www.asqc.org 414-272-8575	Quality Manager, Technician, Reliability Engineer, Mechanical Inspector, Quality Engineer, Quality Asst.	35 series, 55 series, or related training	YES	Minimum of 2 yrs experience, up to 10 yrs experience	DEPH Chpt 11
Board of Certified Safety Professionals (BCSP) www.bcsp.com 217-359-9263	Certified Safety Professional	55 series, or related training and assignments	YES	Associate's degree in safety or bachelor's in any field, 4 yrs experience	DEPH Chpt 12
American Board of General Dentistry (ABGD) www.agd.org 312-440-4306	Certified General Dentist	91E	YES	Minimum 2 yrs experience or 1 yr with 600 hours	DEPH Chpt 13
Cardiovascular Credentialing International (CCI) www.cci-online.org 1-800-258-4914	Certified Cardiographic Technician, Registered Cardiovascular Technologist, Registry Exams	91 series	YES	Minimum 2 yrs experience with associate's degree or bachelor's degree	DEPH Chpt 14
Certified Technical Trainer (CTT) www.chauncey.com/survey 1-800-258-4914	Certified Technical Trainer	Related training, assignments/additional skill identifier	YES, Computer delivered, video	Minimum 2 yrs field experience	
Dental Assisting National Board (DANB) www.ada.org/direct/org/ si_danbo.htm 312-642-3368	Certified Dental Asst., Oral and Maxilloficial Surgery, Dental Practice Management Asst., Orthodontic Asst.	91E	YES	Graduate of dental program, 2 yrs experience or 3500 hrs in 2-yr period. Adult CPR	DEPH Chpt 15

Certification Agency	Types of Certification	NER/NEC	Exam?	Courses/ Training	Other
The Education Institute of the American Hotel/Motel Association (EIAH&MA) www.ahma.com/index.htm 1-888-575-8726	Certified Hotel Administrator, Food/Beverage Exec., Hospitality Housekeeping Exec., Human Resources Exec., etc.	94 series and 91M	YES	Hospitality associate's degree or 3 yrs experience	DEPH Chpt 31
The National Registry of Emergency Medical Technicians (EMT) www.nremt.org 614-888-4484	Emergency Medical Technician– Basic, Intermediate, and Paramedic	91 series	YES	State license and C level CPR	DEPH Chpt 16
Electronics Technicians Association International (ETA-I) www.eta-sda.com 765-653-8262	Associate Electronic Tech, Electronics Journeyman Tech, Senior/Master Electronics Tech, Fiber Optic Installer, (FCC) Commercial Operator License Exam	33, 35, 44, 45, 52, 55, 63 and 93 series	YES	Minimum 2 yrs full-time experience	DEPH Chpt 17
Food Protection Certification Program (FPCP) www.chauncey.com/cgprgind.htm 609-720-6535	Food Protection Certification	91R, 91S, 92 and 94B	YES, Dantes funded	2 yrs experience	DEPH Chpt 18
Institute for Certification of Computing Professionals (ICCP) www.iccp.org 847-299-4227	Certified Computing Professional, Associate Computing Professional	55, 77 and 92 series or related training or assignments	YES	4 yrs experience or master's degree for certified professional	DEPH Chpt 19
Institute of Certified Professional Managers (ICPM) http://cob.jmu.edu/icmp	Certified Manager	96 and 98 series and any MOS meeting certification criteria	YES, 3 parts	4 yrs experience as a manager	DEPH Chpt 20
Institute for Personal Finance (IPF) 602-912-5331	Accredited Financial Counselor, Certified Housing Counselor	Any 75 or 79 series	YES	Minimum 2 yrs as a financial counselor and full-time experience	DEPH Chpt 5

CERTIFICATION AGENCY	TYPES OF CERTIFICATION	NER/NEC	EXAM?	COURSES/ TRAINING	OTHER
American Association of Bio-analysts (AAB) (formerly the Credentialing Commission of the International Society for Clinical Laboratory Technology (ISCLT)) 314-241-1445	Registered Medical Technologists, Laboratory Tech, Physicians Office Laboratory Tech	91K	YES	Minimum associate's degree with 3 yrs full-time experience	DEPH Chpt 21
The Liaison Council on Certification for the Surgical Technologist (LCC-ST) www.ast.org/lcc.htm 1-800-707-0057 x225	Certified Surgical Technologist, Certified First Assistant	91D	YES	Graduate of accredited program	DEPH Chpt 22
The National Association of Radio and Telecommunications Engineers, Inc. (NARTE) www.kmxnet.com/narte 508-533-8333	Telecommunication Class I-IV, EMC-Engineering Tech, ESD-Engineering Tech, and FCC-All elements (commercial) Entry-level tech/engineers	31 series, 36M, 98 series, 35E, 52D 88 series	YES	Education and minimum 2 yrs experience	DEPH Chpt 23
National Association of Social Workers (NASW) www.naswdc.org 202-408-8600	Academy of Certified Social Workers	71M	YES	Membership, master's degree with 2 yrs full-time experience	DEPH Chpt 24
National Board for the Certification of Orthopaedic Technologists (NBCOT) www.nbcot.org 301-990-7979 ext 3131	Certified Orthopaedic Technologist	91H	YES	Occupational therapy degree and fieldwork	DEPH Chpt 25
National Board for Respiratory Care (NBRC) www.nbrc.org 913-599-4200	Certified/Registered Respiratory Therapy Tech, Certified/Registered Pulmonary Function Tech, Perinatal/Pediatric Respiratory Care Specialist	91V	YES	Graduate from respiratory therapy education program	DEPH Chpt 26

CERTIFICATION AGENCY	TYPES OF CERTIFICATION	NER/NEC	EXAM?	COURSES/ TRAINING	OTHER
National Institute for Certification in Engineering Technology (NICET) www.nicet.org 1-888-476-4238	Associate Engineering Tech, Engineering Tech, Senior Engineering Tech	51 series	YES	Bachelor's degree	DEPH Chpt 27
The National Institute for the Certification of Healthcare Sterile Processing and Distribution Personnel (NICHSPDP) www.njcc.com/~multico/nichspdp 1-800-555-9765	Certified Sterile Processing and Distribution Tech, Supervisor, and Manager	92 series and 76J	YES	Associate's degree	DEPH Chpt 28
International Association of Administrative Professionals (IAAP) (formerly Professional Secretaries International (PSI)) www.gvi.net/psi 816-891-6600	Certified Professional Secretary	71 and 75 series	YES, 3 part	No degree then 4 yrs experience, associate's with 3 yrs experience, bachelor's with 2 yrs experience	DEPH Chpt 29
Society of Broadcast Engineers (SBE) www.sbe.org 317-253-1640	Broadcast Technologist, Broadcast Engineer, Senior Broadcast Engineer, Professional Brodcast Engineer	98 and 31 series	YES	Academic degree or professional field experience	DEPH Chpt 30

AIR FORCE RESERVE CERTIFICATION MATRIX

CERTIFICATION AGENCY	TYPES OF CERTIFICATION	NER/NEC	EXAM?	COURSES/ TRAINING	OTHER
Association of Boards of Certification (ABC) Environmental Occupations 515-232-3623	Distribution, Water treatment, Wastewater Treatment, Collection, Analysis, Industrial Wastewater, etc.	3E4X1, 4B0X1	YES, Class I, II, III, and IV	College courses, 1-4 yrs site experience	DEPH Chpt 2
American Board of Industrial Hygiene (ABIH) Board of Certified Safety Professionals (BCSP) Joint Committee for Certification of Occupational Health and Safety Technologists www.bcsp.com/joint.htm 217-359-9263	Occupational Health and Safety Technologist	1S0X1, 4B0X1	YES	Associate's degree in safety and health or a bachelor's degree in any field	DEPH Chpt 3
American Council on Exercise (ACE) www.acefitness.org 619-535-8227	Aerobic Instructors, Personal Trainers, Lifestyle and Weight Management Consultant	3M0X1, 34MX, 4D0X1	YES, Overseas only	Valid adult CPR	DEPH Chpt 4
American Medical Technologist (AMT) www.amt1.com 847-823-5169 ext 213	Registered Medical/Dental Asst., Med Technologists, Medical Lab Technician, Registered Phlebotomy Technician	4F0X1, 4H0X1, 4N0X1, 4T0X3, 4Y0X2, 4T0XX, 47XXX	YES	Minimum associate's degree, graduate of medical program	DEPH Chpt 6
American Nurses Credentialing Center (ANCC) www.nursingworld.org 1-800-284-2378	Registered Nurse, Certified Registered Nurse, Certified Specialist	46XXX	YES	Education beyond basic nursing course	DEPH Chpt 7
National Institute for Automotive Service Excellence (ASE) www.asecert.org 703-713-3800	Master/Auto Tech, Master/ Medium/Heavy Truck Tech, Master/Auto/ Body Tech, Master/Engine Machinist Tech, School Bus Tech	2T3XX, 2T4XX	YES, Dantes funded	Minimum of 2 yrs experience	DEPH Chpt 8

CERTIFICATION AGENCY	TYPES OF CERTIFICATION	NER/NEC	EXAM?	COURSES/ TRAINING	OTHER
American Speech-Language-Hearing Association (ASHA) www.asha.org 301-897-5700	Certificate of Clinical Competence	None Listed	YES	Master's degree and field experience	DEPH Chpt 9
Association of State and Provincial Psychology Boards (ASPPB) www.nationalregister.com/ asppros.htm 334-832-4580	Psychologist	42PXX	YES	Make application to the state or provincial psychology licensing board	DEPH Chpt 10
American Society for Quality Control www.asqc.org 414-272-8575	Quality Manager, Technician, Reliability Engineer, Mechanical Inspector, Quality Engineer, Quality Asst.	8B000, personnel teaching quality on a full basis	YES	Minimum of 2 yrs experience, up to 10 yrs experience	DEPH Chpt 11
Board of Certified Safety Professionals (BCSP) www.bcsp.com 217-359-9263	Certified Safety Professional	1S0X1	YES	Associate's degree in safety or bachelor's in any field, 4 yrs experience	DEPH Chpt 12
American Board of General Dentistry (ABGD) www.agd.org 312-440-4306	Certified General Dentist	47XX(X)	YES	Minimum 2 yrs experience or 1 yr with 600 hours	DEPH Chpt 13
Cardiovascular Credentialing International (CCI) www.cci-online.org 1-800-258-4914	Certified Cardiographic Technician, Registered Cardiovascular Technologist, Registry Exams	4F0X1, 4H0X1, 4N0X1	YES	Minimum 2 yrs experience with associate's degree or bachelor's degree	DEPH Chpt 14
Certified Technical Trainer (CTT) www.chauncey.com/survey 1-800-258-4914	Certified Technical Trainer	3S2X1, 8B000, 8B100	YES, Computer delivered, video	Minimum 2 yrs field experience	DEPH Chpt 15
Dental Assisting National Board (DANB) www.ada.org/direct/org/ si_danbo.htm 312-642-3368	Certified Dental Asst., Oral and Maxilloficial Surgery, Dental Practice Management Asst., Orthodontic Asst.	47XX(X), 4Y0X2	YES	Graduate of dental program, 2 yrs experience or 3500 hrs in 2-yr period. Adult CPR	DEPH Chpt 15

CERTIFICATION AGENCY	TYPES OF CERTIFICATION	NER/NEC	EXAM?	COURSES/ TRAINING	OTHER
The Education Institute of the American Hotel/Motel Association (EIAH&MA) www.ahma.com/index.htm 1-888-575-8726	Certified Hotel Administrator, Food/Beverage Exec., Hospitality Housekeeping. Exec., Human Resources Exec., etc.	3M0X1, 34MX	YES	Hospitality associate's degree or 3 yrs experience	DEPH Chpt 31
The National Registry of Emergency Medical Technicians (EMT) www.nremt.org 614-888-4484	Emergency Medical Technician– Basic, Intermediate, and Paramedic	4F0X1, 4N0X1	YES	State license and C level CPR	DEPH Chpt 16
Electronics Technicians Association International (ETA-I) www.eta-sda.com 765-653-8262	Associate Electronic Tech, Electronics Journeyman Tech, Senior/Master Electronics Tech, Fiber Optic Installer, (FCC) Commercial Operator License Exam	1A5XX, 2A1X2/4, 2A4X1, 2E4X1, 2E2X1, 2E8X1, 2M0XX, 2P9X1, 4A2X1	YES	Minimum 2 yrs full-time experience	DEPH Chpt 17
Food Protection Certification Program (FPCP) www.chauncey.com/cgprgind.htm 609-720-6535	Food Protection Certification	3M0X1, 34MX, 4D0X1, 4E0X1	YES, Dantes funded	2 yrs experience	DEPH Chpt 18
Institute for Certification of Computing Professionals (ICCP) www.iccp.org 847-299-4227	Certified Computing Professional, Associate Computing Professional	3C0X2, 3C2X1, 3C3X1, all AFFSC's for associate level	YES	4 yrs experience or master's degree for certified professional	DEPH Chpt 19
Institute of Certified Professional Managers (ICPM) http://cob.jmu.edu/icmp	Certified Manager	Any AFSC meeting certification criteria	YES, 3 parts	4 yrs experience as a manager	DEPH Chpt 20
Institute for Personal Finance (IPF) 602-912-5331	Accredited Financial Counselor, Certified Housing Counselor	6F0X1, 6F0x2, 6F1x1, 65FX	YES	Minimum 2 yrs as a financial counselor and full-time experience	DEPH Chpt 5

CERTIFICATION AGENCY	TYPES OF CERTIFICATION	NER/NEC	EXAM?	COURSES/ TRAINING	OTHER
American Association of Bio-analysts (AAB) Board of Registry (formerly the Credentialing Commission of the International Society for Clinical Laboratory Technology (ISCLT)) 314-241-1445	Registered Medical Technologists, Laboratory Tech, Physicians Office Laboratory Tech	4T0XX	YES	Minimum associate's degree with 3 yrs full-time experience	DEPH Chpt 21
The Liaison Council on Certification for the Surgical Technologist (LCC-ST) www.ast.org/lcc.htm 1-800-707-0057 ext 225	Certified Surgical Technologist , Certified First Assistant	4N1XX, 45XX, 46XXX	YES	Graduate of accredited program	DEPH Chpt 22
The National Association of Radio and Telecommunications Engineers, Inc. (NARTE) www.kmxnet.com/narte 508-533-8333	Telecommunication Class I-IV, EMC-Engineering Tech, ESD-EngineeringTech FCC-All elements (commercial) Entry-level tech/ engineers	All 2Es and 3Cs	YES	Education and minimum 2 yrs experience	DEPH Chpt 23
National Association of Social Workers (NASW) www.naswdc.org 202-408-8600	Academy of Certified Social Workers	42S3	YES	Membership, master's degree with 2 yrs full-time experience	DEPH Chpt 24
National Board for the Certification of Orthopaedic Technologists (NBCOT) www.nbcot.org 301-990-7979 ext 3131	Certified Orthopaedic Technologist	4N1X1C	YES	Occupational therapy degree and fieldwork	DEPH Chpt 25
National Board for Respiratory Care (NBRC) www.nbrc.org 913-599-4200	Certified/Registered Respiratory Therapy Tech, Certified/Registered Pulmonary Function Tech, Perinatal/Pediatric Respiratory Care Specialist	4H0X1	YES	Graduate from respiratory therapy education program	DEPH Chpt 26

CERTIFICATION AGENCY	TYPES OF CERTIFICATION	NER/NEC	EXAM?	COURSES/ TRAINING	OTHER
National Institute for Certification in Engineering Technology (NICET) www.nicet.org 1-888-476-4238	Associate Engineering Tech, Engineering Tech, Senior Engineering Tech	3E0XX, 3E1X1	YES	Bachelor's degree	DEPH Chpt 27
The National Institute for the Certification of Healthcare Sterile Processing and Distribution Personnel (NICHSPDP) www.njcc.com/~multico/nichspdp 1-800-555-9765	Certified Sterile Processing and Distribution Tech, Supervisor, and Manager	4Y0XX, 4N1XX	YES	Associate's degree	DEPH Chpt 28
International Association of Administrative Professionals (IAAP) (formerly Professional Secretaries International (PSI)) www.gvi.net/psi 816-891-6600	Certified Professional Secretary	3S0X1, 3A0X1, 4A0X1	YES, 3 part	No degree then 4 yrs experience, associate's with 3 yrs experience, bachelor's with 2 yrs experience	DEPH Chpt 29
Society of Broadcast Engineers (SBE) www.sbe.org 317-253-1640	Broadcast Technologist, Broadcast Engineer, Senior Broadcast Engineer, Professional Brodcast Engineer	2EX54	YES	Academic degree or professional field experience	DEPH Chpt 30

SPONSORING ORGANIZATIONS

The following organizations sponsor certification programs. To learn the specifics of each program, visit *www.voled.doded.mil/dantes/cert/Calendar.htm*.

NATIONAL CERTIFICATION PROGRAMS

American Association of Bioanalysts (AAB) Board of Registry

American Board of General Dentistry (ABGD)

American Board of Industrial Hygiene (ABIH) Board of Certified Safety Professionals (BCSP) Joint Committee for Certification of Occupational Health and Safety Technicians

American Council on Exercise (ACE)

American Medical Technologist (AMT)

American Nurses Credentialing Center (ANCC)

American Society for Quality (ASQ)

American Speech-Language-Hearing Association (ASHA)

Association of Boards of Certification (ABC)—Uniform Program for Reciprocity

Association of State and Provincial Psychology Boards (ASPPB)

Board of Certified Safety Professionals (BCSP)

Cardiovascular Credentialing International (CCI)

Certified Technical Trainers (CTT)

Dental Assisting National Board (DANB)

Educational Institute of the American Hotel & Motel Association (EIAH&MA)

Electronics Technicians Association International (ETA-I)

Institute for Certification of Computing Professionals (ICCP)

Institute for Personal Finance (IPF)

Institute of Certified Professional Managers (ICPM)

International Association of Administrative Professionals® (IAAP)

The Liaison Council on Certification for the Surgical Technologist (LCC-ST)

The National Association of Radio and Telecommunications Engineers (NARTE)

National Association of Social Workers (NASW)

National Board for the Certification of Orthopaedic Technologists (NBCOT)

National Board of Respiratory Care (NBRC)

The National Environmental Health Association (NEHA)

National Institute for Automotive Service Excellence (ASE)

National Institute for Certification in Engineering Technology (NICET)

The National Institute for the Certification of Healthcare Sterile Processing and Distribution Personnel (NICHSPDP)

The National Registry of Emergency Medical Technicians(EMT)

Society of Broadcast Engineers (SBE)

United States Navy Certification Board (USNCB) Alcohol & Drug Program

Appendix B

CAREER TRANSITION RESOURCES

GENERAL CAREER RESOURCE WEBSITES

www.fedjobs.net
Federal Jobs.net. Best federal jobs site on the web. Comprehensive free instruction on landing a federal job. Plus links to key civil service and other federal websites, and access to full-text civil service Qualification Standards.

www.iccweb.com
Internet Career Center. Comprehensive career site with job postings, professional counseling, plus links to scores of other job search sites to meet specific needs. Also visit the Gonyea Online Career Center (Keyword: Gonyea)

www.monster.com
The Monster Board. A career network job seekers can use to expand their careers, providing continuous access to the most progressive companies, plus interactive job search tools.

www.careermosaic.com
Career Mosaic. Full-service job search site just added *www.headhunter.net* as an allied partner.

www.hotjobs.com
Hot Jobs.com. High-end full-service job listing site breaks down search into nearly two dozen field specific career channels.

www.damngood.com
Damn Good Resumes. By Yana Parker, author of the best-selling *Damn Good Resume Guide*. Resume how-to and more.

www.careerpath.com
Career Path.com. Aggregates help-wanted ads from over 100 daily newspapers.

www.campus.aol.monster.com/careersteps/preparing
Articles and quizzes on various job search topics. Resume how-tos and sample cover letters.

www.10minuteresume.com
10 Minute Resume. Online forms and instructions help you write, print, e-mail, and fax your resume directly from the website.

www.manpower.com
Manpower. Online site for a temp and temp-to-permanent placement service.

www.usacareers.opm.gov
USACAREERS. Sponsored by the Office of Personnel Management. Self-assessment, career planning, career transitioning, workforce reengineering, and job searching for federal employees or those entering civil service.

www.brassring.com
Brass Ring.com. Live and Web-based recruiting solutions links employers and job seekers.

www.careerbuilder.com
Career Builder.com. Mega Job Search (SM) capability gives job seekers a "one-stop-shop" solution by providing access to more than two million job postings.

MILITARY-RELATED CAREER RESOURCE WEBSITES

www.destinygrp.com
The Destiny Group. The Destiny Group has revolutionized the military placement industry by making direct access to its database of thousands of individuals with military experience available to corporate clients.

www.military.com
Military.com. Offers a new career channel with career search tips and advice, including military-to-civilian skill-matching tool. Job listings powered by the Destiny Group.

www.content.monster.com/military
Articles, links, and resources on transitioning from military to civilian work.

www.acap.army.com
Army Career and Alumni Program. Army military-to-civilian career transition site.

www.taonline.com
Transition Assistance Online. Military-to-civilian transition site. Resume help. Job listings.

www.veteran.net
Veterans.net. Multi-interest site for veterans. Includes civilian employment and links to veterans service organizations and benefits resources.

www.voled.doded.mil/dantes/ttt
Troops-to-Teachers. provides referral assistance and placement services to service members and civilian employees of the Department of Defense who are interested in beginning a second career in public education as teachers or teacher's aides.

www.dmdc.osd.mil/ot
Operation Transition. Sponsored by the Department of Defense, Operation Transition provides the Transition Bulletin Board (TBB), an automated system which contains a listing of job want ads and other useful information to separating/retiring military and federal civilian personnel and their spouses.

www.hire-quality.com
Employment and networking services sponsored by the American Legion.

www.interviewing.com/military/indes.htm
Career services for military personnel entering the civilian workforce. Offers success stories, research manuals, and job listings.

www.usdoj.gov/cops/gpa/grant_prog/troop_cops/default.htm
Troops-to-Cops. The Troops to Cops 99 program is designed to encourage the hiring of recently separated military veterans to serve as law enforcement officers.

CORPORATE/ EXECUTIVE RECRUITERS

The following recruiters specialize in placing military personnel.

www.bradley-morris.com
Bradley-Morris. Bradley-Morris specializes in placing military officers and enlisted candidates in management and technical jobs.

www.cameron-brooks.com
Cameron-Brooks. Specializes in placing Junior Military Officers into development careers in the business world.

www.careerdevelop.com
Career Development. Junior Military Officer placement company.

www.leadersinc.com
Leaders, Inc. Serving many types of worldwide companies, places Junior Officer and enlisted candidates in manufacturing, service, sales, and engineering jobs.

For more than 20,000 more sites, search www.google.com *using the following search terms alone or in combination. (Be sure to include all quote marks):* "job search," "career search," resume, career, and job listing.

CAREER CHANGE BOOKS

Bolles, Richard Nelson. *What Color Is Your Parachute?* (NY: Ten Speed Press, 2000).

BOOKS ON RESUME AND COVER LETTER DEVELOPMENT

Beatty, Richard H. *175 High-Impact Cover Letters* (NY: John Wiley & Sons, 1996).
———. *175 High-Impact Resumes* (second edition)(NY: John Wiley & Sons, 1998).

Betrus, Michael, and Block, Jay A. *101 Best Cover Letters* (NY: McGraw-Hill Professional Publishing, 1999).

———. *101 Best Resumes* (NY: McGraw-Hill, 1997).

———. *101 More Best Resumes* (NY: McGraw-Hill, 1999).

Career Press (editor). *101 Great Resumes* (NY: Career Press, 1995).

Enelow, Wendy. *1500+ Keywords for $100,000+ Jobs* (NY: Impact Publications, 1998).

Farr, J. Michael. *America's Top Resumes for America's Top Jobs: A Complete Career Handbook* (Indianapolis: JIST Works, 1997).

Fein, Richard. *101 Quick Tips for a Dynamite Resume* (NY: Impact Publications, 1998).

Hill, Beverly. *40 Minute Power Resume* (NY: Renaissance Ink Press, 1999).

Ireland, Susan. *The Complete Idiot's Guide to the Perfect Resume, Second Edition* (Malibu, CA: AlphaBooks, 2000).

Parker, Yana. *The Damn Good Resume Guide: A Crash Course in Resume Writing (3rd edition)* (NY: Ten Speed Press, 2000).

Potter, Ray. *100 Best Resumes for Today's Hottest Jobs* (NY: Arco Publications, 1998).

Rice, Craig Scott (introduction). *The $100,000 Resume* (NY: McGraw-Hill, 1998).

Rich, Jason R. *Great Resume* (NY: LearningExpress, 2000).

Schwab, John E. *6 Weeks or Less: The Job You Really Want, Guaranteed* (spiral edition)(April Day Books, 1998).

Appendix C

On the following pages you will find a series of resumes created for actual transitioning servicemembers. Chronological, functional, and combination resume formats are all represented. Among these samples you will find a range of servicemembers with different career objectives, military career histories, levels of education, and skills sets. You'll also find examples of effective achievement statements throughout these sample resumes. Read these samples to see how these servicemembers translated and marketed their military experience to create winning resumes that are targeted and comprehensible to civilian employers.

These samples can help you see how the different types of resume format work to best represent the servicemembers' careers. As you begin to write your own resume, you can use these samples to generate ideas, discover the right format for your career, and find effective language for the civilian job market.

NORMAN ALONZO COX
1480 Oro Vista Road #122
San Diego, CA 92154
(619) 575-2065

OBJECTIVE: Position in **Mail Processing, Delivery and Distribution**.

SUMMARY: **Top-rated Navy veteran with eight years experience in mail handling, processing and distribution,** including sorting, packaging, customs declarations, classified material handling, mail tracing and customer service. **Over four years supervisory experience.** Dedicated and honest; committed to delivering top-quality service.

EDUCATION   **Business Administration,** Southwestern College, Chula Vista, CA, 1992 - Present. **GPA 3.8.** Expect to complete degree Fall 1995.

**PROFESSIONAL
EXPERIENCE:**   **Postal Clerk/Outgoing Mailroom Supervisor**   **April 1992 - Present**
                      U.S. Navy   San Diego, CA

As Outgoing Mailroom Supervisor, direct and coordinate seven subordinates in receipt and delivery of mail to a large military complex. Schedule shifts, make work assignments and provide input for employee performance evaluations. Coordinate staff training and development. Stress quality customer service and attention-to-detail in all mailroom operations.

Receive, scan, proofread, serialize and distribute correspondence and directives received from executive-level management. Maintain and standard distribution list on computer data base. Ensure all addressees on distribution list receive appropriate correspondence.

As Official Mail Courier, responsible for control, accountability, pickup, and delivery of official postage. Maintained custody and accountability for over $3000 in stamp stock.

                      Postal Clerk   **July 1986 - April 1992**
                      U.S. Navy   San Diego, CA

Packaged, processed and labeled over 7000 pieces of registered, certified, and express mail for distribution to over 280 Pacific fleet units weekly. Performed and supervised postal counter work, including selling stamps, processing international money orders and collecting and remitting COD charges. Collected and remitted postage meter funds. **Established mail transportation schedules and routes and supervised/trained employees in postal operations.** Prepared and distributed local postal reports/records.

Audited and reviewed postal facility inspection reports. Prepared summaries for submission to district office. Performed general clerical duties, such as mail sorting and distribution and record maintenance. **Operated two-ton truck in completion of mail delivery routes and handled parcels up to 70 pounds.** Advised patrons on packaging and preparation of customs declarations. Improved accountability for registered and certified mail by reorganizing facility tracking procedures.

**CLERICAL
SKILLS:**   Windows, WordPerfect 5.1, data base management. Type 30 wpm.
                      Operate scanners, postage meters, scales, photocopiers, fax machines.

CONNIE COLTER
1490 Saturn Boulevard
San Diego, CA 92154
(619) 424-7684

OBJECTIVE: Position as a **Systems Administrator/Analyst** with special emphasis in employee training.

SUMMARY: **Computer Systems Analyst and Administrator with over ten years experience**
coordinating and supervising the development, installation, and integration of large-scale
computer systems. Specializes in coordinating employee training programs to speed systems
integration. **An award-winning technician specifically recognized for exceptional
performance by the U.S. Joint Chiefs of Staff and the Office of the Secretary of Defense.**

PROFESSIONAL   <u>Data Entry Technician</u>   **December 1993 - March 1994**
EXPERIENCE: George W. Sharp, Inc.   Charleston, SC

At this government contract firm specializing in supply processing, processed supplies from
decommissioning Navy units and supply system inventory overages. Performed data entry on
over 1500 line items daily with an error rate of less than .001%. Worked extensively in
customer service in processing large-scale physical turn-ins of supplies and equipment.
Specially selected to process large supply turn-ins because of data entry speed and accuracy.

<u>System Administrator/Analyst</u>   **March 1983 - November 1993**
U.S. Navy   Washington, D.C. & Charleston, SC

Performed automated data processing and electronic data processing system analysis.
Implemented computer maintenance and diagnostic programs and designed input/output
requirements for systems and subsystems. Conducted extensive employee training in
system/software use and ensured quality of computer output. Implemented data file and data
base management. Directed configuration and installation of hardware and software.

Specific Accomplishments

- As System Security Administrator, directed 20 personnel in the operation of four Honeywell
  mainframes, 65 remote terminals and associated peripherals. Provided technical assistance to
  system users and devoted extra hours to ensuring customer satisfaction. **Awarded the Navy
  Achievement Medal for exceptional technical performance.**

- Supervised the maintenance and continuous operation of four major computer subsystems,
  resulting in over one full year of uninterrupted system availability.

- As System Administrator for the Joint Staff Support Information System Network, developed,
  installed and conducted training on the computer system serving U.S. Joint Chiefs of Staff (JCS)
  operations. System was comprised of 39 Wang minicomputers with over 1600 work stations.
  Awarded the Joint Service Commendation Medal for technical achievements.

- Independently maintained a complex program providing computer system and software training
  for over 1600 Joint Chiefs of Staff personnel. **Tailored existing corporate system/software
  training programs to meet organizational needs.** Scheduled and coordinated all training.
  Personally conducted extensive employee training in system usage and troubleshooting, as well
  as training in specific software usage.

(Continued)

CONNIE COLTER (619) 424-7684

PROFESSIONAL EXPERIENCE: (Continued)	• Developed utility programs to edit and remove erroneous data from supply status tapes. **Saved over 20 man-hours a week and eliminated suspensions of operations.**
	• Developed numerous software applications to increase system and administrative efficiency.
	• Developed and implemented procedures to maintain optimum network security.
	• **Researched power, hardware and software requirements and coordinated with contractors to install/de-install new systems with minimum interruption to system users.** Inspected proposed system sites and provided time- and money-saving guidance. Tailored system configuration and installation according to individual organizational requirements.
	• Produced graphic products and data base summaries in support of major international studies and analyses for the Office of the Secretary of Defense.
EDUCATION & TECHNICAL TRAINING:	Computer Systems Administration School, U.S. Navy. COBOL/FORTRAN Programming Language Training, U.S. Navy. Advanced Data Processing School, U.S. Navy
	Completed over 600 hours of training in IBM-compatible software, including WordPerfect, Lotus 1-2-3, Harvard Graphics, DOS, and PC Tools.
REFERENCES:	Gladly furnished.

THOMAS P. DAWSON ·
1441-C Sun King Road
San Diego, CA 92126
(619) 271-9035

OBJECTIVE:

Position in **Facilities** or **Maintenance Management**.

SUMMARY:

Top-rated Maintenance Management Specialist with over eight years experience directing maintenance of buildings, facilities, and equipment. Extensive supervisory experience and outstanding organizational skills. Prioritizes heavy workloads with exceptional results. Consistently develops time- and money-saving solutions to major maintenance problems.

PROFESSIONAL
EXPERIENCE:

Maintenance Management Supervisor	**4/92 - Present**
Marine Corps Reserve Center	San Diego, CA

Supervise administrative support of maintenance procedures for $30 million in equipment, including vehicles, heavy construction equipment, refrigeration/power generation equipment, weapons, food service and communications equipment. Scope of responsibilities includes administrative oversight of nine military reserve sites nationwide encompassing a total of 900 personnel.

- Supervise preparation and modification of spreadsheet reports for all sites detailing equipment maintenance and repair parts ordering/shipping status. Provide guidance for remote sites regarding reporting accuracy and deadlines. Reconcile nationwide spreadsheet discrepancies and provide reports for senior management regarding current maintenance status on all equipment.

- Arrange equipment service requests with agencies nationwide to perform tasks not achievable within individual units.

- Maintain liaison with supply department to ensure repair parts/equipment on order is expedited to destination sites. Focus on waste minimization by coordinating disposal/reuse of excess equipment with supply department.

- Coordinate ordering and distribution of technical manuals and directives for all sites. Coordinated a two-year project to upgrade nine technical libraries.

Maintenance Management Supervisor	**4/89 - 3/92**
Naval Air Station Memphis Marine Corps Reserve Center	Millington, TN

Supervised facility maintenance for six buildings on a major naval installation. Directed two personnel in a variety of maintenance support functions, including survey and requests for repair of safety hazards, power generator maintenance, environmental work conditions, sanitation, and minor building repairs.

- Coordinated all associated administrative activities, including equipment status reports and supply acquisition.

- Directed all personnel training in the areas of administration, technical publications ordering and storage, and occupational safety.

EDUCATION
& TECHNICAL
TRAINING:

Business/General Studies, Miramar College, San Diego, CA, 8/93 - Present. **GPA 3.33**.
Leadership and Management School, 9/91. (130 hours).
Hazardous Material Handling Course, 2/90. (8 hours).
Maintenance Management School (Supervisory Level), 5/89. (120 hours).
Maintenance Management School (Fundamentals), 4/87. (160 hours).

J. WILLIAM GREENE

365 Alameda Boulevard
Coronado, CA 92118
(619) 435-1783

OBJECTIVE: Position in **Human Resources Management**.

SUMMARY: Top-rated naval officer and proactive manager with twenty years experience in human resources administration, staff development and program management. Proven ability to troubleshoot programs, develop solutions, and manage resources to meet or exceed organizational goals.

EDUCATION: **M.S. Management**, Salve Regina College, Newport, RI, 3/85.
M.A. National Security & Strategic Studies, Naval War College, Newport, RI, 3/85.
B.A. Mathematics, Northwestern University, Evanston, IL, 6/74.

PROFESSIONAL **Naval Line Officer/Aviator** 1974 - 1994
EXPERIENCE: U.S. Navy Locations worldwide

Human Resources Administration

- Successfully managed diverse organizations of 50 to 150 employees; built highly productive work teams through superior training, total quality management and open channels of communication.

- **Oversaw all labor force issues**, including personnel assignments, work-hours, career development, technical training, counseling and referral.

- Successfully functioned as Internal Management Control Officer: increased work force efficiency by reviewing organizational structure and workload distribution. **Redistributed tasking to maximize employee productivity.**

- Appointed and trained quality review teams to assess progress toward organizational goals.

- **Streamlined administrative procedures** and ensured accurate documentation of departmental actions by conducting comprehensive record reviews.

Training & Development

- Conducted zero-base reviews of staff development programs. Evaluated unit goals and analyzed quality of program materials, presentation, time lines, and qualification requirements. **Upgraded quality of training and enabled divisional training departments to function more effectively** by automating large portions of their reporting systems.

- Worked with civilian contractors to develop program lesson texts for a self-paced aviation ground school. Functioned as subject matter consultant in the development of specific aviation training devices to facilitate student pilot learning. **Increased training program efficiency, reduced live instructor time, and provided students with an easier transition to a more advanced aircraft.**

- Developed formal examinations and informal quizzes to monitor aviator currency and test their aircraft knowledge. Through consistent attention to professional development, contributed to squadron's reputation as having the most knowledgeable and professional SH-3H pilots in the entire Navy.

(Continued)

J. WILLIAM GREENE   (619) 435-1783

PROFESSIONAL   **Program & Resource Management**
EXPERIENCE:
(Continued)   • Managed complex information system encompassing location and mission of all Naval
                          Special Warfare Units worldwide. Improved timeliness and accuracy of the reporting
                          network.

                          • **Researched and edited Joint Chiefs of Staff Special Operations publications.** Played
                          integral role in the production of several publications, participating in the production
                          process from first draft to final publication and Navy-wide dissemination. In addition,
                          researched and drafted Naval Special Warfare organizational instructions.

                          • Reorganized aviation refresher training program to schedule the use of Marine Corps
                          resources more effectively. **Saved thousands of dollars in flight hours and man-hours.**

                          • **Developed comprehensive 'security of operations' checklist** for use by subordinate
                          organizations in developing security procedures, including facility security measures and the
                          safeguarding of information.

                          • Established and chaired a committee on occupational safety. Implemented employee
                          training programs and reporting procedures. **Reduced to near-zero the number of safety
                          violations and incidents/accidents both on and off the job.**

HONORS   **Navy Commendation Medal, 1992.**
& AWARDS: For superior management and strong leadership in evaluating and training aviation units for
                          deployment to Operation Desert Storm.

ROGER C. PAGEL

434 8th Street
Imperial Beach, CA 91932
(619) 424-6906

OBJECTIVE

A position in **Sales**.

SUMMARY

Award-winning Navy Recruiter with in-depth experience in sales, marketing, prospecting and network development. Highly successful communicator and closer. Consistently exceeded monthly and annual quotas by up to 240%. Solid technical and supervisory background. Dedicated to top quality customer service.

PROFESSIONAL EXPERIENCE

U.S. Navy, 1976 - Present

Recruiting/Sales

Successfully completed Naval Recruiting School, a 180-hour course covering sales and marketing techniques, including prospecting, marketing, product/service information, and closing. As a Recruiter/Canvasser, built prospect list through community research, cold calling, public contact, and canvassing of likely sources including schools, local businesses, and career counselors. Effectively communicated Navy features and benefits to prospects. Painted verbal pictures to contrast the advantages of buying the product (the Navy) versus the disadvantages of not buying.

- Led district recruiting force in sales, **consistently exceeding monthly quota by 25 - 40%**.
- Over a one year period, exceeded district monthly contract average by over 240%.
- **Ranked number one of 69 production recruiters. Named Recruiter of the Year in 1990**.
- Awarded the Navy Achievement Medal as approved by the Secretary of the Navy for excellence in recruiting.
- **Meritoriously advanced in rank based on superior performance.**

Communication/Marketing

Generated leads by presenting public service talks at schools and civic organizations. Distributed marketing materials. Contacted students nearing high school graduation, as well as recent graduates, via direct mail. Followed up mailings with cold calls. Developed a network of referral sources, including school counselors, current recruits awaiting departure and business owners.

- Proved extremely effective in direct public interaction, **consistently setting appointments with 25% of all contacts**.
- Through ongoing positive client relations, **maintained zero percent monthly loss rate (cancellations) versus the district average of 13%**. This is especially significant because the time from closing until recruits report to boot camp can span up to one year.

Management/Technical

As a Navy Construction Mechanic, managed, motivated and trained teams of up to 50 employees. Responsibilities included performance counseling and evaluation, shift scheduling and workload distribution. Developed professional training materials and delivered lectures. Provided career development information based on extensive knowledge of Navy career programs. **Assisted in managing a $600,000 budget**.

Maintained, diagnosed and repaired a wide range of construction and material handling equipment, as well as truck/automotive systems. In-depth expertise in the following: gas/diesel engines, power trains, chassis and component assemblies, hydraulic valves and cylinders, fuel injection systems, general/special purpose test equipment, electrical systems, ignition systems, hydraulic/air/vacuum braking systems. Extensive experience in heavy equipment repair.

EDUCATION AND TRAINING

Naval Recruiting School, U.S. Navy, 1987. (180 hours).
Construction Mechanic School (Basic & Advanced), U.S. Navy, 1985. (960 hours).
Leadership and Management Training, U.S. Navy, 1982. (80 hours).

DOUGLAS L. COOKE
6042 Rancho Hills Drive
San Diego, CA 92139
(619) 470-2419

OBJECTIVE: Position as a **Special Agent** with the Federal Bureau of Investigation.

SUMMARY:
- **Navy SEAL** with in-depth experience in intelligence operations.
- Currently attending **Egyptian Arabic language training**.
- Secret security clearance updated 3/26/92.
- Experienced in **undercover/electronic surveillance, investigation, and apprehensions of felony theft** suspects.

EDUCATION: **B.A. Psychology**, Salisbury State University, 5/87.

PROFESSIONAL   <u>U.S. Navy SEAL</u>   **7/90 - Present**
EXPERIENCE: SEAL Team Three   Naval Amphibious Base Coronado, CA

Successfully completed one of the most demanding training programs in the U.S. military and earned designation as a SEAL Operator. Excelled in operations involving photographic intelligence, small unit tactics, urban assault, small arms handling and demolitions.

- Specially selected by Commanding Officer to attend an intensive training course in the Egyptian Arabic language in preparation for work with Arab allies.
- As platoon weapons coordinator, effectively managed and maintained weapons and explosives inventory. Received Letter of Commendation from force commander.
- Successfully completed Defense Mapping Systems course covering the latest digital and satellite imagery technology for use in intelligence operations.
- Achieved diverse weapons qualifications, including .45, .357 and 9 mm hand guns.

Managed inventory of intelligence-related products, including classified publications and software, geopolitical case studies, and photography equipment. Worked closely with foreign special forces counterparts, training foreign operators in special warfare skills and participating in joint operations.

<u>Store Detective</u>   **11/87 - 11/89**
Ames Department Stores, Inc.   Salisbury, MD

Conducted investigations of internal theft and shoplifting, including undercover/electronic surveillance and apprehension of suspects. Coordinated installation of surveillance equipment with store managers. Gathered and analyzed evidence, including videotape and register tapes. Interrogated suspects, and coordinated arrest and detention with local law enforcement agencies. Elicited signed confessions. Wrote reports detailing investigation procedures, evidence on hand, and case resolution. Testified in district and circuit courts.

- Coordinated large "sting" operations involving the apprehension, interrogation and arrest of multiple suspects. This impacted internal theft tremendously, resulting in large recoveries of stolen funds and reductions in losses related to employee theft.
- District led region in recovery of funds lost to internal theft. Recognized as key contributor. Awarded Store Detective of the Month, 11/89.
- Received training in Wicklander, Zulawski and Associates interview and interrogation techniques.

ADDITIONAL   **Arabic Language Course,** Berlitz International, Inc., 1995.
MILITARY   **Photo Intelligence/Reconaissance,** U.S. Navy, 1994.
TRAINING: **Special Combat Aggressive Reactionary Systems (S.C.A.R.S.),** U.S. Navy, 1992/1994.

ROBERT S. HAYMAN

221 Calla Avenue   Imperial Beach, CA 91932   (619) 423-5692

OBJECTIVE

A **Senior Analyst Position** in a Defense Contractor Corporation.

SUMMARY

Top-rated Naval Special Operations (SEAL) Officer and senior intelligence analyst with proven successful experience in intelligence production/analysis, tactics, long-range and intermediate planning, special operations and training. Expert in budget process and data base analysis. Holds a U.S. government clearance for special classified information.

EDUCATION

Defense Intelligence College, **M.S. Strategic Intelligence,** 1987.
(Concentration in Latin American Foreign Affairs)

University of Virginia, **B.A. Biology,** 1976.

Significant Military Courses:
Basic Underwater Demolition/SEAL Course, 1977 and Basic Airborne Course, 1974.

PROFESSIONAL EXPERIENCE

Tactics

- As Third Fleet Staff member, formulated campaign policy precedents directly affecting employment of Naval Special Warfare Forces, Army Special Operations Forces, and conventional U.S. Army Forces.

- Developed new Naval Special Warfare targeting strategy for Third Fleet operational plans that effectively integrated warfare systems from all U.S. military services.

- Developed SEAL platoon tactics for striking high priority targets using weapons that provide safe firing distances, significantly reducing SEAL operator vulnerability to detection/counteraction by the enemy.

Intelligence Production/Analysis

- Managed a division of Special Operations personnel and intelligence analysts providing direct support to approximately 2,000 SEAL field personnel in the Pacific and Persian Gulf regions. Developed and produced intelligence information for 36 intelligence studies. Established new milestones for quality control of Naval Special Warfare intelligence studies that increased production by 50%.

- Produced finished hard copy documents containing analysis and edited photographs based on all-source intelligence methods and products.

- Represented the Commander-in-Chief U.S. Pacific Fleet at theater-level targeting conferences. Represented theater-level naval commanders at Special Operations Command conferences on intelligence support for the targeting process which addressed intelligence architecture, analysis methodologies and new equipment.

- Defined theater requirements for Special Operations Forces intelligence production based on extensive special operations and tactical employment experience. Developed special expertise in intelligence study analysis to support special operations in the Asian, Pacific Ocean and Middle Eastern regions.

ROBERT S. HAYMAN   (619) 423-5692

Research & Documentation

♦ Produced a Naval Special Warfare Analyst Guide with in-depth procedures and step-by-step mechanics for constructing and updating a Naval Special Warfare Target Intelligence Study. These procedures were implemented in all military services throughout the Pacific theater.

♦ Drafted a Naval Special Warfare Operations chapter for multi-national combined exercise agreements which focused on integration of coalition nations' special forces and conventional forces during low intensity conflicts.

♦ Developed detailed Naval Special Warfare force employment schedule for a major multi-national exercise. Schedule was so effective that it was adopted as the main scenario for all future exercises.

♦ Wrote an organizational manual for a major training school detailing unit/department/division structure, functional areas, and oversight responsibilities. Assisted in editing tactical handbooks and fleet tactical employment guides (TACMEMOs).

Data Base & Budget Process Analysis

♦ Prepared the Naval Special Warfare CINC's Preparedness and Readiness document (CSPAR), an executive-level capability assessment, for the budget review process at the Joint Staff and Department of Defense levels.

♦ Proficient in accessing and applying intelligence research methodology and analysis of data from the Defense Intelligence Agency On-line System and Community On-line Intelligence System.

♦ Represented Naval Special Warfare Commander in Cost and Operational Effectiveness Analyses (COEAs) of mine countermeasures and small craft programs over an eight month period.

Special Operations/Training

♦ Developed and presented long range training plans to ensure operational readiness of the Navy's Special Warfare Forces (4,000 SEALs and 2,500 support personnel).

♦ Planned and coordinated Special Operations support for 15 fleet and joint major training exercises.

♦ Trained 250 students in the intensely rigorous Basic Underwater Demolition/SEAL course. As Senior SEAL Instructor, taught diving physics and physiology, combat diving techniques, explosives handling and techniques, small arms training, land navigation, and small unit tactics.

♦ Coordinated and supervised special training for foreign naval forces, and special operations training for local and national law enforcement agencies , including the Federal Bureau of Investigation.

HONORS & AWARDS

Navy Commendation Medal, 1993: Superior executive management leading to significant improvements in organizational productivity and financial accountability.

Navy Commendation Medal, 1991: Exceptional achievements in integrating Naval Special Warfare missions into major military exercises.

Navy Commendation Medal, 1989: Superb professional performance and exemplary leadership as a Senior Intelligence Analyst.

RONNIE G. MADORE
7689 Jade Coast Road
San Diego, CA 92126
(619) 271-5180

OBJECTIVE: Position in **Inventory/Supply Management** or **Purchasing**.

SUMMARY: **Top-rated senior supply manager with over 15 years experience in all facets of inventory and supply management.** Personally developed and implemented automated supply programs serving entire military service branches. Expert troubleshooter; pinpoints inefficiencies in material control systems and develops cost-saving solutions.

PROFESSIONAL
EXPERIENCE: **Supply Manager**   **July 1979 - July 1994**
United States Marine Corps   Locations worldwide

In-depth experience in the performance, management, analysis, and improvement of the following:

Financial accounting	*Material control/expediting*	*Purchasing*
Property accounting	*Supply systems design*	*Vendor research*
Warehousing	*Stock control*	*Quality assurance*
Shipping/receiving	*Facility design/maintenance*	*Technical research*
Receipt processing	*Records and returns*	*Account auditing*
Supply systems analysis	*Information systems*	*Packaging*

Specific Achievements

- Worked with contractors and senior military officers in developing a comprehensive integrated supply system to serve the entire Marine Corps. Conducted one year of extensive technical research and troubleshooting/analysis of existing systems to develop an automated system which **reduced man-hours, increased accountability, cut training costs, and significantly reduced spending.** System was so successful it is now being adapted for U.S. Army use.

- As Information Systems Chief, managed a comprehensive computer information system housing all available Marine Corps accounting data, including personnel, supply, financial, and transportation information. Established access authorization for system users, limited access according to user clearances, and suspended authorization for use.

- Conducted thousands of hours of initial and staff development training in basic and advanced supply management, stock control, warehousing, accounting, and automated systems usage. **Personally responsible for training over 5000 supply specialists.**

- As a Supply Maintenance Analysis Team inspector, conducted detailed inventory and accounting audits of military supply facilities. Ensured proper system maintenance, accountability, inventory validity, and documentation. Provided procedural guidance and recommended changes to improve efficiency and cut costs.

- Reorganized an entire warehouse, including an inventory valued at over $2 million. Revised facility layout and accounting systems to **provide faster material access, improved equipment maintenance and increased accountability.**

RONNIE G. MADORE   (619) 271-5180

**PROFESSIONAL
EXPERIENCE:**
(Continued)

- At one installation, saved thousands of dollars in unexplained equipment losses by developing an automated accounting system to track base property.

- As Supply Administration Chief, developed spreadsheet programs to ensure accurate and efficient collection and compilation of unit supply allowance data. Improved data accuracy and reduced reporting errors 15 percent. **Decreased man-hours required to perform data compilation by 40 percent.**

- Developed, implemented, evaluated and upgraded numerous computer programs to increase operational efficiency, **Implemented the first Marine Corps use of Local Area Networks (LANs) in transmitting supply information.**

- Directed and monitored the successful redistribution of millions of dollars in supplies and equipment tied to the current military reorganization and reduction in force.

**HONORS
& AWARDS:**

Received numerous personal recognition awards for achievements in supply management, logistics, personnel training, systems design/analysis and leadership, including:

Meritorious Service Medal, 1994
Navy Commendation Medal, 1988.
Navy Achievement Medal, 1985.
Navy Achievement Medal, 1983.

Received numerous awards for military service, including:

Combat Action Ribbon, Desert Shield/Desert Storm, 1991.
Humanitarian Service Medal, Bangladesh Relief Effort, 1991.

**TECHNICAL
TRAINING:**

Consumer Level Supply Management Course, U.S. Marine Corps, 1984.
Supply Administration School, U.S. Marine Corps, 1979.
Stock Control School, U.S. Marine Corps, 1979.

REFERENCES: Gladly furnished.

DENNIS K. MEDLOCK
504G Big Bend Way
Ocenaside, CA 92054
(619) 967-8525

SUMMARY:

Top-rated firefighter with over 18 years technical and managerial experience. Advanced through ranks from turret operator to Officer-in-Charge of an Aircraft Rescue and Firefighting unit at a large category military airfield. Experience ranges from on-scene coordination of major firefighting operations to administration and management of airfield and structural firefighting facilities.

**LICENSES
& CERTIFICATES:**

Fire Officer III, Department of Defense
Fire Instructor II, Department of Defense
Airport Firefighter, Department of Defense
Firefighter I, State of South Carolina
Nationally Registered Emergency Medical Technician (To recertify January 1995).

**PROFESSIONAL
EXPERIENCE:**

Fire Officer/Instructor   **1977 - Present**
United States Marine Corps   Stations worldwide

- As Crew Chief, coordinated and directed operations at airfield, structural and brush fires. Analyzed mishaps, determined appropriate firefighting agents, and directed crew/equipment deployment. Expert in use and deployment of all firefighting agents.

- As Officer-in-Charge, directed and motivated teams of up to 76 firefighters. Managed all personnel matters, including professional development and training, scheduling, workload planning, performance appraisal, pay and incentives, leave, promotions, and disciplinary action.

- Planned and controlled a $265,000 annual operating budget. Managed all material assets, including plant property and vehicles. Prepared and forwarded administrative reports on mishaps and incidents.

- Performed technical training in all phases of aircraft firefighting and rescue operations and basic structural firefighting. Coordinated with outside agencies for mutual aid and training. Conducted airport and structural fire prevention inspections.

- Equipment qualifications include: P19-A, commercial and tactical forklifts to 10,000 pounds, and rescue and salvage cranes to 55 tons. Familiar with all types of breathing apparatus.

- Instrumental in Camp Pendleton, CA flood recovery operations where flood damage was estimated at $130 million. Simultaneously managed normal airfield rescue and firefighting operations.

- Received numerous personal recognition awards for superior job performance in firefighting, rescue and salvage operations.

**EDUCATION
& PROFESSIONAL
DEVELOPMENT:**

A.S. Business Management, University of South Carolina, 1/87.
Firefighter Health and Safety, U.S. Air Force, 4/90. (24 hours).
Advanced Fire Protection Technology, U.S. Air Force, 4/90. (80 hours).
Structural Firefighting, U.S. Air Force, 12/88. (104 hours). **Honor graduate**.
Firefighter I Course, State of South Carolina, 3/86. (360 hours).
Aircraft Rescue and Firefighting, U.S. Marine Corps. 9/77. (200 hours).

RAY DELAROSA
5532 Redding Road
San Diego, CA 92115
(619) 583-0408

OBJECTIVE: Position as an Instructor or Technician in communications/electronics.

SUMMARY: **Top-rated Communications Technician and Technical Instructor with over 14 years experience in communications technical support and employee training.** Last held Top Secret security clearance. Solid supervisory background with exceptional motivational and organizational skills.

PROFESSIONAL EXPERIENCE:

<u>**Assistant Manager/Instructor**</u>   **1991-1993**
Pro Gym   Biloxi, MS

Planned, organized and implemented a comprehensive fitness center program designed to enhance human relations and promote harmony and teamwork in the local community.

<u>**Communications Technical Instructor/Technician**</u>   **1977-1991**
U.S. Air Force   Locations worldwide

Technical:

Operated, tested, maintained and repaired state-of-the-art airborne communications equipment associated with EC-130 and EC-135 Early Warning aircraft. Systems included point-to-point, air-to-ground, long distance and satellite communications equipment such as radio transceivers in all frequency bands, secure/nonsecure digital systems, and teletypes. Provided technical support for all system components, including antennas, multiplexers, uplinks/downlinks, and control panels, using general and special purpose test equipment. Monitored and controlled telecommunications transmissions, reception, terminal and processing equipment. Enforced strict security restrictions in conjunction with classified communications. Developed and administered long-range preventive maintenance programs.

Instruction & Training:

As a Technical Instructor, trained technicians and operators in teletyping, airborne communications equipment, cognizant agencies, publications and security requirements. Taught air/ground and point-to-point systems operations. Trained students in use of a newly released Unisys module in preparation for Operation Desert Storm. Employed a variety of instructional techniques and aids, including lectures and lab work. Supervised and critiqued students and observed/reported factors affecting morale. Provided individualized assistance and maintained related documentation. Used diplomacy and effective communication skills in training foreign nationals.

Supervision & Management:

Managed, trained and motivated teams of up to 15 employees in a technical environment. Directed all work force functions, including scheduling, on-the-job training, and performance evaluation. Provided counseling and guidance on personal issues, often referring employees to helping resources. Promoted individual growth by providing professional development opportunities in challenging job assignments.

EDUCATION & TECHNICAL TRAINING:

Aeronautical Technology, Embry-Riddle University. (93 hours).
Airborne Communications Systems, U. S. Air Force, 1977-1990. (800 hours).
Technical Instructor Course, U.S. Air Force, 1985. (240 hours).
Satellite Communications, U. S. Air Force, 1980. (80 hours).

B. DELORIS DAVIES

1320 Vass Road   Spring Lake, NC 28390   (910) 497-4684

OBJECTIVE

Position as a **Diet Technician/Food Service Supervisor**.

SUMMARY

- **Five years experience in diet therapy,** food service management and staff development.
- Results-oriented manager; pinpoints problems and develops viable solutions.
- Exceptional interpersonal skills; **promotes positive morale through effective communication**.

PROFESSIONAL EXPERIENCE

Diet Therapy & Client Relations

Assisted registered dietitian and other health professionals in **planning, implementing and evaluating nutrition care** in health care facilities. Consulted with clients to determine nutrition needs and completed scheduled and requested follow-up. **Developed, implemented and revised nutrition care plans,** verified implementation of nutrition prescription for individual clients, and monitored client tolerance of nutrition care. Accurately performed documentation, including diet sheets, client nutrition care cards, and medical records.

- Developed and implemented client relations program, including administration, case charting, and regular consultation. **Improved facility nutrition program by individualizing client care.**
- Stressed attention to individual client needs/preferences and own availability for follow-up, improving client morale and client-staff relations. Researched client suggestions and concerns, and responded with immediate information.

Supervision & Management

Managed, motivated and trained 23 food service employees, including shift scheduling, work assignment and performance evaluation. Directed food preparation, dining room service, equipment maintenance, sanitation, and stock management. Directed and supervised tray preparation as per diet order or request. **Assisted in ongoing quality assurance program,** including food preparation and storage standards, sanitation, and employee medical screening. Met with health team members to integrate nutrition care. **Assisted consulting dietitian in developing material for in-service training**. Ordered supplies, and recommended purchases to accommodate changing client needs. Participated in food service employee interview/selection and conducted new employee orientation.

- Reorganized food service work procedures and developed new shift schedules, **improving efficiency and smooth operations, and eliminating crisis management**.
- Boosted work place morale with a "secret pal" program, **reducing employee turnover by 50%.**
- Upon assuming this position, **immediately reduced state inspection discrepancies** from five to ten each visit to zero.

EDUCATION & TRAINING

Diet Therapy Technician School, U.S. Air Force. (520 hours).
Diet Therapy Specialist Training, U.S. Air Force. (680 hours).
Leadership Development Course, U.S. Air Force. (160 hours).

WORK HISTORY

1/93 - 4/95:	**Diet Technician/Food Service Supervisor**, St. Paul's Episcopal Home, San Diego, CA.
12/82 - 6/92:	**Training Technician/Diet Therapist**, U.S. Air Force.

MARY T. MILAR
9919 Rio San Diego Drive #32
San Diego, CA 92108
(619) 280-2333

SUMMARY: **Top-rated Navy professional** with successful experience in personnel and program management. Exceptional troubleshooter. Demonstrated ability to pinpoint inefficiencies and develop cost-effective solutions. **Mature, reliable and dedicated** to delivering top quality service.

**PROFESSIONAL
EXPERIENCE:**

1/94 - Present **NAVAL AIR STATION NORTH ISLAND, San Diego CA**

<u>**Assistant Program Manager, NALCOMIS Training, Commander Naval Air Force Pacific**</u> - In this congressionally-mandated program, coordinate and schedule implementation of NALCOMIS, a computer-automated maintenance tracking system, in Pacific Fleet aviation units. **Establish action plans and milestones,** and schedule implementation training for 45 sites annually. Coordinate required schools for unit personnel, as well as hardware/software installation and data base collection. NALCOMIS is revolutionizing logistics support and production management in naval aviation maintenance and is being systematically implemented fleet-wide via this program.

- Coordinated quarterly Integrated Logistics Support Management Team conference. Promoted inter-service and Navy-wide information exchange on the NALCOMIS system.

12/91 - 12/93 **NAVY SUPPORT FACILITY, British Indian Ocean Territory Diego Garcia**

<u>**Quality Assurance Officer**</u> - Directed industrial quality control programs. Monitored unit maintenance operations and performed periodic audits to ensure compliance program specifications. Managed, motivated and trained seven program inspectors. Developed work schedules/assignments and evaluated employee performance.

- During critical transition period involving 90% personnel turnover, ensured all of new inspectors were thoroughly trained and ready to work when production began.
- **Designed and implemented a quality assurance tracking system** to ensure all required inspections were completed on time.

<u>**Production Manager**</u> - Directed and coordinated production efforts of 50 maintenance personnel. Planned operations, made work assignments based on technical expertise, monitored progress, **troubleshot inefficiencies** and inspected completed work. Estimated time, material and manpower requirements.   Led production teams to achieve consistently outstanding scores on audits and quality assurance inspections.

- Rewrote standard operating procedures for production control, **improving currency of information and training efficiency**.
- Developed and implemented qualification program for production control shift supervisors, **speeding training process and improving work quality** among newly qualified personnel.

Additional experience includes Maintenance Administration Supervisor (8 years), involving in-depth administrative/human resources duties. Also held Data Analyst position (2 years).

**EDUCATION
& TRAINING:**
Senior Management Fundamentals, U.S. Navy, 2/95. (Nonresident course).
Total Quality Management (Revised Course), U.S. Navy, 2/94. (24 hours).
Leadership and Management, U.S. Navy, 4/92. (40 hours).
Total Quality Management Fundamentals, U.S. Navy, 7/90. (100 hours).

LORETTA L. CALDWELL
15235 Avenida Rorras
San Diego, CA 92128
(619) 451-0968

OBJECTIVE: Nursing position in Operating Room, Trauma Unit, or Emergency Room.

SUMMARY:
- Over 16 years experience in Nursing, skilled in treatment, supervision, and training.
- Reliable and consistent professional; warm, empathetic, and sensitive to patient's needs.
- Consistently recognized for outstanding performance, organizational and managerial ability.
- Registered Nurse, State of Hawaii, (1994 - present).
- Pediatric Advanced Life Support (PALS) Certificate, March 1995.
- Operating Room Specialty Course, U.S. Army, El Paso, TX, 1978.
- Bachelor of Science, Nursing, University of Portland, Portland, OR, 1975.

PROFESSIONAL **Surgical Nurse (Operating Room)**   **1994 - 1995**
EXPERIENCE: Shriner's Hospital for Crippled Children   Honolulu, HI

Coordinated surgical procedures using doctors' preference cards and extensive knowledge of Operating Room policies and procedures. Performed physical assessment of pre-operative, intra-operative and post-operative patients. Utilized highly developed organizational skills in the set-up of multiple surgical procedures. Established supply levels for ordering, organized supplies on hand, and organized instruments according to procedural needs. Proven effectiveness with patients from varied ethnic and socio-economic backgrounds, demonstrating awareness of cultural and family dynamics.

- Developed program for pre-operative visits, including orientation tour, physical examination, and post-operative procedures resulting in a higher standard of care.
- Reviewed and re-wrote policy and procedures for Operating Room and PACU.
- Created Locator File for all sterile and non-sterile supplies, instruments, and equipment.
- Demonstrated ability to work under stress in a fast paced environment.

Community Service   **1992 - 1994**
Schofield Barracks   Honolulu, HI

Provided crisis intervention for over 300 families. Served as liaison with local community and referred those in need to appropriate resources. Planned, organized, and hosted community holiday celebration with over 500 in attendance. Awarded Certificates of Achievement and Appreciation, and was nominated for Volunteer of the Year.

Independent Contractor   **1991 - 1992**
MEDEX   Washington, DC

Worked as a consultant for insurance companies, providing on-site physical assessments and blood work. Utilized outstanding organizational, scheduling, and time management skills and ability to work independently. Demonstrated excellent people skills and professionalism, assessing up to 30 clients in a two day period.

Head Nurse (Operating Room)   **1990 - 1991**
Womack Army Hospital   Fort Bragg, NC

Voluntarily returned to active duty, U.S. Army Nurse Corps, during Persian Gulf War. Managed eight operating rooms and a staff of 25 personnel. Assigned duties and coordinated cases for 15 surgeons among six surgical services. Effectively handled stress and diffused tension caused by war, and a staff entirely comprised of individuals recalled to active duty. Developed a cohesive unit by re-developing policy and ensuring staff followed local procedures.

- Effectively managed large budget, ordered and inventoried drugs, solutions, and equipment.
- Evaluated patient care, staff relations, and efficiency of service.
- Investigated and resolved complaints.

Clinic Nurse   **1988 - 1990**
Primus Health Care Corporation   Fayetteville, NC

Performed triage for up to 200 patients per day in acute minor illness clinic. Provided care and treatment as directed by physician. Administered injections and medications, dressed wounds and incisions, explained physician's instructions to patients, and assisted with emergency and minor surgery.

- Demonstrated highly effective triage skills and ability to interview patients and recognize symptoms, diseases, and illnesses, and their severity.
- Read and interpreted corporate guidelines for contract health care and systematically followed written procedures and criteria for triage assessment.
- Skilled at handling large volume of patients, working in a fast paced, demanding environment, while providing excellent care and developing patients' trust.

O.R. Staff Nurse   **1986 - 1988**
St. John's Hospital   Leavenworth, KS

Provided nursing care to pre-, intra-, and post-operative patients. Prepared equipment and assisted with all types of surgery other than open-heart. Observed patients, recorded significant conditions and reactions and used proper procedures to report any significant conditions, reactions or incidents. Performed physical assessment of patients.

Surgical Nurse   **1984 - 1991**
U.S. Army Reserves   Various Locations

Served as Army Reserve Nurse, working two days per month, plus two weeks a year, at assigned duty stations. Provided physical assessment of patients and assisted in all types of surgery other than open-heart. As Charge Nurse, directed activities of nursing staff, planned and organized services in obstetrics, pediatrics, operating room, and emergency room. Ensured patient needs were met, inspected conditions, and evaluated performance of staff.

Staff Surgical Nurse   **1977 - 1984**
U.S. Army Nurse Corps   Fort Bragg, NC & Nuremberg, Germany

Served as Surgical Nurse, Head Nurse, and Supervising Nurse. Administered nursing programs and directed activities of nursing staff. Initiated studies to evaluate effectiveness of nursing services in relation to objectives and costs. Developed curriculum for O.R. Tech program and taught Phase II practical applications to groups of 5-8 students. Tested, trained, and assessed students in a six week rotating program.

- Established/revised policy and standards of performance, drafted procedure manuals, initiated in-service training, and managed personnel.
- Managed Central Material Supply Section; purchased, set up, and inventoried equipment, instruments and supplies; wrote policy and procedures, and managed large budgets.
- Received two Army Commendation Medals and the Meritorious Service Medal for Outstanding Performance.

Surgical Nurse   **1975 - 1977**
U.S. Navy Nurse Corps   Camp Pendleton, CA

Awarded Navy Nurse Corps Scholarship for outstanding academic achievement, and served two years active duty in Navy Nurse Corps. Provided nursing care to patients in General Surgery and Surgical Intensive Care.

REFERENCES: Outstanding personal and professional references available upon request.

ROBERT S. BROWN IV
3234 Cowley Way #3
San Diego, CA 92117
(619) 275-2821

OBJECTIVE: Position in Supply Management / Inventory.

SUMMARY:
- Top-rated Navy supply specialist with extensive experience in receiving and issuing stock.
- Demonstrated ability in maintaining inventory records, tracking back orders, and handling fast paced supply operations.
- Dedicated and reliable; committed to top-quality performance.

PROFESSIONAL EXPERIENCE:

Storekeeper   **1992 - 1996**
U.S. Navy   San Diego, CA

Supply - Received and inspected incoming stock and distributed items to storerooms or for direct turn over to specified department. Managed storerooms and issued materials, supplies, equipment, and repair parts. Kept back order files in established sequence and released back orders for issue or shipment as stock became available. Issued repair parts for aircraft maintenance and emergency repair operations.

- Assisted with hazardous underway replenishment evolutions including the receipt and distribution of over 2,000 pallets during a six month period.
- Licensed forklift driver, fully proficient in proper loading and transportation procedures to avoid damaging stock.

Inventory - Compiled and maintained records of quantity, type, and value of material, equipment, parts, and supplies stocked in each storeroom. Tracked consumption rate to determine stock supply and need for replenishment. Performed weekly, bi-weekly, and monthly inventories of storerooms. Reviewed files and inspected shelves to identify unused items and recommended disposal of excess stock.

- Managed and served as Assistant Supervisor for up to 11 storerooms located throughout the ship.
- Received Letter of Appreciation for personal contribution to divisional grade of outstanding during major supply management inspection.

Air Transportation - Assigned to aircraft carrier flight deck to greet military VIPs, foreign nationals, and company officials and escort to and from boarding area. Carried and loaded / unloaded baggage and equipment, working under arduous conditions, including extremely rough seas. Ensured safety of passengers and gear and explained safety precautions and loading procedures. Observed military protocol and directed arriving passengers to staging area to meet welcoming party.

- Loaded and unloaded cargo, including equipment and repairables, according to loading schedules.
- Employed proper loading patterns to prevent shifting or damage to materials during transit.
- Verified loaded or unloaded materials against work order or bill of lading.

NOTABLE: Received Superior Performance Awards for annual physical fitness tests, 1992 - 1996. Sang in shipboard choir and gave performances at church functions, 1994.

EDUCATION & TRAINING:

Storekeeper Training, (320 hours), U.S. Navy, 1992.
Associate of Arts, Lees McRae College, Banner Elk, NC, 1990.
Completed over 100 semester hours toward Bachelor's degree including courses in:
Technical Writing   *Mathematics*   *Safety*   *Speech*

JASON E. CLINE

3327 Juanita Street • San Diego, CA 92105
(619) 583-5763
E-mail: 103260.3513@compuserve.com

OBJECTIVE: Position as **LAN/WAN & Server Manager.**

SUMMARY:
- Top-rated veteran with extensive experience in network installation, maintenance, and troubleshooting.
- Certified Banyan Specialist, (pending).
- Held **Secret Security Clearance**.
- Hard working team player, committed to top quality performance.

PROFESSIONAL   **NETWORK SYSTEMS MANAGER**   **1993 - Present**
EXPERIENCE: U.S. Marine Corps   Santa Ana & San Diego, CA

LAN/WAN Manager - Outstanding Network Administrator with demonstrated skill in developing new networks, identifying hardware/software requirements, and determining capability levels. Initially built, then continued to manage and operate large Banyan Vines network for more than 1,000 users. Configured server platforms with EISA, using Network Interface, SCSI, and Banyan ICA cards. Network included over 700 workstations and 15 servers, including:

DEC Prioris XL servers	DECpc XL servers	Dell Power Edge servers
HP Net Server LC	Cisco 4000 routers	3com Netbuilder router

Proficient in the operation and management of Ethernet Local Area Network, including 10 base 2, 10 base5, 10 base T, 100 base T, and FDDI, as well as 3com Linkswitch Hubs, Cabletron Stackable Hubs, Black Box Stackable Mini-Hubs, and AT&T modular jack panels. Managed Wide Area Network consisting of HDLC server to server, TCP/IP server to server, Async server to server, Analog Async Dial-In, and ISDN Async Dial-In. Manage fiber optic network including 3com Link Builder Hubs and Allied Telesis Repeaters.

Supervision & Training - Coordinated and provided training to more than 22 Information System Coordinators on all aspects of their jobs. Supervised and provided training on the configuration of Banyan Vines in small systems including installation of Network Interface Cards with jumper settings or NDIS drivers.

- Coordinated a Computer Help Desk to efficiently handle heavy trouble calls and provide service to ensure user satisfaction.
- Install, maintain, and provide user assistance on a variety of software on more than 800 small systems, including all versions of DOS, Windows 95, Windows 3.1 and 3.11 for Workgroups, and Lotus Smart Suite.

Information Security Manager - Manage network security of Banyan Vines network and 3270/SNA host connection to high security mainframes. Created and maintained more than 50 user accounts on Kansas City, Camp Pendleton, and Quantico mainframes connected to the worldwide Marine Corps Data Network.

AVIATION TECHNICIAN   **1992 - 1993**
U.S. Marine Corps   Santa Ana, CA

Troubleshot, repaired, and maintained the Flight Control Computer and hydraulic / structural systems on the F/A-18D aircraft. Attained qualifications in record time, earned GSE licenses and pursued Plane Captain qualifications. Consistently upgraded and maintained all qualifications. Maintained maintenance records, updated publications, and upgraded tool control program for Quality Assurance Inspections.

Continued...

JASON E. CLINE　　　　　　　　　　　　　　　　　　　(619) 583-5763
(Continued)

TECHNICAL
TRAINING:　　　　**Vines Problem Solving**
　　　　　　　　　　Banyan Certified Education Center, Irvine, CA, 1996.

　　　　　　　　　　Advanced Vines Administration
　　　　　　　　　　Banyan Certified Education Center, Irvine, CA, 1995.

　　　　　　　　　　Basic Vines Administration
　　　　　　　　　　Banyan Certified Education Center, Irvine, CA, 1994.

　　　　　　　　　　Hydraulic / Structural Maintenance - F/A-18
　　　　　　　　　　U.S. Navy, Lemoore, CA, 1993.

　　　　　　　　　　Aircraft Maintenance - Hydraulics
　　　　　　　　　　U.S. Navy, Memphis, TN, 1993.

REFERENCE:　　　Outstanding personal and professional references available on request.

PAUL N. BEVERLY

2588 Euclid Avenue
San Diego, CA 92105
(619) 262-4727

OBJECTIVE: Position as an **Electrician**.

SUMMARY: **Highly skilled electrician with in-depth experience in the troubleshooting, maintenance and repair of avionics systems.** Exceptional technician, leader and organizer. Equally adept in maintenance/repair and overall project oversight roles. Background includes production management, quality control and staff technical training.

PROFESSIONAL   <u>**Marine Electrician**</u>   **1995 - Present**
EXPERIENCE: NASSCO   San Diego, CA

Repair and modify a wide range of electrical systems and components, including power distribution systems, motor generators, voltage/frequency regulators, switchboards, turbine generators, controllers, power and lighting circuits, diesel generators, and AC/DC systems. Plan wiring and installation of equipment, fixtures, and control mechanisms, including junction boxes, circuit breakers, and fuse boxes. Proficient in splicing, wire-stripping, and soldering.

<u>**Aviation Electronics/Production Supervisor**</u>   **1977 - 1994**
U.S. Navy   San Diego, CA

<u>**Maintenance & Repair**</u> - Performed and supervised advanced maintenance and repair work on a wide range of aircraft electrical and electronics systems, including navigation, power distribution, instrumentation, engine, lighting, landing gear, auto pilot, flap control and associated systems.   Troubleshot analog and digital circuitry to component level. Read and interpreted schematics, blueprints and block diagrams. Proficient in the use of all general and special purpose test equipment.

- Personally troubleshot and repaired aircraft simulators, **saving thousands in outside contractor costs.**

<u>**Production Supervision & Quality Control**</u> - Managed production efforts, including **workload planning, time and manpower estimates, material planning/acquisition, work assignments and quality control.** Inspected job phases to ensure compliance with technical specifications and safety requirements. Planned and supervised preventive maintenance cycles. **Monitored and enforced occupational safety programs** and maintenance of shop equipment and work spaces. Completed maintenance documentation and reports.

- Trained and qualified over 30 quality assurance inspectors, **increasing overall shop productivity.**
- Systematically reduced repair backlog at each shop managed by **analyzing and improving work procedures.**
- Prior to ship deployment, brought all avionics systems to full operational readiness in half the allotted time.
- Provided expert management of a repair parts program supporting 31 aircraft. **Improved accounting processes and local self-sufficiency.**

TECHNICAL   **Inertial Navigation Systems School**, U.S. Navy, (80 hours).
TRAINING: **Aircraft Electrical and Instrument Systems**, U.S. Navy, (80 hours).
                     Aviation Electrical Intermediate School, U.S. Navy, (1040 hours).
                     Aviation Maintenance Quality Control Training, U.S. Navy, (80 hours).
                     Leadership and Management Training, U.S. Navy (120 hours).

GARY S. MINTER
2716 46th Street
San Diego, CA 92105
(619) 264-7668

SUMMARY:
- **Top-rated** Navy explosives technician with experience in intelligence operations, physical security and Secret Service technical support.
- **Mature and reliable.** Demonstrated exceptional performance in high-pressure situations.

PROFESSIONAL
EXPERIENCE:

SENIOR EXPLOSIVE ORDNANCE DISPOSAL TECHNICIAN   **6/89 - Present**
U.S. Navy   U.S. and Overseas

<u>Explosives and Secret Service Support</u> - As a Senior Technician, implement in-depth knowledge of foreign and domestic explosive ordnance in location, identification, render safe and disposal procedures. **Provide technical support to U.S. Secret Service** during presidential and other VIP visits to California. Swept sites, vehicles, and travel routes for explosive devices; secured areas verified as safe. **Perform physical security duties.** Provided close support for Navy SEALs and Naval Intelligence Service during Gulf War. **Collect and interpret intelligence information** and plan strategies based on projected target actions.

- **Discovered and disposed of three potentially hazardous packages** during President Clinton's visit to Los Angeles following the Northridge earthquake. Commended by Commanding Officer and Department of the Treasury.
- Under low visibility conditions, cleared South Korean harbor routes of moored mines using electronic and underwater manual search techniques. Commended by fleet admiral.
- **Qualified small arms expert.**
- Achieved qualification as Range Safety Officer for demolitions and small arms.
- Mixed-gas and SCUBA dive supervisor and RAM air parachutist. First aid/CPR certified.

<u>Leadership & Management</u> - Management experience includes mission planning, personnel motivation, and staff development and training. Perform quality control inspections of systems and equipment, and provide training/supervision on systems usage.

- Worked with marine mammals associated with Navy special projects. Supervised 14 technicians in developing the only U.S. marine mammal moored mine hunting system (MK-4). Assisted in research and development of deep ocean recovery systems and devices/methods for worldwide transport of dolphins. Commended by fleet admiral.

AIRCREWMAN, ANTISUBMARINE WARFARE   **8/83 - 5/89**
U.S. Navy   San Diego, CA

Flew anti-submarine warfare missions aboard naval helicopters. Duties included intelligence analysis, sonar target identification and tracking, acoustic analysis, and intelligence reporting. Qualified search and rescue swimmer.

- Located and tracked Soviet nuclear submarine in Indian Ocean.
- As rescue swimmer in adverse sea conditions, performed heroically in the recovery of a downed A-4 pilot.

EDUCATION
& TECHNICAL
TRAINING:

Senior Explosive Ordnance Disposal Technician Training, U.S. Navy, 12/94.
Army Airborne, RAM Air/Water Insertion Parachutist Training, 1991, 1993. (200 hours)
Explosive Ordnance Disposal Technician Basic, U.S. Navy, 12/90.
Dive School, U.S. Navy, 7/89. (12 weeks).
Survival, Evasion, Resistance and Escape (SERE), U.S. Navy, 7/83. (80 hours).
Desert Survival Training, U.S. Navy, 7/83. (220 hours)
Leadership and Management, U.S. Navy. (120 hours)

KEVIN J. CARSON
1122 Alaska Street
El Paso, TX 79915
(915) 591-9605

OBJECTIVE: Position as a **Boiler/Pump Repair Technician**.

SUMMARY: Top-rated repair technician with in-depth experience in operation, maintenance, and repair of, turbo generators, condensate circulating water systems, compressed air potable water auxiliary systems, and lube oil systems. Solid background in hazardous material handling and environmental control procedures, preventive maintenance planning, and quality assurance. Mature, reliable used to working under stress, and dedicated to top quality craftsmanship.

PROFESSIONAL **BOILER TECHNICIAN**   **1987 - 1996**
EXPERIENCE: U.S. Navy   Various Locations U.S. and Overseas

PRIVATE   **1986 - 1987**
U.S. Army National Guard   U.S. Locations

Technical - Installed, maintained, troubleshot and repaired high-pressure/low pressure systems and components including:

1200 PSI steam systems	600 PSI steam systems
70K GPD distilling unit	100K GPD distilling unit
High pressure air compressor	Low pressure air compressor
Potable water auxiliary system	Heat exchangers
Steam turbine generators	Forced draft blowers
Valve/valve operators (all types)	Evaporators
Pumps (centrifugal, rotary / screw-type, sliding shoe)	Saltwater coolers
Condensers	Boilers

Calibrated and aligned pumps using special calibration, and precision measuring devices. Sample of tools familiar with include:

Torque wrenches	Venier Micrometers	Cylinder liner pullers
Pressure gauges	Piston pullers	Conventional hand tools
Electric/pneumatic tools	Fire/safety equipment	Flaring tools
Calibration tools/equipment's	Metalworking tools	Chemical/Water Testing Kits

As Shop Supervisor , coordinated work assignments and managed performance of overhaul technicians at the Pump Repair and Overhaul Shop, SIMA, San Diego. Performed initial inspection, repair, overhaul, and alignment of various Main and Auxiliary Propulsion Pumps and Turbines for ships homeported in San Diego, CA. Supervised up to 10 Boiler Technicians, assigned jobs, monitored work in progress, and evaluated performance. Completed and trained assigned individuals in use of maintenance data forms, system diagrams, procedures of working in high temperatures and consistent environment of dust and noise

- Assisted USS Chandler (DD-996) in overhaul of 2 time stringent repairs on #1 Sonar Static Pump and #2 Lube Oil service Pump in record time enabling ship to rapidly meet commitments.

- Assisted USS Coronado (AGF-11) in repair of #2 Salt Water Service Pump, and #7 Turbine Fire Pump, enabling ship to return to Operational status.

- Assisted USS Denver (LPD-9) in CASREP overhaul and installation of #1 Emergency Diesel Engine Lube Oil Service Pump allowing ship to get underway with equipment operating at peak efficiency.

Water Analysis - Performed boiler water and feed water sample extraction and analysis. Tested water for pH, chloride, alkalinity, conductivity and additional factors. Detected contamination, isolated cause and determined appropriate type and dosage rate of chemical response. Monitored results and kept detailed logs and records throughout process. Also tested and treated potable water.

Hazardous Material - As the Damage Control Supervisor, trained ship crew personnel in hazardous material handling and disposal including EPA, DOD, and local directives and guidelines. Received, issued, stored, and controlled hazardous materials and ensured proper disposal of hazardous waste. Managed Material Safety Data Sheets; and tracked HAZMAT use to ensure return and proper disposal of hazardous waste.

HONORS & AWARDS:

Letter of Appreciation, from Commanding Officer, SIMA, San Diego, for superior performance in supervision and repair/maintenance in the Pump Shop.
Letter of Commendation, from Commander Middle East Forces, for Outstanding performance in damage control and burnerman duties in support of Operation Desert Storm.
Letter of Commendation, from Commanding Officer, USS Horne (CG-30), for Outstanding performance as burnerman and in support of damage control during Operation Desert Storm.

EDUCATION & TRAINING:

Licensed Forklift (15K) Operator
Craftsman, U.S. Navy, 1996
Firefighting (Refresher), U.S. Navy, 1996
Fire Fighting Team Leader Qualification, 1991
Gauge Calibration Qualification, U.S, Navy, 1991
1200 PSI MMR Upper/Lower Level Qualification , U.S. Navy, 1991
Advanced Damage Control Qualification, U.S. Navy. 1991
Fundamentals of Respiratory Protection, U.S. Navy, 1990
Heat Stress, U.S. Navy, 1989
Maintenance, Material Management Qualification, U.S. Navy, 1988
Boiler Technician Class "A" School, SSC Great Lakes, IL, 1987
High School Graduate

DAVID SCOTT DACUS

2865 Worden Street
San Diego, CA 92110
(619) 226-4674
DSDacus@aol.com

OBJECTIVE: Position as a **Maintenance Technician.**

SUMMARY:
- Results-oriented professional with proven success in electronics systems maintenance, computer systems maintenance and engineering, and technical supervision.
- Exceptional troubleshooting skills; pinpoints problems rapidly and accurately.
- Dedicated, responsible and committed to delivering top quality service.

PROFESSIONAL   **Maintenance Technician**   **June 1986 - Present**
EXPERIENCE: U.S. Navy   San Diego, CA

Electronics -   Perform and supervise analysis, maintenance and repair of analog, digital, electrical, and electromechanical systems and components, including:

Digital data systems	Audio and video systems	Displays
Radar transmitters/receivers	Fiber optics	Communication systems
Indicators	Microwave systems	Measuring equipment

Additional systems include **integrated circuits, I/O cards, digital-to-analog converters, multiplexers, LAN PC workstations, and computer interface systems.** Extensive experience in cabling installation and termination, and component-level PC maintenance. Coordinate multi-level preventive maintenance programs. Troubleshoot to component level and perform all circuit repairs, including microminiature. Read and interpret schematics, blueprints and block diagrams. Also experienced in a wide range of electromechanical, electrohydraulic and pneumatic systems.

- Served as Radar Maintenance Supervisor aboard the USS Rushmore during Operation Restore Hope. Performance was cited by management as a key factor in mission success.
- Researched and wrote electronics systems casualty control manual for a large naval unit; manual included emergency troubleshooting/repair guidelines for more than 100 systems.

Computer Systems - Expert in configuration, maintenance and component-level repair of mini- and microcomputer systems, and large capacity disk drives. Experienced in assembly and repair of a wide range of systems from casing to the smallest components, including:

386/486 micros	High speed data buss	Print servers
Multiport/dual control	LAN interfaces	Fiber optics
IBM RS/6000	Multiplexers	RISC Processors

- Installed and maintained all hardware, software and cabling for a Banyan Vines LAN supporting 80+ PC workstations.

Production/Project Management - Supervise and coordinate production efforts, including **workload planning, time and manpower estimates, material planning and acquisition, work assignments and quality control.** Perform quality control inspections. Experienced classroom instructor - conduct basic and advanced technical training for new or less experienced employees.

EDUCATION   **B.S. Workforce Education & Development**, Southern Illinois University.
& TECHNICAL   Expected completion 1996.
TRAINING: **Electronics Mechanic National Apprenticeship Program**, U.S. Dept. of Labor.
                   Microminiature Repair, U.S. Navy.
                   Secure Satellite Communications, U.S. Navy, 9/92.
                   Electronics Technician School, U.S. Navy, 7/87.

Appendix D

PROFESSIONAL ASSOCIATIONS AND TRADE
ORGANIZATIONS

ARTS

**American Society of
Cinematographers**
1782 North Orange Drive
Hollywood, CA 90028
Phone: 213-969-4333
Fax: 213-876-4973
E-mail: ascmag@aol.com
Category: Performing Arts

**American Society of Composers
Authors & Publishers**
ASCAP Building
One Lincoln Plaza
New York, NY 10023
Phone: 212-621-6000
Fax: 212-721-0955
E-mail: info@ascap.com
Website: www.ascap.com
Category: Arts

**Professional Photographers of
America Inc.**
57 Forsyth Street N.W.
Suite 1600
Atlanta, GA 30303
Phone: 404-522-8600
Fax: 404-614-6400
Category: Arts

BUSINESS AND TRADE

**American Association of Professional
Landmen**
4100 Fossil Creek Boulevard
Fort Worth, TX 76137-2791
Phone: 817-847-7700
Fax: 817-847-7704
Category: General Business

American Production and Inventory
  Control Society Inc.
500 West Annandale Road
Falls Church, VA 22046-4274
Phone: 703-237-8344
Fax: 703-534-4767
Category: General Business

American Society for Industrial Security
1655 North Fort Myer Drive
Suite 1200
Arlington, VA 22209-3198
Phone: 703-522-5800
Fax: 703-243-4954
Category: General Business

American Society for Nondestructive
  Testing Inc.
1711 Arlingate Lane
P.O. Box 28518
Columbus, OH 43228-0518
Phone: 614-274-6003
Fax: 614-274-6899
Category: General Business

American Society for Quality Control
611 East Wisconsin Avenue
P.O. Box 3005
Milwaukee, WI 53201-3005
Phone: 414-272-8575
Fax: 414-272-1734
Category: General Business

American Society for Training and
  Development
1640 King Street
Box 1443
Alexandria, VA 22313
Phone: 703-683-8100
Fax: 703-683-8103
Category: Business

American Society of Corporate
  Secretaries Inc.
521 Fifth Avenue
New York, NY 10175
Phone: 212-681-2000
Fax: 212-681-2005
Category: Business

American Society of Landscape
  Architects
4401 Connecticut Avenue N.W.
Washington, DC 20008-2302
Phone: 202-686-2752
Fax: 202-686-1001
Category: General Business

Association of Corporate Travel
  Executives
515 King Street, Suite 330
Alexandria, VA 22314
Phone: 703-683-5322
Fax: 703-683-2720
E-mail: info@acte.org
Website: www.acte.org
Category: Travel

Business Professionals of America
5454 Cleveland Avenue
Columbus, OH 43231-4021
Phone: 614-895-7277
Fax: 614-895-1165
E-mail: bpa@ix.netcom.com
Website: www.thomson.com/partners/
  bpa/default.html
Category: Business

Federation of International Trade
  Associations
1851 Alexander Bell Drive
Reston, VA 20191-4345
Phone: 703-620-1588
Fax: 703-391-0159
E-mail: info@fita.org
Website: www.fita.org
Category: Trade

Iron and Steel Society Inc.
410 Commonwealth Drive
Warrendale, PA 15086-7512
Phone: 412-776-1535
Fax: 412-776-0430
E-mail: mailbag@issource.org
Website: www.issource.org
Category: General Business

ISA-The International Society for Measurement and Control
67 Alexander Drive
P.O. Box 12277
Research Triangle Park, NC 27709
Phone: 919-549-8411
Fax: 919-549-8288
E-mail: info@isa.org
Website: www.isa.org
Category: Business

Meeting Professionals International
4455 LBJ Freeway
Suite 1200
Dallas, TX 75244-5903
Phone: 214-702-3000
Fax: 214-702-3070
Category: Business

National Association of Professional Surplus Lines Offices Ltd.
6405 North Cosby
Suite 201
Kansas City, MO 64151
Phone: 816-741-3910
Fax: 816-741-5409
E-mail: napslo@microlink.net
Website: www.microlink.net
Category: Business

National Board of Boiler and Pressure Vessel Inspectors
1055 Crupper Avenue
Columbus, OH 43229-1183
Phone: 614-888-8320
Fax: 614-888-0750
E-mail: chomer@nationalboard.org
Website: www.nationalboard.org/index.html
Category: General Business

National Fire Protection Association
1 Batterymarch Park
P.O. Box 9101
Quincy, MA 02269-9101
Phone: 617-770-3000
Fax: 617-770-0700
E-mail: library@nfpa.org
Website: Library@NFPA.org.
Category: General Business

National Guild of Professional Paperhangers
910 Charles Street
Fredericksburg, VA 22401
Phone: 540-370-4503
Fax: 540-370-0015
Category: Design

Printing Industries of America Inc.
100 Daingerfield Road
Alexandria, VA 22314
Phone: 703-519-8100
Fax: 703-548-3227
Category: Manufacturing

Professional Services Council
8607 Westwood Center Drive
Suite 204
Vienna, VA 22182-7506
Phone: 703-883-2030
Fax: 703-883-2035
Category: Business

Professional Women in Construction
342 Madison Avenue, Room 451
New York, NY 10173
Phone: 212-687-0610
Fax: 810-490-1213
Category: Trade

Regulatory Affairs Professionals Society
12300 Twinbrook Parkway Suite 630
Rockville, MD 20852
Phone: 301-770-2920
Fax: 301-770-2924
Category: Business

The Society of Competitive Intelligence
  Professionals
1700 Diagonal Road Suite 520
Alexandria, VA 22314
Phone: 703-739-0696
Fax: 703-739-2524
E-mail: scip@dc.infi.net
Category: Business

Society of Consumer Affairs
  Professionals in Business
801 North Fairfax Street, #404
Alexandria, VA 22314-1757
Phone: 703-519-3700
Fax: 703-549-4886
Category: Business

Society of Industrial and Office
  REALTORS
700 11th Street N.W.
Suite 510
Washington, DC 20001-4511
Phone: 202-737-1150
Fax: 202-737-8796
E-mail: sior@access.digex.net
Category: Real Estate

Travel Industry Association of America
1100 New York Avenue N.W.
Suite 450
Washington, DC 20005-3934
Phone: 202-408-8422
Fax: 202-408-1255
E-mail: feedback@tia.org
Website: www.tia.org
Category: Travel

COMMUNICATIONS

Society for Technical Communication
901 North Stuart Street
Suite 904
Arlington, VA 22203-1854
Phone: 703-522-4114
Fax: 703-522-2075
E-mail: stc@tmn.com
Category: Communications

Society of Telecommunications
  Consultants
13766 Center Street
Suite 212
Carmel Valley, CA 93924
Phone: 408-659-0110
Fax: 408-659-0144
E-mail: stchdq@att
Category: Telecommunications/General
  Business

COMPUTERS AND ELECTRONICS

DPMA Assn. of Information Systems Professionals
505 Busse Highway
Park Ridge, IL 60068-3191
Phone: 847-825-8124
Fax: 847-825-1693
E-mail: 70430.35@compuserve.com
Category: Computers

Institute of Electrical and Electronics Engineers Lasers and Electro-Optics Society
445 Hoes Lane
Piscataway, NJ 08854
Phone: 908-562-3892
Fax: 908-562-8434
Category: Electronics

ISHM-The Microelectronics Society
1850 Centennial Park Drive
Suite 105
Reston, VA 22091
Phone: 703-758-1060
Fax: 703-758-1066
E-mail: ishm@aol.com
Category: Electronics

Network and Systems Professionals Association
7044 S. 13th Street
Oak Creek, WI 53154
Phone: 414-768-8000
Fax: 414-768-8001
E-mail: jerry@naspa.net
Website: www.naspa.net
Category: Computers

ENGINEERING AND SCIENCE

American Association of Professional Sales Engineers
55969 Jayne Drive
Elkhart, IN 46514-1325
Phone: 219-522-4837
Fax: 219-522-4837
Category: Engineering

American Helicopter Society
217 North Washington Street
Alexandria, VA 22314
Phone: 703-684-6777
Fax: 703-739-9279
Category: Aviation

The American Nuclear Society
555 North Kensington Avenue
LaGrange Park, IL 60526
Phone: 708-352-6611
Fax: 708-352-0499
E-mail: nucleus@ans.org
Website: www.ans.org
Category: Science

American Society for Information Science
8720 Georgia Avenue
Suite 501
Silver Spring, MD 20910
Phone: 301-495-0900
Fax: 301-495-0810
E-mail: asis@cni.org
Website: www.cni.org
Category: Science

American Society for Photogrammetry
and Remote Sensing
5410 Grosvenor Lane
Suite 210
Bethesda, MD 20814-2160
Phone: 301-493-0290
Fax: 301-493-0208
E-mail: asprs@asprs.org
Website: www.asprs.org/asprs
Category: Science

American Society of Heating
Refrigerating and Air-Conditioning
Engineers Inc.
1791 Tullie Circle N.E.
Atlanta, GA 30329-2305
Phone: 404-636-8400
Fax: 404-321-5478
E-mail: ashrae@ashrae.org
Website: www.ashrae.org
Category: Engineering

The American Society of Mechanical
Engineers
345 East 47th Street
New York, NY 10017
Phone: 212-705-7722
Fax: 212-705-7739
E-mail: infocentral@asme.org
Website: www.asme.org
Category: Engineering

American Society of Safety Engineers
1800 East Oakton Street
Des Plaines, IL 60018-2187
Phone: 847-699-2929
Fax: 847-296-3769
E-mail: 73244.562@compuserve.com
Category: Engineering

The Ecological Society of America
2010 Massachusetts Avenue N.W., #400
Washington, DC 20036
Phone: 202-833-8773
Fax: 202-833-8775
E-mail: esahq@esa.org
Website: www.esa.org
Category: Science

The Geological Society of America
3300 Penrose Place
P.O. Box 9140
Boulder, CO 80301
Phone: 303-447-2020
Fax: 303-447-1133
E-mail: admin@geosociety.org
Website: www.geosociety.org
Category: Science

Materials Research Society
9800 McKnight Road
Pittsburgh, PA 15237
Phone: 412-367-3003
Fax: 412-367-4373
E-mail: info@mrs.org
Category: Science

National Society of Professional
Engineers
1420 King Street
Alexandria, VA 22314-2715
Phone: 703-684-2800
Fax: 703-836-4875
Category: Engineering

Refrigeration Service Engineers Society
1666 Rand Road
Des Plaines, IL 60016-3552
Phone: 847-297-6464
Fax: 847-297-5038
E-mail: rses@starnetinc.com
Website: www.starnetinc.com
Category: Engineering

Robotic Industries Association
900 Victors Way
P.O. Box 3724
Ann Arbor, MI 48106
Phone: 313-994-6088
Fax: 313-994-3338
Category: Engineering and Science

Society for Industrial and Applied
Mathematics
3600 University City Science Center
Philadelphia, PA 19104-2688
Phone: 215-382-9800
Fax: 215-386-7999
E-mail: siam@siam.org
Website: www.siam.org
Category: Education

The Society of American Military
Engineers
607 Prince Street
Alexandria, VA 22314
Phone: 703-549-3800
Fax: 703-684-0231
Category: Military/Engineering

Society of Automotive Engineers
400 Commonwealth Drive
Warrendale, PA 15096-0001
Phone: 412-776-4841
Fax: 412-776-5760
E-mail: sae@sae.org
Category: Engineering

The Society of Exploration
Geophysicists
8801 South Yale
Post Office Box 702740
Tulsa, OK 74170-2740
Phone: 918-497-5500
Fax: 918-497-5557
Category: Science

The Society of Naval Architects and
Marine Engineers
601 Pavonia Avenue
Suite 400
Jersey City, NJ 07306
Phone: 201-798-4800
Fax: 201-798-4975
Category: Engineering

The Society of the Plastics Industry Inc.
1275 K Street N.W.
Suite 400
Washington, DC 20005
Phone: 202-371-5200
Fax: 202-371-1022
Category: Engineering and Science

EVENTS AND MARKETING

Association for Wedding Professionals
1601 Fulton Avenue
Suite 8A
Sacramento, CA 95825
Phone: 800-242-4461
Fax: 916-482-2025
Category: Events

Professional Convention Management
Association
100 Vestavia Parkway
Suite 220
Birmingham, AL 35216-3743
Phone: 205-823-7262
Fax: 205-822-3891
Category: Events and Marketing

Public Relations Society of America
33 Irving Place
New York, NY 10003-2376
Phone: 212-995-2230
Fax: 212-995-0757
E-mail: hq@prsa.org
Website: www.prsa.org
Category: Marketing

Society for Marketing Professional
  Services
99 Canal Center Plaza
Suite 250
Alexandria, VA 22314-1588
Phone: 703-549-6117
Fax: 703-549-2498
Category: Marketing

FINANCE

American Society of Appraisers
P.O. Box 17265
Washington, DC 20041
Phone: 703-478-2228
Fax: 703-742-8471
E-mail: asainfo@apo.com
Website: www.apo.com
Category: Finance

Financial Managers Society Inc.
230 West Monroe Street
Suite 2205
Chicago, IL 60606
Phone: 312-578-1300
Fax: 312-578-1308
Category: Finance

National Association of Professional
  Insurance Agents
400 North Washington Street
Alexandria, VA 22314-9980
Phone: 703-836-9340
Fax: 703-836-1279
E-mail: patbo@pianet.com
Website: www.pianet.com
Category: Finance

Reinsurance Association of America
1301 Pennsylvania Ave. N.W.
Suite 900
Washington, DC 20004
Phone: 202-638-3690
Fax: 202-638-0936
E-mail: 6483431@mcimail.com
Category: Finance

Robert Morris Associates—The
  Association of Lending and Credit
  Risk Professionals
One Liberty Place
1650 Market Street
Suite 2300
Philadelphia PA 19103
Phone: 215-851-9100
Fax: 215-851-9206
Category: Financial Services

Society of Financial Services
  Professionals
270 S. Bryn Mawr Avenue
Bryn Mawr, PA 19010
Phone: 610-526-2500
Fax: 610-527-4010
E-mail: custserv@financialpro.org
Website: www.financialpro.org
Category: Finance

GOVERNMENT

**American Society for Public
Administration**
1120 G Street N.W.
Suite 700
Washington, DC 20005-3885
Phone: 202-393-7878
Fax: 202-638-4952
E-mail: dcaspa@ix.netcom.com
Category: General Business

National League of Cities
1301 Pennsylvania Avenue N.W.
Suite 550
Washington, DC 20004
Phone: 202-626-3000
Fax: 202-626-3043
E-mail: pa@nlc.org
Website: www.nlc.org
Category: Government

HEALTH-RELATED

**American Association of Occupational
Health Nurses—AAOHN**
2920 Brandywine Road
Suite 100
Atlanta, GA 30341
Phone: 770-455-7757
Fax: 770-455-7271
E-mail: aaohn@aaohn.org
Website: www.AAOHN.org
Category: Health

**American Professional Practice
Association**
292 Madison Avenue
New York, NY 10017
Phone: 212-949-5900
Fax: 212-949-5910
Category: Health

**American Society for Healthcare
Environmental Services**
One North Franklin
Chicago, IL 60606
Phone: 312-422-3860
Fax: 312-422-4572
E-mail: Webmaster@ASHES.org
Website: www.ashes.org/
Category: Health

**Associated Bodywork & Massage
Professionals**
28677 Buffalo Park Road
Evergreen, CO 80439
Phone: 800-458-2267
Fax: 303-674-0859
E-mail: expectmore@abmp.com
Website: www.abmp.com
Category: Health

Association for the Advancement of
  Health Education—AAHE
1900 Association Drive
Reston, VA 20191-1599
Phone: 703-476-3437
Fax: 703-476-6638
E-mail: aahe@aahperd.org
Website: www.aahperd.org/aahe/
  aahe.html
Category: Health

Association of Academic Health
  Centers—AAHC
1400 16th Street N.W.
Suite 720
Washington, DC 20036
Phone: 202-265-9600
Fax: 202-265-7514
E-mail: scurry@acadhlthctrs.org
Website: www.ahcnet.org
Category: Health

Association of Clinical Research
  Professionals
1012 14th Street N.W.
Suite 807
Washington, DC 20005
Phone: 202-737-8100
Fax: 202-737-8101
E-mail: office@acrpnet.org
Category: Health

California Association of Hospitals and
  Health Systems
1201 K Street, Suite 800
Sacramento, CA 95812-1100
Phone: 916-443-7401
Fax: 916-552-7596
E-mail: membership@calhealth.org
Website: www.cahhs.org
Category: Health

IDEA The International Association of
  Fitness Professionals
6190 Cornerstone Court East
Suite 204
San Diego, CA 92121-3773
Phone: 619-535-8979
Fax: 619-535-8234
Category: Health

National Association of Pharmaceutical
  Manufacturers
320 Old Country Road, #205
Garden City, NY 11530
Phone: 212-838-3720
Fax: 516-741-3699
Category: Health

National Association of Social Workers
  Inc.
750 First Street N.E.
Suite 700
Washington, DC 20002
Phone: 202-408-8600
Fax: 202-336-8310
E-mail: nasw@capcon.net
Website: naswca.org/jobsjun1.html
Category: Health

HUMAN RESOURCES

Human Resource Planning Society
317 Madison Avenue
Suite 1509
New York, NY 10017
Phone: 212-490-6387
Fax: 212-682-6851
Category: Human Resources

National Association of Temporary and
Staffing Services
119 South Saint Asaph Street
Alexandria, VA 22314-3319
Phone: 703-549-6287
Fax: 703-549-4808
E-mail: natss@aol.com
Website: www.natss.com/staffing
Category: Employment

Professionals in Human Resources
Association
888 S. Figueroa Suite 1050
Los Angeles, CA 90017-5459
Phone: 213-662-7472
Fax: 213-622-7450
Website: www.pihra.org
Category: Human Resources

NATURAL RESOURCES

American Bureau of Metal Statistics
400 North Main Street
Suite 6
Manahawkin, NJ 08050
Phone: 609-597-3375
Fax: 609-597-6625
E-mail: info@ambs.com
Website: www.abms.com
Category: Metals

American Forest and Paper Association
1111 19th Street N.W.
Suite 800,
Washington, DC 20036
Phone: 202-463-2700
Fax: 202-463-2785
E-mail: Info@afandpa.org
Category: Paper

Association of Petroleum Re-Refiners
P.O. Box 584
Buffalo, NY 14231-0584
Phone: 716-631-8246
Fax: 716-631-8246
Category: Recyclers

Association of Post-Consumer Plastic
Recyclers
1275 K Street N.W. #501
Washington, D.C. 20005
Phone: 202-371-5336
Fax: 202-371-0616
Category: Recyclers

Gypsum Association
810 First Street N.E. #510
Washington, D.C. 20002
Phone: 202-289-5440
Fax: 202-289-3707
E-mail: info@gypsum.org
Category: Geology

Lead Industries Association Inc.
295 Madison Avenue
New York, NY 10017
Phone: 212-578-4750
Fax: 212-684-7714
E-mail: miller@leadinfo.com
Website: www.leadinfo.com
Category: Metals

Society for Mining Metallurgy and
Exploration Inc.
P.O. Box 625002
Littleton, CO 80162-5002
Phone: 303-973-9550
Fax: 303-973-3845
E-mail: smenet@aol.com
Category: Metals

Solid Waste Association of North
America
1100 Wayne Avenue
Suite 700
P.O. Box 7219
Silver Spring, MD 20910
Phone: 301-585-2898
Fax: 301-589-7068
Category: Environment

Southern Forest Products Association
P.O. Box 641700
Kenner, LA 70064-1700
Phone: 504-443-4464
Fax: 504-443-6612
Category: Environment

PUBLISHING

American Society of Newspaper Editors
11690B Sunrise Valley Drive
Reston, VA 20191
Phone: 703-648-1144
Fax: 703-476-6125
E-mail: asne@aol.com
Category: Publishing

Society of Professional Journalists
16 South Jackson Street
P.O. Box 77
Greencastle, IN 46135-0077
Phone: 317-653-3333
Fax: 317-653-4631
E-mail: spj@interneteci.com
Website: www.interneteci.com
Category: Publishing

RECREATION AND HOME

American Professional Pet Distributors
225 E. Sixth Street
St Paul, MN 55101
Phone: 612-293-9317
Fax: 612-293-9470
Category: Pets

Professional Association of Diving
Instructors
1251 East Dyer Road
Suite 100
Santa Ana, CA 92705-5605
Phone: 714-540-7234
Fax: 714-540-2609
Category: Sports

Appendix E

CIVIL SERVICE RESOURCES

PERIODICALS LISTING FEDERAL JOBS

Federal Career Opportunities—Federal Research Service, P.O. Box 1059, Vienna, VA 22183; 1-800-822-5627. E-mail: info@fedjobs.com. A biweekly publication listing thousands of currently available federal jobs. $39 for a 3-month subscription. Also check the website and federal jobs search engine at www.fedjobs.com.

Federal Jobs Digest—Breakthrough Publications, P.O. Box 594, Millwood, NY 10546; 1-800-824-5000. Website: www.jobsfed.com. Biweekly listing of federal job vacancies in a newspaper format. $34 for 6 biweekly issues.

Federal Times—6883 Commercial Drive, Springfield, VA 22159; 1-800-368-6718. Website: www.federaltimes.com. $52/year; $29.95 for 6 months. A weekly newspaper; publishes several hundred federal vacancies.

FEDERAL JOB HOTLINES

USA JOBS Automated Telephone System—The federal government job national hotline numbers are:

912-757-3000, 202-606-2700, TDD 912-744-2249. There are also 16 Office of Personnel Management (OPM) Centers across the country. Each has its own hotline number:

Note: This service does not list all vacancies. Agencies with direct-hire authority advertise their openings through their human resources departments.

Atlanta, GA	404-331-4315
Chicago, IL	312-353-6192
Dayton, OH	937-225-2720
Detroit, MI	313-226-6950
Honolulu, HI	808-541-2791
Huntsville, AL	256-837-0894
Kansas City, MO	816-426-5702
Norfolk, VA	757-441-3355
Philadelphia, PA	215-861-3070
Raleigh, NC	919-790-2822
San Antonio, TX	210-805-2402
San Francisco, CA	415-744-5627
Seattle, WA	206-553-0888
Twin Cities, MN	612-725-3430

United States Postal Service—The following toll-free numbers offer information on job vacancies at the U.S. Postal Service: *National Vacancies:* 800-JOB-UPS. *Local opportunities:* 800-276-5627.

FEDERAL JOBS WEBSITES

www.federaljobs.net
Federal employment career center that will assist you with your civil service job search and guide you step by step through the process. Includes a list of more than 200 federal employment websites.

www.fedjobs.com
Federal Research Service. Lists thousands of federal job openings. Searchable by GS series, grade, location, eligibility, agency, or combination of the above.

www.law.vill.edu/Fed-Agency/fedwebloc.html
Federal Web Locator. One-stop shopping for federal government information on the Internet. A service of the Villanova Center for Information Law and Policy.

www.fedworld.gov
FeDWorld. Downloads source files from USA JOBS. Allows searching by job category and type as well as immediate downloading and viewing of some vacancy announcements.

www.healthcarejobs.org
Health Care Jobs Career Center. Good place to explore health care service occupations in the private sector. Also lists federal health care job openings.

www.usajobs.opm.gov
USA JOBS. Operated by the Office of Personnel Mangaemenet. Provides access to the national federal jobs database, full text job announcements, and answers to questions frequently asked about federal employment.

FEDERAL DEPARTMENT INTERNET WEBSITES

Not all federal openings are listed in cross-agency databases. Sometimes you have to go directly to the source. You can connect to most federal agencies by visiting the website of the department which administers that agency. Department websites are listed below. For a comprehensive listing of agency employment websites, visit *www.federaljobs.net*.

Department of Agriculture (*www.usda.gov*)

Department of Commerce (*www.doc.gov*)

Department of Defense (*www.hrsc.osd.mil/empinfo.htm*)

Department of Education (*www.ed.gov*)

Department of Energy (*www.doe.gov*)

Department of Health and Human Services (*www.hud.gov*)

Department of Interior (*www.doi.gov*)

Department of Justice (*www.usdoj.gov*)

Department of Labor (*www.dol.gov*)

Department of State (*www.state.gov*)

Department of Transportation (*www.dot.gov*)

Department of Treasury (*www.ustreas.gov*)

Department of Veterans Affairs (*www.va.gov*)

White House (*www.whitehouse.gov*)

OTHER GOVERNMENTAL AGENCIES

Central Intelligence Agency (www.odci.gov/cia)

Environmental Protection Agency (www.epa.gov)

Federal Communications Commission (www.fcc.gov)

Office of Personnel Management (www.opm.gov)

United States Postal Service (www.usps.gov)

Index